HOL[

GERMANY

Antwerp

Schelde

Brussels

Meuse

Namur

Mons Charleroi

Maubeuge

BELGIUM

LUXEMBOURG

Sedan

Aisne

Montmédy

Moselle

Reims

Meuse

Verdun

Metz

Marne

St. Mihiel

Contents

SUMMING-UP

MAPS

ILLUSTRATIONS

Credit List

Mrs. Ashmore: 26
Australian War Memorial: 60
Mrs. L. L. Blake: 34
Squadron-Leader Bricker: 77
Geoffrey Burnand: 51
Department of Defence, Canberra: 59
Mrs. Fraser Evans: 64
Flight International: 7, 12, 13, 14, 17
Imperial War Museum: 10, 16, 18, 22, 23, 25, 28, 29, 30, 31, 32, 33, 35, 36, 37, 38, 39, 44, 45, 48, 49, 50, 52, 53, 55, 56, 65, 66, 69, 71, 72, 73, 76, 78, 79, 80
Institution of Royal Engineers: 3, 4, 5, 19, 20
Lieutenant-Colonel C. J. B. Jarrett: 61, 62, 63
Group Captain A. S. Mann: 74
Brigadier P. W. Mead: 41
Ministry of Defence, UK: 24, 40
Museum of Army Flying: 6, 47, 54, 70
Mrs. Parham: 43
Public Record Office: 21, 68
Royal Aeronautical Society: 2, 8, 9, 11
Royal Air Force Museum: 15
Royal Artillery Institution: 42, 46
Charles J. Russhon: 57, 58
Group Captain G. H. Sellers: 75
Mrs. D. Sole: 27
South African National Museum of Military History: 67

Introduction

The best way to explain this book is to describe how it happened. Jack Parham was its inspiration and must here be briefly introduced. Son of a Wiltshire farmer, an army officer, a man of many interests which included equitation, flying and later sailing, he made two notable contributions (recorded in this book) to the Allied success in the Second World War. He was a genius, less in the solving of complex problems than in the revelation of simple solutions which others had never perceived.

With Major E. M. G. Belfield he wrote *Unarmed into Battle,* the story of the air observation posts in the Second World War. After I had published *Soldiers in the Air,* about post-war army flying, Jack Parham suggested to me that a third volume was needed, chronologically preceding *Unarmed into Battle* and telling the story of previous efforts (from 1785 to 1939) to provide soldiers with air observation. He, by then, had failing eyesight and did not feel he could attempt the task. I told him that I would attempt it as soon as I retired from a somewhat demanding job I had at the time. He immediately gave me a copy of Snowden Gamble's *The Air Weapon,* from which I subsequently derived great pleasure and much assistance, as I invariably did from my many discussions with Jack Parham. He agreed to my using the title of this book – one he had used for a lecture in 1965. But, soon after I started to write, Jack Parham died. This was a sad parting for all his friends, and I must add here how much I felt the lack of his experience and wise advice.

As the book took shape, the problem of its boundaries arose. Once my researches had reached the First World War, I found myself immersed in studies not only of the growing expansion of Royal Flying Corps observation and reconnaissance, but also of the appearance of more aggressive roles and, in 1918, the rationalisation of air observation, not as one means of acquiring information but, surprisingly, as one function of flying. I did not intend my book to become a wide emanation from the balloon at Fleurus to cover the whole situation of naval, air force and (such as it was) army flying in 1939. On the other hand I could hardly omit the R.F.C.'s observation and reconnaissance for the Army from the background story of the Air O.P.s.

The year, 1939, with impending war and the three reconnaissance imponderables of the Autogiro, the *Lysander* and the Air O.P. concept, did not seem a very good point at which to end the story; 1945 seemed better. Perhaps I should not be able to divorce the Royal Air Force from my further studies. As I continued, my motives changed. I began to understand how the R.A.F.'s role of reconnaissance for the Army had been forced out of the limelight by the roles of fighting and bombing, more spectacular and satisfying to the R.A.F.'s desire for independence. I learnt too of the vast ignorance, both among air force and army writers of the efforts, achievements and devotion of the army co-operation and tactical reconnaissance squadrons of the Royal Air Force and felt the need for them to be adequately recorded, as Parham and Belfield had recorded those of the Air O.P.s.

This book has therefore become a history of air observation and reconnaissance for the British Army from 1785 to 1945, embracing balloons, kites and aeroplanes, the Royal Engineers, the Air Battalion, the Royal Flying Corps, the Royal Air Force and the Air O.P.s. Except where their stories march with that theme, this book makes no attempt to cover naval aviation or reconnaissance primarily for naval or air force purposes.

I write separately about my sources and have acknowledged there the kind and lavish help provided by very many individuals. There remain two minor matters to mention.

First I must refer to the frequently mentioned functions of 'observation' and 'reconnaissance'. I have generally used 'observation' to describe an individual's surveillance of a particular place or small area, either from a point of vantage on the ground or from a balloon or aeroplane flying in a restricted zone. I have used 'reconnaissance' to describe a deeper or wider search for information.

Secondly there is the matter of military and other decorations. After much consideration and several false starts, I finally decided to omit decorations when naming individual soldiers and airmen. This decision was in no way the result of egalitarian emotions but rather of the intolerable disturbance of the even flow of the English language by the decorations of the more senior officers.

PETER MEAD

Sources

---◇---

I started my investigations with Snowden Gamble's *The Air Weapon* and, before I had finished, I had read a further 166 books and a number of pamphlets, unpublished manuscripts, and articles from many journals. I had also studied some 150 Public Record Office files. A complete bibliography (though omitting individual designations of Public Record Office files) appears at the end of this book, to which references in the text may be linked.

Snowden Gamble's book on the pre-1914 period is outstanding, but I also derived much information from Brigadier Broke-Smith's *History of Early British Military Aeronautics* and Harald Penrose's *British Aviation, the Pioneer Years*. Colonel Waller's excellent manuscript history of the *Royal Engineers' Operations in South Africa, 1899–1902* has the most convincing information of the balloon operations of that time.

In the First World War period, I found Brigadier-General Sir James Edmonds's *Official History of Military Operations, France and Belgium* a sheet anchor. Sir Walter Raleigh's and H. A. Jones's volumes on *The War in the Air* are, of course, the recognised authority on the work of the Royal Flying Corps and Royal Air Force in the First World War and they contain a vast quantity of well-authenticated fact. The service atmosphere of the years following the war, during which period the work was written, may, however, have influenced their distinct bias in emphasis upon the fighting, and even the scarcely developed bombing, roles as compared with those of tactical, photographic and artillery reconnaissance. Christopher Cole's *Royal Flying Corps, 1915–1916,* a collection of operational communiqués of those years, was very useful in restoring the balance, while Brigadier-General E. C. Anstey's manuscript, *History of the Royal Artillery from 4th August, 1914,* contains much of value on the R.F.C.'s artillery observation role and Major Neumann's *The German Air Force in the Great War* gives very clearly the view from the other side of the hill. I was fortunate to be able to use the personal experience of Colonel R. MacLeod and Basil E. Catchpole, the former with Third Wing, R.F.C. on the Somme and the latter an artillery pilot of the R.F.C. and R.A.F. in 1918.

The period of the Second World War presented me with more problems than did the periods before it. With a few exceptions, the

Official Military Historians almost ignored air reconnaissance, seeming to regard it as a routine affair – like the soldiers' breakfasts, perhaps, a necessary preliminary to battle but hardly worthy of mention. Air force chroniclers, with one exception, concentrated on the aggressive roles. The exceptions were, admittedly, notable, General Playfair's four Official volumes on *The Mediterranean and Middle East,* Air Commodore Millington's *The Unseen Eye* (on air reconnaissance in north-west Africa and Italy) and the accounts of two of the Australian Official Historians, Lionel Wigmore and David Dexter, *The Japanese Thrust* and *The New Guinea Offensives,* respectively. The Air Observation Post story was well told in Parham and Belfield's *Unarmed into Battle* and more Air O.P. information was obtained from Brigadier A. L. Pemberton's authoritative volume on the Second World War's *Development of Artillery Tactics and Equipment.* For all these, there were many gaps, to fill which I had resort to the Royal Air Force Squadron, Wing and Group Operational Record Books in the Public Record Office.

I was lucky to be able to supplement these by discussions and correspondence with a large number of individual soldiers and airmen who had served, mostly in the air reconnaissance field, during the Second World War; these I have listed, with many other helpers, after the Bibliography. Many of them I traced through the kindness and competence of the A.R.8 (Air) branch of the Ministry of Defence and the Directorate of History in the Department of Defence in Ottawa. It would be invidious to particularise here but I would wish to record that very many of those who helped were extremely busy men, who nevertheless devoted an inordinate amount of time to answering my questions and to introducing me to further contacts. I am most grateful to them all.

I made myself a nuisance to a number of libraries and similar institutions which I have also listed after the Bibliography. I would like to pay a particular tribute to the staff of the Portugal Street branch of the Public Records Office, who delved swiftly and successfully for the great mass of files which I requested, and made it appear an interesting, almost exciting task. I acknowledge the particularly heavy load I placed on the Royal Artillery library, chiefly because of its adjacency to my home, and thank Major R. St. G. G. Bartelot, Miss Wood and the staff for their kindness. Without the ready help of Mr. E. H. Turner of the Air Historical Branch of the Ministry of Defence I should hardly have known where to start, and, among many other friendly, helpful and enthusiastic librarians, I must mention particularly Mr. C. A. Potts of the Ministry of Defence Central Library and Mr. F. S. White of the Adastral Library.

I must conclude with a note on illustrations. I feel these to be an important part of this particular book, especially the portraits of those who became prominent in the air reconnaissance field and, despite or perhaps because of that, have been in danger of becoming forgotten warriors. I have acknowledged much help from various museums, societies and institutes, among which the help given by Mr. M. Willis of the Imperial War Museum and Mr. D. C. Bateman of the Air Historical Branch was exceptional. Great kindness was shown me by many relatives, in making portraits available or in some cases in long and extensive research to locate such portraits. To all I am most grateful. Invidious though it may be to mention particular occasions, I feel I must mention the prolonged and successful detective work of Guy M. Burnand which resulted in the running to earth of a photograph of his relative, Lewis, and a comparable operation in the United States by Charles J. Russhon to obtain a copy of the air photograph with which he, as observer and photographer, had saved the 1944 Chindit operation from initial disaster.

PETER MEAD

CHAPTER 1

The Eye

———◇———

'Now anyone with experience of life in the forward area of battlefields knows
that here is an area where life is stripped down to very real 'realities' and that, away
out ahead of all other priorities, comes the question 'what is the enemy doing,
where exactly is he and where exactly are my people?' '
MAJOR-GENERAL JACK PARHAM, letter to the *Royal United
Service Institution Journal* of August 1966

Man is an aggressive animal; in this particular era we do not need,
surely, to substantiate this statement. Understanding of robust team
games and sports, and of less friendly forms of physical conflict, is
general; it is not a large mental step to a superficial understanding of the
clash of armed forces in battle.

Before such clash occurs, however, and throughout the subsequent
struggle, the contestants have another problem forever before them, the
problem of seeing their enemy, of knowing where to aim their blows, of
knowing how he aims his blows and of maintaining contact with friends
and allies. To this problem also there used to be a peace-time counter-
part, but modern life has blurred it. Children may tiptoe through the
woods in games of hide-and-seek but adults in cities are rarely confronted
by physical difficulties in locating and identifying their friends and
enemies. It is not instinctive, therefore, to recognise the urgent and
elemental need of soldiers, and of military units and formations, for
information, for observation, for reconnaissance.

Jeremy Taylor, in *This Band of Brothers*, one of the very few books with
Reconnaissance as its central theme, has put this matter very simply:

Since man first went to war he has employed the art of reconnaissance. If a man goes to war by himself, his first act is to turn himself
into a reconnaissance unit and go and see how the land lies and
whether his opponent can be taken off guard and laid out with the
knob-kerry from behind. When a number of men on each side engage
in war, the job of those men told off for reconnaissance work becomes
more complicated and divorced from the main business of fighting.
The knob-kerry needed for the *coup-de-grace* is now much larger, and
too heavy to be carried by the few men worming their way through
the bushes for a sight of the strength of the enemy. They need eyes,
not knob-kerries; a cunning for concealment and a good turn of speed
to get the news back, so the main force knows what to do.[1]

As long ago, probably, as the thirteenth century B.C., when the
Israelites had reached Kadesh in their wanderings, Moses sent a
reconassance party into South Canaan.[2] Its report, coupled with well
founded doubts as to the morale of his people, decided Moses against a
direct approach. When Joshua, his successor, eventually led his people

across Jordan from the east and against the defended town of Jericho, his first action was to send spies into the city. After Jericho, Joshua's next attempt was against Ai and failed at first because an inadequate reconnaissance had reported that city to be only lightly held.[3]

Biblical references to reconnaissance are not, however, so frequent as might be supposed from these early examples. It soon became recognised as a fact of war and was only mentioned when reconnaissance or the lack of it had spectacular consequences.

Speed was an obvious requirement of successful reconnaissance and it was natural therefore to enlist the horse's aid. The first cavalry units were no doubt small parties of unarmed men, horsed to help them evade capture and to bring back information quickly. Encounters with the enemy, inevitable whenever reconnaissance needed to be bold, led to the carrying of swords and sometimes bows and arrows; thus equipped, cavalry began to be used in larger numbers for related tasks such as the protection of flanks, of commanders' reconnaissances or of foraging parties. It was but a step hence to the use of formed bodies of armed cavalry to disrupt the enemy by shock action and to pursue them from the field.

An early example of a successful reconnaissance was that of Alexander the Great before the battle of Arbela, in Mesopotamia (331 B.C.). He spent part of the day before the battle, with a cavalry escort, viewing the position of the Persians, under Darius. He noticed that the ground in front of the position had been levelled, correctly deduced the enemy's intention of using chariots decisively and tailored his tactics to that threat.

Hannibal, in his long struggle against Rome, used heavy cavalry, armed with sword and spear, for shock action and his Numidian light cavalry for reconnaissance and harassing. His victory at Lake Trasimene (217 B.C.), however, which with Cannae established him in Italy for thirteen years, was less the result of his own reconnaissance than of the entire neglect of it by his opponent, Flaminius. The latter marched his army confidently into a horseshoe of hills with the lake at its open end; Hannibal's troops held the hills and his Numidians closed the gap – between hill and lake – after the Romans had passed through; the result was a massacre.

Interesting contrasts in reconnaissance are provided by the events of the autumn of A.D. 1066, in England. Harold of England, the mobility of whose levies was matched by the efficiency of his intelligence organisation, was awaiting a Norman invasion in the south when he was informed of the successful invasion of the north-east by Harald Hardrada of Norway, assisted by dissidents under Tostig, and of their defeat at Fulford of the Earls of Northumbria and Mercia. By 25th September, five days after that battle, Harold of England had marched north, collecting reinforcements en route, and had fallen upon his enemies at Stamford Bridge, seven miles east of York. The latter had taken no protective measures and sent out no patrols; completely surprised, the

Norwegians and their allies were utterly defeated and their leaders slain. Four days later, William of Normandy landed at Pevensey; on 1st October Harold set out for London and, after a short pause, continued south towards the Normans. William, however, had sent cavalry patrols well forward and was as thoroughly informed of English movements as was Harold of his. The two armies met on the well-known ground of Senlac, to the discomfiture of the English.

By the Middle Ages the cavalry of the European armies, designed originally for seeing, became more interested in killing. Heavily armoured knights, sometimes with lances, began to exercise an important influence in battle; they were unsuitably accoutred for reconnaissance, for which light cavalry was usually provided. The achievements of the latter, less easy to describe, less readily related to an ultimate victory and less exciting to audience or reader, have been less lavishly recorded than the cavalry charges. We shall find similar trends in the development of 'air cavalry'.

During the Thirty Years War (1618–48) and the clashes between Prussia and Austria a century later, there was considerable development in the 'shock' role of cavalry, incorporating for a period (and without great success) the use of firearms. The facts of war, however, prevented the arts of reconnaissance from being entirely neglected and the Austrians, in the eighteenth century, seem to have made something of a speciality of them. Denison described their cavalry as 'quite incapable of withstanding in the open plain the impetuous rush of the serried squadrons of the Prussian king; but in scouting, reconnoitring, and covering the front of an army, . . . more than a match for their opponents'.[4] Frederick the Great himself, it seems, recorded the Austrians' successes in cutting his communications, discovering all that passed in his camp and preventing his own patrolling.

For a final example of the results of faulty reconnaissance we may move forward to the South African War of 1899–1902 and to the Battle of Colenso. The Boers, under Botha, held with some 7,000 men the line of the Tugela River, a massif of broken hill country to the north and the one notable hill to the south of the river, Hlangwhane. The British General Buller approached from the south, with 19,000 men, on 14th December, 1899. 'The river', as the Official History somewhat naively records, 'because of the difficulty of approaching it, had not been systematically reconnoitred.[5] The maps provided were both inadequate and inaccurate. Buller did not, it seems, consider a preliminary operation to capture the vantage point of Hlangwhane; he examined the enemy's position through a telescope and that was that. A preliminary crossing was planned at a ford some four miles to the west, after which frontal attacks were to be made on Colenso in the centre, where there was a bridge, and on Hlangwhane on the right. The preliminary operation came to grief when the map, the ground and the allotted Kaffir guide disagreed as to the position of the ford, leaving the British infantry on the river bank under fire from well concealed Boer riflemen and artillery.

In the centre an advance was made down an open slope in full view of the Boers and the British field artillery was deployed, too far forward, in this same open country. In due course Buller ordered a general withdrawal, Boer casualties being twenty-seven, British over a thousand.

Failure to obtain information (often because of the superiority of enemy covering forces) or failure to convey to the commander information which has been obtained (usually because of faulty communications) results in a situation at the seat of command well described as the 'fog of war' – often, though not always, a preliminary to defeat.

The experiences of Wellington, Blücher and Napoleon in the Waterloo campaign afford interesting examples of the fog of war. Wellington and Blücher were alert to the probability of their adversary attempting to separate and defeat them in detail; they were resolved not to be separated – but separated they were. On the morning of 15th June, 1815, the Prussian I Corps was attacked on the river Sambre by French forces advancing towards Charleroi; the report of this did not reach Wellington, in Brussels, until 3 p.m. Another message, from Mons, was dispatched at 9.30 a.m. and arrived late in the evening.[6] Wellington was no doubt sensitive regarding his right flank which covered his base communications, and it was not until midnight that he ordered his reserve to move south from Brussels.[7] This delay contributed to the British delay in concentrating at Quatre Bras and thus to Blücher's isolation at Ligny on 16th June.

Blücher's force was driven off the field that evening, but no intelligence of this reached Wellington. During the night which followed, enemy were found on the road east of Quatre Bras and there was rumour that a message from Blücher had been intercepted. At 7 a.m. on the 17th intelligence was received (accidentally, according to Von Muffling, Blücher's representative with Wellington)[8] that Blücher was retreating upon Wavre. Wellington thereupon withdrew to the Waterloo position. He left at Hal a force of 18,000 men, to cover Brussels from a possible French move around his western flank. With better intelligence this detachment might not have been necessary.

These failures of intelligence or of its transmission pale into significance beside Napoleon's 'loss' of Blücher after the battle of Ligny. He sent Grouchy off, a little tardily, in Blücher's pursuit; Grouchy never caught up with him or with a knowledge of the situation. He eventually reached Wavre on the evening of 18th June (the fight at Waterloo, ten miles to the west, being by now in full swing) and was engaged there by the Prussian III Corps. Blücher had reached Wavre twenty-four hours earlier, had exchanged messages with Wellington and, early on the 18th, had set out with two corps to fall upon Napoleon's right flank.

A notorious example of fog of war was the situation of the German General Headquarters at Luxembourg during the battle of the Marne in September 1914. Liddell Hart well describes their inadequate communications and transport, the reluctance of the army commanders to report anything but successes (which they exaggerated) and von Moltke's

complete ignorance at the crisis of the battle of the movements and
location of his First Army.[9] The result, as we shall see in a later chapter,
was the mission of a mysterious Colonel Hentsch and the order for a
general German withdrawal.

Another example, again provided by the Germans who had however
by no means a monopoly of fogs of war, was the situation of General
Liman von Sanders in his headquarters at Nazareth in North Palestine
on 19th and 20th September, 1918. He had expected Allenby's offensive
to fall on the eastern flank and, on the night of the 18th, this attack
began. On the following morning the main blow was struck, however,
in the coastal sector, a breakthrough quickly achieved and the British
cavalry launched through the gap. The R.A.F. however, had bombed
and put out of action the main Turco-German telegraph and telephone
exchange at El Afule, as a result of which silence fell between von
Sanders and his subordinate commanders. Early on the 20th, the silence
still unbroken, von Sanders hurriedly left Nazareth as the British cavalry
entered.

The few examples given in this chapter of good and bad reconnaissance
may have served to indicate the Army's all-pervading need for information. Bad reconnaissance has led to spectacular military failures; good
reconnaissance has only rarely led, in itself, to spectacular events. Good
reconnaissance, however, gives a commander a regular, small advantage
and, in battle, it is the sum of these small advantages that gives victory.

Intelligence, which dispels the 'fog of war', is not, of course, obtained
solely through the medium of the human eye; the human ear has always
had a part to play, particularly since the invention of wireless with the
opportunity it gave for the interception of enemy transmissions. Here
we are concerned, however, with human eyes which, assisted by clari-
fying devices such as telescopes and binoculars or recording devices such
as cameras, have up to now been the principal means of obtaining
tactical information – the eyes of spies, of observers at points of vantage,
of reconnaissance patrols. We have seen, in this chapter, something of
the part played by eyes in the winning of battles and thus of wars; in the
following chapters we shall see the steps by which some of the eyes of the
British Army gradually moved into the air, and how they fared there.

The Eye on the Hill

———————◇———————

'I will lift up mine eyes unto the hills; from whence cometh my help.'
Psalm 121

Soldiers have always been attracted to the higher places. Before the days
of long-range weapons, high ground gave certain advantages to a
defensive position; stones and boulders were easier to roll downhill than
to hurl upward, arrows were easier to aim, those attackers who reached
the summit might be weary and would certainly be at some disadvantage
vis à vis the axemen or spearmen striking down at them.

There would be advantages to be gained from the extra observation
from the higher ground, anyhow by day, although the final approach of
an enemy to a summit position might be concealed by the conformation
of the slope to a greater extent than on the flat. Observers were certainly
posted on high ground on an enemy's probable approach route to give
warning, often by the well-known method of lighting fires on the peaks.

With the introduction of firearms, and with the increase in the size of
armies, commanders needed to occupy a point of vantage whence they
could assess the progress being made by the rival forces and determine
how and when and where to intervene. An early example of such an
observation post, quoted in many a history book, was Edward III's
windmill at Crecy. Burne writes of it: 'though not centrally situated (it)
allowed an uninterrupted view of the whole position and of the French
advance.'[1]

The great Duke of Marlborough, not unnaturally, took endless pains
to select his command posts at positions where observation was best and
it is interesting to learn how he combined good observation with military
genius and decisiveness of action. Here is his famous descendant and
biographer on a short phase of the Battle of Blenheim.[2]

Marlborough, who had lately been watching the battle from the
rising ground behind Unterglau, attended by his retinue, now came
quickly forward, passed the burning villages, crossed the (river) Nebel
by a causeway, and took personal control at the danger point. He led
forward three Hanoverian battalions from Holstein-Beck's reserve.
He made Colonel Blood bring a battery of cannon across the streamlet
. . . Meanwhile Marlborough had sent a personal message to Prince
Eugene asking for the use of Fugger's brigade.

Here, from the same pen, is a word-picture of the same great general
at Ramillies.[3]

Marlborough with his staff and retinue must at this time have been on the high ground . . . practically opposite to Villeroy and the Elector, though somewhat further south . . . Measuring and timing the forces now launched, he was entitled to the same assurance of success as he had felt before the final attack at Blenheim.

Forthwith he began the simple yet superb manoeuvre to which all the preliminaries had led, namely, the transference of all his cavalry to the left wing . . . Leaving Cadogan to enforce Orkney's withdrawal and to re-arrange the right, he ordered eighteen squadrons of that wing to trot across the rear of his infantry attack on Ramillies to the support of Overkirk's cavalry attack. He galloped on ahead of them with his personal staff.

The Duke of Wellington, a century later, acquired and used commanding ground in a very similar way. Here are two short extracts from Napier on the Battle of Talavera.[4]

Sir Arthur Wellesley from the summit of the hill on his left viewed the whole field of battle.

When the guards first made their rash charge, Sir Arthur, foreseeing the issue of it, had ordered the forty-eighth down from the hill, although a rough battle was going on there, and at the same time he directed Cotton's light cavalry to advance. These dispositions gained the day.

And we cannot leave Wellington without Philip Guedalla's description of the decisive moments at the Battle of Salamanca,[5] where 'forty thousand men were defeated in forty minutes'.

Wellington was 'stumping about and munching' in a little farmyard among the brown cottages of Los Arapiles, lunching apparently of alternate bites of chicken and glances at the French through a telescope . . . The Peer's lunch was interrupted by a final look towards the French. 'By God,' he suddenly exclaimed, 'That will do' – and scandalised Alava by flinging far over his shoulder the leg of chicken which he had been eating in his fingers. Then he cantered up the hill for a more comprehensive view, and the whole field was spread before him . . . 'Mon cher Alava,' he said cheerfully, 'Marmont est perdu', and rode off to launch the attack.

Of course a commander could not guarantee to find an all-embracing viewpoint on every battlefield through every phase of the battle, so, besides counting upon reports sent back to him from the forward units and formations, he often used the services of aides or 'gallopers' from his staff both to discover for him the situation in a given area and to convey his orders to subordinate leaders. An outstanding example of the drawbacks of this system was the failure in communication between Lords Raglan and Lucan at Balaclava, which led to the charge of the Light Brigade.

As armies increased in size and mobility commanders needed to inform themselves of what was happening in wide ares of countryside to their front and flanks. It was one of the roles of cavalry to reconnoitre, moving from one point of vantage to another. Dragoons were mounted infantry and could usefully picquet heights which dominated enemy approaches to a defensive position; light infantry carried out a similar role in closer proximity to the main position or to the main column on the move.

In the second half of the nineteenth century there came a great revolution in gun manufacture. For two hundred years there had been little change. Suitable projectiles had been loaded through the muzzles of smooth-bored iron guns mounted on wooden carriages and fired, by the application of flame or flint-spark, to an effective range of about 1,400 yards. By the beginning of the twentieth century, however, artillery, including that of the British Army, was equipped with breech-loading, rifled, steel guns, on relatively light metal carriages, with a range of 4,000 yards.

British gunners were slow to appreciate the tactical implications of these rapid developments. It needed the South African War to persuade them that, if the extra range obtained by the gun designers was to obtain an accurate engagement of a hostile target at that range, then it was no longer practicable for a battery commander to observe fire from the vicinity of the guns and give his orders to the latter by megaphone. The Boer artillery and riflemen demonstrated that guns needed to be, and, thanks to the invention of smokeless propellant-charges, could be concealed under cover, a little further back than customary, using some of that extra range to compensate. This made the British battery commander's job more difficult than ever, particularly as battery signallers, for some inconceivable reason, had been abolished in 1899. The solution was, of course, the observation post (O.P.), consisting essentially of a gunner officer in a position with visual command over the enemy-held area and with communication to the guns.

Once the penny had dropped, the gunners quickly became organised. Methods of indicating targets to batteries far out of sight of them, methods of laying guns without visual reference to targets, methods of passing fire-orders from O.P.s to gun positions by Semaphore, Heliograph, Lamp and Telephone – all were quickly developed. Back came the signallers. Progressive gunners took to the hills with equal enthusiasm to that of the light infantry, and inventive genius continued to be expended, right up to 1914, on a variety of 'observation ladders' for attachment to pack-saddles or carts, to give the extra command when no hills were available.

During the Great War the Army as a whole began to appreciate the advantages, quite apart from gunnery, of having this network of observers, with their now excellent communications extending back to artillery sub-units, units and headquarters, each one of which was closely linked with the infantry or cavalry units whom they were supporting or, further back, with the divisional and corps headquarters. The gunner network became the principal channel of information based on Observation – as distinct from Reconnaissance.

Long before this, however, the eye had taken to the air.

The Eye in the Air

———◇———

'Nothing,' replied the artist,
'will ever be attempted, if all possible objection must first be overcome.'
SAMUEL JOHNSON: '*Rasselas*'

Basil Collier suggests that the Chinese may have used man-lifting kites for battle-reconnaissance some two thousand years ago.[1] They were pioneers in kite-flying and it would indeed have been strange if they had not extended their researches into the carriage of voluntary or impressed passengers, and thus into the realm of military observation. Once the aeronautical design problem had been solved, no further difficulty confronted the military user; it is surprising, therefore, that almost eighteen hundred years went by before air-observers went into battle in the western world and that, when they did, it was not by kite but by balloon.

The French were in the forefront of balloon, as of much subsequent aeronautical, development. Two brothers, Joseph-Michel and Étienne-Jacques de Montgolfier, who were papermakers, designed and produced the first practicable balloons, activated by hot air. On 19th September, 1783, a sheep, cockerel and duck ascended from Versailles in a wicker basket beneath one of these balloons and on 15th October (if we discount for lack of evidence the Chinese kite-flyers) Jean-Francois-Pilâtre de Rozier became, in General Parham's words, 'the first chap to get an artifical view from the air', making an ascent in a captive balloon from the Faubourg Saint-Antoine, Paris.[2] Two days later he took up with him André-Giroud de Villette; this ascent was possibly of greater significance than the former one to the art of aerial observation, for de Villette subsequently recorded his impressions in a letter to *Le Journal de Paris*, including this (translated) extract:

'From that moment I was convinced that this apparatus, at little cost, could be made very useful to an army for discovering the position of its enemy, its movements, its advances, its dispositions, and that this information could be conveyed by a system of signals, to the troops looking after the apparatus.'[3]

This inspired a number of similar, and other very different, suggestions for the warlike employment of balloons.

Development of the hot-air balloon had severe limitations, however, and we should therefore look back a few more years to the most important date for the balloon, May 1776, when the physicist Henry Cavendish announced his discovery of the density of hydrogen (as it came to be called) – lower than that of any other known element. Parallel with the Montgolfiers' experiments, others, notably Barthélemy-Faujas de Saint-Fond and the chemist Jacques-Alexandre-César Charles, were wrestling with the problems of association between hydrogen and balloon-fabrics and the even more stubborn one of generating hydrogen in a suitable manner to inflate balloons. On 1st December, 1783, two and a half months after de Rozier's first ascent, Charles, and one of two instrument-maker brothers called Robert, made a 'free' ascent from the Tuileries and landed twenty-seven miles from Paris two hours later.

This was spectacular, but it was not the first free ascent, de Rozier and the Marquis d'Arlandes having made a five-mile and twenty-five-minute flight ten days previously – in their 'Montgolfière'. In the rivalry between the hot-air 'Montgolfières' and the hydrogen 'Charlières', the latter gradually drew ahead, however.

An Italian, Vincenzo Lunardi, seems to have made the first extended balloon flight in Great Britain, from the Honourable Artillery Company's Moorfields ground in September 1784, a controlled twenty-mile flight with an intermediate landing. James Sadler, the first Briton to contribute appreciably to the art, flew both hot-air and hydrogen balloons in 1784 and 1785, including one flight of fifty miles. The first British soldier to make a balloon ascent was Major John Money. He had been a Cornet of the 6th Inniskilling Dragoons but on promotion to Captain in 1770 transferred to the 9th Regiment of Foot and took part in Burgoyne's ill-fated Saratoga campaign in the American War of Independence, where he was taken prisoner and held until the end of the war. Money made his first balloon ascent on 3rd June 1785, together with George Blake (apparently representing the Royal Navy) and the balloon's owner, Jonathan Lockwood. They made the ascent from Tottenham Court Road in London and were forced down near Abridge, Essex. Joint-service co-operation suffered a setback when it became apparent that either Blake or Money would need to step out if the flight was to continue. They drew lots and Blake lost. The other two continued the flight to a point near Maldon, a total distance of forty miles. A subsequent solo flight by Money ended in his fortunate rescue after descending into the sea twenty miles off Great Yarmouth.

In Snowden Gamble's view, the first British suggestions for the military employment of balloons had been in a pamphlet *The Air Balloon: Or a Treatise on the Aerostatic Globe, Lately invented by The celebrated Mons. Montgolfier of Paris*, published as early as November, 1783.[4] They had included their use for reconnaissance and for aerial command posts. It is to be feared, however, that to the British people in general balloons were a bit of a joke.

Returning to France, we must mention particularly the name of Jean-Pierre Blanchard, who made a cross-channel flight in January 1785 and later a continental flight of three hundred miles. Militarily, ballooning developed at a rate which may surprise students of modern defence planning, research and development. After the French Revolution, her armies were in disarray and soon confronted by a hostile combination of Austria and Prussia; in these circumstances the Committee of Public Safety acted with commendable foresight in getting together in 1793 a 'Commission Scientifique' to advise them on measures which might help France over her many military difficulties. This commission included at least four individuals who had been involved in ballooning either from the aeronautical or chemical aspect.

On 14th July, 1793, the Commission Scientifique reported to the Committee of Public Safety that a number of captive balloons should be supplied to the armies of the Republic for reconnaissance – as quickly as possible. The Committee agreed, but stipulated that the existing process for producing hydrogen, involving sulphuric acid, should not be used because of the acute shortage of sulphur for gunpowder. Lavoisier, who had helped to develop the sulphuric acid method of producing balloon-hydrogen, and who was himself a member of the Commission Scientifique, now proposed a fresh method based on the analysis of water by passing steam over red-hot iron. A young chemist, Jean-Marie-Joseph Coutelle, was given the job of developing a practical and efficient adaptation of this method to the operation of balloons in the field. By mid-October he had completed his task and was sent to Maubeuge to sell the idea of the military balloon to Général de Division Jourdan, Commander of the Army of the Moselle.

Jourdan, expecting to be attacked at any moment, showed character-istic military reluctance to receive a 'trials organisation' on the battle-field, and Coutelle returned. It was decided to conduct further exper-iments and, to that end, Coutelle was alloted space at the Château de Meudon, which, with its grounds, had recently been appropriated by the Committee of Public Safety as a Military Trials establishment. He was also given a clever assistant, Nicolas-Jacques Conté. Together they succeeded, by the early spring of 1794, in producing a servicable generator of hydrogen and in demonstrating to the Committee that a balloon could quickly be inflated and simply and reliably launched, that observations of military value could be made from it and that com-munication between balloon and ground could be conducted by means of message bags and ground panels. Coutelle was thereupon com-missioned as a captain of artillery and authorised to raise, at Meudon, a 'Compagnie d'Aérostiers' (Aeronaut Company).

A high proportion of the rank and file of the company were to have had training in skilled trades; it was evidently already understood that a good air effort demands a good ground organisation. On 10th April, 1794, less than nine months after the original report of the Commission Scientifique, Coutelle was ordered forward to Maubeuge with a skeleton party to see if they could be of help to the French force besieged in that town, which they entered after infiltrating the Austrian forces. After losing three of the party killed during an irrelevant participation in a sortie by the garrison, but no doubt improving their image thereby, they erected their hydrogen generator and filled and launched their balloon, *L'Entreprenant*, a free translation of which might be 'Enterprise'. The pamphlet *Revue Historique No. 49, La Campagne de 1974 à l'Armée du Nord* contains copies of the sortie-reports of Coutelle and his observers;[5] they are highly professional and full of information, largely about the enemy's artillery and working-parties. Though the balloon was 'holed' by gunfire it was not put out of action.

Coutelle, ordered to move the balloon to the support of Jourdan, who was about to invest Charleroi, manhandled it fully inflated over the walls of Maubeuge at 2 a.m. and across twenty miles of country by the following evening. On the next day, 25th June, General Morlot, of Jourdan's staff, observed from the balloon for many hours. On the 26th the Austrian garrison capitulated, just as the Duke of Coburg arrived to raise the siege; battle was joined at Fleurus, Jourdan being successful. The balloon was employed, but to what effect is uncertain. Morlot seems to have observed once again, not always very accurately according to Jourdan, who claimed that the balloon's only essential service was to astonish the enemy. Reports from the latter however indicated their conviction that the balloon had been successful and that the French had changed their dispositions as a result of observations from it.[6] Coutelle made no extravagant claims. 'I shan't say,' as Tissandier quotes him and the present author freely translates, '. . . that the balloon won the battle of Fleurus . . . What I can say is that, being trained to use my glasses in spite of the oscillation and swaying due to the wind, I was able to distinguish infantry, cavalry and artillery, their movement and, in general, their numbers.'[7]

Soon afterwards l'Entreprenant was damaged, but was repaired in time to take part in the forcing of the passage of the River Ourthe, south of Liège. It has been suggested that the French enveloping movement, which followed the river crossing, resulted from quick intelligence from the balloon and that a captured enemy officer remarked to his captors that 'one would have supposed that the French general's eyes were in our camp'.[8] This remark, and the Austrian reactions to the balloon at Fleurus, illustrate a significant tendency (which we shall notice from time to time) for the efforts of enemy air observers to be more readily appreciated than those of one's own. The French army now advanced to the Rhine, and Coutelle took the opportunity to form a base store and workshop for the balloon operations. Among other balloons constructed at Meudon were two of elongated shape, one of which was tried out, but rejected, on the Liège front.[9]

Three days before the battle of Fleurus orders had been given for the raising of a second Compagnie d'Aérostiers at Meudon and in October 1794 the 'École Nationale Aérostatique de Meudon' was formed for the training of aérostiers. Conté was appointed director, while the two companies were increased in strength, both of men and balloons, and grouped under command of Coutelle as battalion commander.

In April 1795, the second company joined General Pichegru's Army of the Rhine and Moselle, under Coutelle's command. Operating the balloon *L'Entreprenant*, this company took part in the siege of Mainz and, in 1796, marched with Général de Division Moreau to Augsburg. The French generals were not impressed with the value of the aérostiers to the army, however, and they were allowed to lapse into virtual inactivity. The First Company, meanwhile, took part in Jourdan's advance beyond the Rhine and was captured by the Austrians at Wurzburg in September 1796.

The personnel of the First Company were released from captivity under treaty terms, and were re-equipped. In 1798, under Coutelle, they sailed to join Napoleon's expedition to Egypt but Nelson sank the ship with the balloon and stores in Aboukir Bay, and that was the end. Between 1799 and 1801 the whole of the French military balloon organisation was disbanded, and with it – in France and elsewhere – military interest in balloons virtually disappeared for fifty years.

After the scientific and organisational brilliance with which the French launched their balloon service, its early and complete collapse was surprising. It was, of course, the beginning of something rather complex – a compound of aeronautics, observation and communication. Perhaps, as General Parham has suggested, the idea was 'oversold' by the aérostiers; the French generals, fighting their own battles, saw nothing inherently difficult in the balloons and expected better results. Jourdan once complained that the balloon observers could see no farther than the enemy's front line, and it is noticeable that they operated at heights of no more than 800 to 1,200 feet – due perhaps to cable limitations. Administratively, the balloon companies were certainly awkward to handle.

In two years, however, one would have expected the aérostiers to have got over their teething troubles. That they had not, one must probably ascribe to the shape of the spherical balloon; moored in a wind, it would oscillate to and fro, causing at least inaccurate observation and at worst acute air-sickness and a risk of structural failure.

If the French military leaders had lacked the vision to build on the very enterprising start their aérostiers had made, the British military leaders had evinced not the slightest desire even to experiment in that direction. Only John Money, undeterred by the narrowness of his escape from drowning, kept agitating for the military observation balloon. A restless and explosive character, he was an early advocate of the British Army's need for 'chasseurs' (light infantry) for use in close country. He offered his services, in 1790, to the Belgian rebels against the Austrians and, as a Major-General, commanded a force of about 5,000 in the final (unsuccessful) operations. In 1803 he dedicated to the Secretary at War a *Short Treatise on the Use of Balloons and Field Observators in Military Operations*, in which he wrote as follows:

I would not consult old Generals whether balloons or field obser- vators[10] could be of use to the army, for I know what the answer would be, 'that as we have done hitherto very well without them, then

we may still do without them', and so we did without light artillery,
riflemen and telegraphs, &c., and not till we had ocular demonstrations
of their use were they adopted.' [11]

For this shaft (which did not, it seems, impair his eventual advancement to full general), and for his personal enterprise in the air, we must
rate John Money the first pioneer of the British Air Observation Post.

With the coming of peace in 1815 ballooning seems to have been
established as a sport; there was little official recognition that it had
anything to do with war. Nor is there much record of pressure on the
military authorities to adopt balloons for observation, though one or two
suggestions envisaged bombing from balloons; a less promising role, one
would have thought.

Quite early in the century Sir George Cayley had made a deep study
of the science of heavier-than-air flight, supported by tests with models
on 'whirling arms'. He published the results in periodic treatises and
before 1810 seems to have built and launched a full-sized, but unmanned,
glider. Some forty-two years later he built his last glider, in which his
coachman may have been an involuntary, and certainly uncontrolling,
passenger. William Henson and John Stringfellow designed and experimented with powered models.

Henry Coxwell, an experienced balloonist, made prolonged but unsuccessful efforts to persuade the War Office to use balloons in the Crimea
and elsewhere,[12] and in 1855 General (as he became) Henry Lefroy, one
of the most scientific of British soldiers, proposed that a balloon be
manufactured for experiments by the Royal Engineers. The latter
proposal was put to a Select Committee whose youngest member was a
boy of sixty-four years, and its fate can be imagined. At the same time
Frederick Abel, F.R.S. designed a means of producing hydrogen by the
interaction of zinc and sulphuric acid, but failed to interest the War
Office.

Meanwhile a French clockmaker, Pierre Jullien, produced a model
airship with two clockwork propellors and this inspired Henri Giffard to
build and fly a powered airship, 144 feet long with a 3 h.p. steam
engine. This first powered flight was made, from Paris needless to say,
on 24th September, 1852.

In the American Civil War the Federal forces employed a small
number of balloons, operated by non-military and reputedly not very
co-operative aeronauts. As in the case of Coutelle's balloons, it is difficult
to find in the general histories references to the performance of the
Federal balloons; one is driven to conclude that they achieved few
positive results. Early in the war an artillery bombardment, with balloon
observation and some pretty complicated signal arrangements, was
planned against the Confederate outposts after the first battle of Bull
Run; it may well have actually taken place. Later, in the battles of the
Yorktown Peninsula, at least one shoot of this kind actually occurred.

The electric telegraph was, at this period, used from air to ground and was, on one occasion it seems, connected with the line to Washington, which became in direct receipt of the balloonists' battle reports. The stability of the spherical balloon was once again in question and, soon after the Peninsula battles, the Federals discontinued its use.

A Confederate general, writing of Gettysburg, however, indicates the sort of 'negative' result which Air observation posts have (often unwittingly) achieved.[13] 'I was particularly cautioned', he writes, 'in moving the artillery, to keep it out of sight of the signal station upon Round Top,' and he adds the footnote:

This suggests the remark that I have never understood why the enemy abandoned the use of military balloons early in 1863, after having used them extensively up to that time. Even if the observers never saw anything they would have been worth all they cost for the annoyance and delays they caused us in trying to keep our movements out of their sight. That wretched little signal station up on Round Top that day caused one of our divisions to lose over two hours, and probably delayed our assault nearly that long. During that time a Federal corps arrived near Round Top and became an important factor in the action which followed.

The Confederates, incidentally, could operate only one balloon at a time, first a hot-air balloon and then a multicoloured coal-gas balloon, by tradition made from the silk dresses of the patriotic ladies of Richmond. It was captured in due course but the ladies of Richmond seem to have obliged once more.

Captain F. Beaumont, of the Royal Engineers, had been in 1861 a military observer with the Federal forces and had returned to England stimulated by the possibilities of balloons and anxious so to stimulate the War Office. He was joined in this endeavour by a brother officer, Lieutenant George Edward Grover, a determined individual with financial resources which he was prepared to expend on his cause.

Grover sent a paper on the employment of military balloons to the Ordnance Select Committee, whose secretary happened to be that same Henry Lefroy, who, seven years previously, had unsuccessfully proposed the manufacture of an experimental balloon for the Royal Engineers. The committee reported in February 1862 that the employment of balloons as one of the resources of modern warfare was not in doubt, nor had they many problems still to solve. To solve them, they wished to conduct trials in the summer. The War Office, however, cleverly wasted a year by calling for the experiences of a number of other armies in the operation of balloons, receiving in reply a variety of pessimistic reports. The committee reiterated their request for trials and, after some argument, the War Office agreed to experimental ascents by Coxwell, assisted by Beaumont and Grover and with the active participation of members of the Select Committee, at Aldershot and later at Woolwich.

Two years now passed while Frederick Abel conducted experiments in materials for the envelopes of balloons and in the generation of hydrogen in bulk. In February 1865, seventy years and eight months after the Battle of Fleurus, the Select Committee reported on the satisfactory outcome of the trials but was not prepared to recommend 'the special preparation of a balloon equipment in times of profound peace'.[14]

Grover made one more effort in 1868, based on successful balloon operations by the Brazilian Army against the Paraguayans; he asked for £100 to be spent on the construction of a gas-generating apparatus large enough for use in the field. The Ordnance Select Committee would not devote time or money to an Inquiry, and the Secretary of State vetoed the £100.

'Nevertheless,' says Gamble of George Edward Grover, 'he, more than any other officer, deserves the title of the 'Father of English military aeronautics!'[15]

Neither side, in the Franco-Prussian war of 1870, achieved much with balloons in the field, but their use by the French in the siege of Paris was spectacular. Three captive balloon stations were set up for reconnaissance and free balloons of various sizes subsequently conveyed from Paris 164 persons, 381 carrier pigeons, five dogs and 3,000,000 letters.[16] Of 65 such balloons, two were lost at sea and five captured by the Prussians. It is not surprising that the French Government reformed, again at Meudon, the military aeronautical establishment which Napoleon had so abruptly abolished seventy-five years before.

The British War Office felt the need for a standing body to which it could refer problems concerning inventions of, and improvements to, engineering equipment, and revived the so-called 'Royal Engineer Committee'; within months this Committee was asked to investigate the advisability of using balloons with the Army in the field. They leant upon a sub-committee which, strangely enough, turned out to consist of Beaumont, Grover and Abel – now Sir Frederick Abel, Bart., K.C.B. The War Office still resisted proposals to buy a balloon, but permitted experiments in gas-generation both by the zinc-and-sulphuric-acid system and by passing steam over red-hot iron.

And now, in 1878, there appeared upon the scene the third and best known of the early pioneers of British military aeronautics – Captain James Lethbridge Templer, of the 2nd Middlesex (later King's Royal Rifle Corps) Militia and already an experienced balloonist. Thirty-three years old in that year, he is described as tall, powerful, dark, of aspect stern and forbidding, not always popular with superiors by virtue of his disregard of regulations and impatience with official delays and restrictions, but a man who usually got his way. Early in 1878 he met Abel at Woolwich; the latter suggested that Templer should place his experience at the disposal of the Army and this suggestion was followed up. The War Office promptly allocated £150 towards the cost of a balloon and authorised Templer and Captain H. P. Lee, Royal Engineers, to carry out experiments. Soon afterwards they agreed to pay the former as a balloon instructor. Only C. Northcote Parkinson could have explained this sudden loosening of the money bags after such long and determined resistance.[17] By August *Pioneer*, the first British military balloon, had been constructed for £71 and had made its first ascent. Templer also experimented in the generation of hydrogen by the 'red-hot iron' method. The War Office, careful to disclaim acceptance of the balloon as Army equipment, nevertheless decided to finance continued experiment. The foot was in the door.

Within a year the Balloon store in the Woolwich Arsenal contained five balloons. In 1880 the War Office carried out vulnerability trials, shrapnel being fired at a balloon with surprisingly unspectacular results.[18] Two years later it was decided that a number of officers and men of the Royal Engineers should be trained in ballooning, and the balloons were removed from Woolwich to Chatham. It was a fortunate decision to confide military ballooning to the Royal Engineers, a clever and, for the times, technical corps, calculated to develop a sound maintenance system for the balloons but at the same time no strangers to the forward part of the battlefield. The training of the aeronauts incorporated aerial reconnaissance, photography and signalling; in 1880, and again in 1882, a balloon detachment took part in the Aldershot manoeuvres. Research of all kinds continued at Chatham; gold-beaters' skin became the standard material for the balloon envelopes; the 'red-hot iron' method of hydrogen generation gave way to the 'sulphuric acid' and 'electrolysis of water' methods.

In 1884 an expedition was sent to Bechuanaland to deal with Boer raiders and to pacify the country, and a balloon detachment accompanied the force. Major Herbert Elsdale, R.E. commanded this first-ever British air unit to go into action and they were favourably reported.

After the death of Gordon and fall of Khartoum in the following year, Templer himself took out a detachment of three balloons to Suakin; as in Bechuanaland the gas was taken out in cylinders. The balloons were used, but high winds hindered operations. Protective observation was, however, provided for columns moving across the desert, and Broke-Smith writes that a 'six-stone Arab, Ali Kerar', sent up by balloon to a height of 2,000 feet, reported big guns to be firing at Suakin, twenty-eight miles away, and that this unlikely report was confirmed as a *feu de joie* in honour of the Khedive's birthday.

In 1886 trials were carried out on the artillery ranges at Lydd, in the observation and correction of artillery fire by balloon observation, and earned commendation from the Ordnance Select Committee. In 1889 a balloon detachment taking part in summer manoeuvres in Aldershot Command had an admitted stroke of luck, a negative reconnaissance report by a Sapper subaltern, B. R. Ward, after a dusk sortie, inspiring a night attack and proving to have been accurate. Shortly afterwards, at a parade for the German emperor who attended the manoeuvres, Lieutenant Ward 'marched past' in the balloon, at about 300 feet altitude.

One or other, or both, of these events led to a pro-balloon report to the War Office from Lieutenant-General Sir Evelyn Wood, who also recommended that the Balloon establishment should move from Chatham to Aldershot, where it would get more realistic training. Four years later this move took place. By now it could be said that the Balloon 'section' and its parent establishment had been fully accepted into the Army fold and made respectable by inclusion in the Army Estimates. Templer had become, in turn, 'Instructor-in-Ballooning' and 'Officer in Charge of Balloons'; he was now a Lieutenant-Colonel. In 1897, when the organisation had settled down in Aldershot, he became 'Superintendent of the Balloon Factory'.

During the last ten years of the century there was steady development in balloon training and equipment. Balloon detachments regularly attended artillery practice-camps and courses were held for the training of officers of all arms and of staff-officers. A *Manual of Military Ballooning* was published. Free-run ballooning (as opposed to tethered or captive) was taught, not only to give aeronauts a sporting chance of landing their captive balloons, should they come adrift, but also as a military art, for reconnaissance or even bombing. Captive balloons could safely operate, it was thought, in winds up to 20 m.p.h., normally at a height of about 1,000 feet, two men being carried under such conditions. Communication with the ground was normally by means of reports and sketches sent down the cable in weighted bags, or by telephone. The transport of a one-balloon section consisted of eight wagons, one for the balloon, cable and hand-winch, one for miscellaneous stores and six for hydrogen in tubes (54 tubes in all). This would enable a well-trained detachment to fill their balloon in twenty minutes.

Such was the situation (in the British Army) on the eve of the South African War. Other developments, however, unrelated to the captive balloon, had taken place in Britain and elsewhere and were relevant to military reconnaissance and the air observation post.

The second half of the nineteenth century had seen some development in the power-driven balloon, 'dirigible' or 'airship'. The associated problems of engine-ignition and the inflammability of hydrogen had not been solved, however, and Count Zeppelin's first large rigid airship was still uncompleted. The British War Office had sanctioned no experiments in this field.

Man-carrying kites, of which more will be written in the next chapter, were under trial by the War Office in the eighteen-seventies and again, on the persuasion of Captain B. F. S. Baden-Powell, Scots Guards, in the eighteen-nineties. A sapper was raised at Pirbright Camp in 1894, soon after which it was decided that kites should be held on Balloon Sections' establishment.

The German Otto Lilienthal, who made more than two thousand glider flights before he was killed in 1896, inspired interest in heavier-than-air flying machines. Hiram Maxim, engineer, designer and show-man, made exhaustive studies and tests of aerofoil sections, both on 'whirling arms' and in a wind tunnel. In 1893 he installed a steam engine in a very large biplane indeed (8,000 lb all-up weight, according to Harald Penrose)[19] which ran along a specially built track, with another higher track designed to restrain it from full flight but through which the machine burst on one occasion for a free flight of 600 feet, with a crew of four.

Percy Pilcher, one of Maxim's team and a builder on Otto Lilienthal's experience, designed, and built and flew a number of gliders. At the time of his death in 1899 – due to structural failure in flight of the last of his gliders – he and Maxim were working on a helicopter design.

No one had yet solved, practically, the problem of exercising lateral control of a winged aircraft in flight, Lilenthal's method of shifting his body position, and thus the centre of gravity of the man-machine combination, having obvious limitations. The most relevant of all aeronautical activities at the end of the century were therefore those of the cycle manufacturers of Dayton, Ohio, Wilbur and Orville Wright who, in 1899, built a biplane glider with an arrangement for countering rolling tendencies by controlled twisting or 'warping' of the wings.

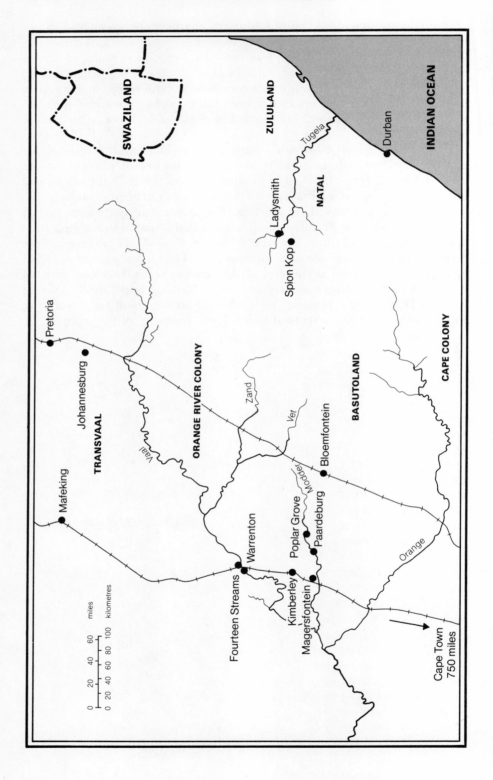

INDIAN OCEAN

SWAZILAND

ZULULAND

Tugela

Durban

Ladysmith

NATAL

Spion Kop

Pretoria

Johannesburg

TRANSVAAL

Zand

Vet

ORANGE RIVER COLONY

Vaal

BASUTOLAND

Bloemfontein

Mafeking

Modder

CAPE COLONY

Poplar Grove

Warrenton

Paardeburg

Orange

Fourteen Streams

Kimberley

Magersfontein

Cape Town
750 miles

miles
kilometres

0   20   40   60
0 20 40 60 80 100

Boers, Balloons,
The Brothers Wright,
and Blériot

———————◇———————

'WAR AIRSHIPS – Nothing to be feared for a long time'
Heading of War Office press hand-out, 23rd July, 1908.

The South African War was the first real military test for British aeronautics. As with the French experiences over a century before, it is extremely difficult to assess the result.

Three Balloon sections were sent out from England, the 2nd Balloon Section arriving at Durban on 26th October, 1899, and the 1st Balloon Section at Cape Town on 22nd November. The 3rd Balloon Section reached Cape Town on 7th March, 1900. Balloon factories were set up both at Cape Town and Durban; hydrogen was produced by them, and also received from England in tubes. During the course of the war the Aldershot Balloon Factory doubled its output and sent, altogether, thirty balloons to South Africa.

The 2nd Balloon Section, under Major G. M. Heath, R.E., reached Ladysmith, took part in the battles outside that town and was besieged with the rest of General Sir George White's force. The balloons regularly came under Boer artillery fire and were hit on several occasions though never thus destroyed. Ascents were made from within the Ladysmith defences for about a month before the gas ran out and, it is claimed, useful information was obtained about enemy positions.[1] Heath, who was to become a General in later years, was awarded the Distinguished Service Order. Rear echelons of this section, which were not besieged in Ladysmith, were organised by Captain G. E. Phillips, R.E. into an improvised balloon section, with the help of Royal Navy and Royal Artillery personnel. This section took part in the battles of Potgeiter's Drift (where Phillips was wounded), Vaal Krantz and possibly Spion Kop – not, unfortunately, Colenso.[2]

The 1st Balloon Section (Captain H. B. Jones, R.E.) came up with General Lord Methuen's advance at the Modder River and took part in the battles of Magersfontein and Paardeberg on 11th December 1899 and 24th February 1900, respectively. At Magersfontein, so the Royal Artillery historian reports, howitzers of the 65th Battery were enabled by balloon observation to search with fire the ground immediately behind the ridge.[3] At Paardeberg there was further artillery co-operation of which the gunners reported: '. . . although communication between battery and balloon was in its infancy much useful information was received.'[4] The balloon did have a major success, however, when

Lieutenant A. H. W. Grubb, R.E. spotted Cronje's laager and sketched it; the information derived from this sketch was the basis of the plan for the attack on the laager, which was followed shortly by Cronje's surrender.

This section was used in the subsequent actions of Poplar Grove and the Vet and Zand Rivers and finally outside Pretoria, after which it ceased to be operational. The Section Commander was awarded a Brevet Majority while his subaltern, Grubb, received the D.S.O., perhaps some indication of the importance of his work at Paardeberg.

The 3rd Balloon Section had in Lieutenant (Temporary-Major) R. B. D. Blakeney a commander with the knack of writing clear and useful operational reports, and he has left behind him a much clearer picture of the Section's activities than exists of any previous balloon operations. The 3rd Section reached Warrenton on 23rd April, 1900, and joined General Sir Archibald Hunter's 10th Division, tasked to march to the relief of Mafeking. Between 23rd April and 5th May a force of infantry and artillery engaged and held the attention of the Boers, in position north of the River Vaal, at Fourteen Streams, while the main body of the division crossed the river further west, defeated the Boer flank guard and forced a general withdrawal from the river line. The Balloon Section provided eyes for the demonstration force opposite the Fourteen Streams position.

On the 24th April the Section was given the following tasks:
a. To reconnoitre the position of enemy camps.
b. To search for alternative gun emplacements or masked batteries.
c. To report on the condition of the piers of the deviation railway bridge over the Vaal (which scouts could not reach).
d. To report any enemy attempt at counterattack on the right flank or rear.

The Observing Officer quickly reported enemy gun positions and the lack of any sign of flank attack. At 10 a.m. telegraphic communication with Kimberley was interrupted and the balloon observer was able to say that the enemy was not responsible for this. By the afternoon detailed information had been given of the enemy's three camps and a 'tolerably accurate estimate' of the damage to the bridges. The effect of our artillery fire was observed, but due to lack of telephone communication it was not possible to control fire. The section's report on the day's operations concluded with a note on the desirability of alternate means of signalling and of much practice.[5]

On the following day small enemy working parties were seen making entrenchments. They were out of range of the field guns and the idea was discussed of getting up a 6-inch gun on a railway truck and directing its fire from the balloon. This plan was set in motion.

Daily thereafter the balloon was used for directing the fire of the 5-inch howitzers of 37th Battery, Royal Field Artillery, at targets unseen from the ground, and for observing enemy movement. Control of fire was reported to be satisfactory, provided the balloon was close to the guns. It seems possible that it was achieved by the simple expedient of shouting down observations of fall of shot with the aid of a megaphone. Broke-Smith states that Captain G. F. MacMunn, Royal Artillery, frequently took part in observation from the balloon; it might be fair to say, therefore, that, while the gunners in South Africa were only now discovering the need for observation posts, the 37th Battery at Fourteen Streams was already using an *air* observation post.

On about 2nd May the 6-inch gun arrived. Two of the enemy's camps were visible only from the balloon and these were now engaged – estimated errors in each round being shouted down by the observing officer. The Section's report claimed success 'beyond anticipation', the sixth shot of each series, on average, going unpleasantly near for the defenders. One of the camps was reported damaged, the other wrecked.

Later the 6-inch gun and the balloon were moved forward a mile, where they were within range of hostile artillery. Three enemy guns opened up – they had been silent since a heavy British artillery bombardment of the 29th. They were well-concealed and used smokeless powder but from the balloon Captain Warry spotted the firing of the first round and directed the 6-inch gun accordingly. The sixth round was reported 'Target' and six more rounds silenced the enemy artillery for the day. The performance was repeated on the following day, after which there was no further enemy artillery activity.

When the main divisional attack developed against the Boer's right flank, north of the river, the enemy's redeployment and the movement of reinforcements were seen and reported by the balloon observers.

This brought to an end the balloon operations of this section, as of the other two sections. The period of guerilla warfare which followed provided little opportunity for these not very mobile units and they were either disbanded or converted to other roles.

But, the reader must ask, what of the great Templer? Did this war provide no outlet for his inventive resource? Indeed it did, providing high farce in the process, for it was discovered that, besides being the greatest British expert on military balloons, Templer had somehow become also the greatest military expert on steam traction engines. And so off to South Africa he went in November, 1899, as Director of Steam Road Transport, together with a shipload of traction engines which were wrecked en route; we need not pursue the story of his activities for the next two years.

Assessment of the achievements of the balloon sections in the South African War is made very difficult by the differing attitudes of authors with aviation interest and those without it. Accounts by former tend to suggest high, even decisive, achievement, but in other accounts (including official ones) balloons are seldom mentioned. Percy Walker claims that there was wholesale military 'prejudice' against balloons,[6] even that the British soldier believed balloon observation to be unfair/tactics against a chivalrous opponent. Soldiers at war, however, are never prejudiced against methods and equipment which help to win battles and prevent casualties, and very quick to understand that it is their business, and that of their commanders, to gain what advantages they can to offset those of their opponent.

The information which has come down to us does not indicate many spectacular achievements by the balloons. In itself, this does not necessarily argue inefficiency; the activities of the technically first-rate artillery observation posts of (for example) the 1914–18 war find little place in subsequent accounts; it is not those O.P.s, nor even the information they sent back, but what the commander did with the information which appears in the military histories. It is significant that the Army Estimates for 1901–02 continued to make provision for balloon sections – on a slightly increased scale – and that those Boer War commanders and other officers who appeared before the Committee on Military Ballooning of 1903–4 (which will be mentioned again) considered that the balloons had served their purpose and should continue to be used.

The balloon sections undoubtedly encountered difficulties. Major B. F. S. Baden-Powell mentioned some of these in an interesting article in *The Aeronautical Journal* of January 1902. South Africa, he believed, was unfavourable country for balloon operations, both by virtue of the rarefied air and turbulence of the high altitudes and also of the excellent ground observation posts to be found.[7] He adversely criticised the balloon sections, however, for a tendency to make their ascents too far back from the front line, whence they could not observe so effectively over the enemy and, in particular, distinguish the false crests and dead ground which deceive the ground observer. Baden-Powell was himself an aeronaut and his criticisms are important. There were other difficulties, however, for which the balloon sections could not altogether be blamed. The need to move their gas from place to place made them somewhat immobile, particularly when – as normally in South Africa – oxen had to be used. Communications were not good, particularly with the gunners, who should have been the chief beneficiaries of the balloons' services but were handicapped, both by having lost their signallers just before the war began and by a revolution in gunnery which they had not fully appreciated and which had confronted them with major changes in the midst of battle.[8] The British Army as a whole did not perform too brilliantly in this encounter and it would be unreasonable to expect a higher standard from a newly created force operating in a strange element than from the rest of the Army.

It is always worthwhile to discover the views of the enemy and here, at any rate, we have the view of one unusual character who fought with the Boers – Colonel Arthur Lynch. Australian-born of Irish and Scottish parents and educated in four Australian and European capitals, a qualified physician and surgeon, he went to South Africa as an English newspaper correspondent, joined the Boers and was made a colonel in their army. He seems to have fought with a Boer Irish Brigade on the Natal front until late in 1900 when he was sent to the United States to seek American support. Thence he went to Paris where, among other things, he lectured on the role of English military balloons in the South African War; we are indebted to Mr. Percy Walker for details of this lecture.[9]

Lynch rated the British military balloon organisation in advance of that of other nations. He paid tribute to the performance of the British balloons both in Natal, on the Modder River and at Fourteen Streams; he claimed that it was through balloon observation that the 'English' overcame the difficulty posed by smokeless powder and were able to locate the Boer batteries, as well as other defences, and from this often divine the Boer intentions. The Boers, he said, hated the balloons – reminder of British scientific advantage in at least one field. Lynch may well have overrated the achievements of the British balloons, but it would appear that the Boers did likewise, to their moral disadvantage. This side-effect, as it were, of aerial observation should not be under-rated.

In 1900 a 4th Balloon Section was formed as part of the British force engaged in the war of the Boxer rebellion in China; fighting had finished by the time it arrived, however. Part of this Section was thereupon moved to India as an experimental unit, where they faced climatic and transport difficulties. Direction of artillery fire was practised at one practice camp, at least, but the balloons do not seem to have made much impact on the army in general and, in 1911, the Section was disbanded. In 1901 the Balloon Factory supplied two balloons for Captain Scott's Antarctic expedition in the *Discovery*; one would have expected them to have been very useful for short-range reconnaissance but Scott was unimpressed by them.[10]

After the South African War the Balloon Sections, back at Aldershot, acquired a separate identity to that of the Balloon Factory, the latter being confined to manufacture, development and research. From 1903 Lieutenant-Colonel J. E. Capper, C.B., R.E. commanded the Balloon Sections – or Balloon Companies as they became two years later. Templer, who had returned from South Africa in 1901, was Superin-tendent of the Factory which, with determined lack of logic, continued to develop steam traction engines as well as balloons.

In 1903 a Committee on Military Ballooning was set up by the War Office 'to report generally upon the extent to which it is desirable to attempt to improve and develop military ballooning, having regard to the experience of two wars and to progress made in this service both by our own country and other nations.' The four military members of the committee were all to become generals, one of them – Lieutenant-Colonel Henry Wilson – Chief of the Imperial General Staff.[11]

This committee took evidence from British commanders in the South African War, from commanders of the balloon sections in that war, from foreign countries and no doubt from Colonel Templer. If the com-manders were not over-enthusiastic, the committee seems to have been in no doubt that observation from the air was now a necessary military art and must continue. French ballooning equipment was thought to be insufficiently robust and German equipment too robust and inclined to be ponderous. Both these countries had been experimenting with dirigibles and Templer, who had visited Paris eighteen months before, had returned convinced that the British should be doing likewise. The Committee on Military Ballooning agreed with him – strongly enough to make a special interim report recommending immediate research into dirigibles by the Balloon Factory, which they invited to cease work on steam traction engines.

In their final report they recommended future organisations and establishments for balloon sections, the formation of a balloon school, the development of an elongated balloon of improved stability, the continued development of man-lifting kites and the further development of photography from the air. This was indeed a forward-looking and enterprising report, but Walker comments on the irony by which almost everything the committee recommended was to be made out-of-date in a short space of time by the continued activities of the Wright brothers.

Man-lifting kites were the obvious accompaniment to observation balloons, the former effective in strong winds when the latter could not safely operate. Although, as we have seen, a soldier had been raised by kite in 1894, it was not until Samuel Franklin Cody started his experiments that we were on our way to a safe and realistic system. A colourful character, Cody had been born in Texas about 1861 (since he seems never to have learnt to read or write, historical exactness is difficult) and graduated as cowboy, horse-breaker and crack rifle shot. He prospected in Alaska for gold – unsuccessfully – and performed in a wild west show. He then came to England with his own music hall turn of the same sort, in which his English wife and his sons played active parts. Between 1892 and 1896 he toured Europe, after which he settled in England, though not naturalised until 1909. He made a lot of money with a successful melodrama, *The Klondyke Nugget*, and with subsequent plays and this enabled him to indulge and expand his hobby of kite-flying. He was an intensely practical man and able, without the most elementary academic education, to grasp and evaluate aeronautical and mechanical detail of an advanced order in his day.

Cody's kites were based on the box-kite, originally developed by an Australian Lawrence Hargrave; Cody added embryonic wings to the horizontal surfaces and the resulting appearance was not unlike one of the early powered biplanes – without the engine. His system was first to launch a 'pilot-kite' on a light line, then a number of 'lifter-kites' on the main cable, spaced out by means of 'stops' at desired positions, and lastly the 'carrier-kite' bearing the observer and his telephone. The observer was able, by means of control lines, to alter the angle of incidence of the carrier-kite's horizontal surfaces to the airflow and thus to make it rise or descend, the observer with it. A normal operating height was about 1,500 feet. Cody sold some of these kites to the Royal Navy in 1903; although they carried out further trials of Cody kites in 1908, both for the elevation of wireless aerials and for observation of submarine objects, they did not adopt them for service.

Encouraged by the Navy's purchase in 1903, however, Cody convinced the War Office in the following year of the need to experiment with his kite-systems, was employed on a temporary basis in demonstrating them and training aeronauts and ground crew and, in 1906, was appointed Chief Instructor in Kiting at the Balloon Factory. In the same year kites were added to the establishment of balloon companies.

Perhaps it was the efficiency of the Cody kite system which discouraged the British Army from following the German development of the *Drachen* balloon. Extra stability was there provided by an elongated shape and by extra vertical surfaces at the stern, and it would be expected to operate in slightly higher winds than could the spherical balloon.

Training with the latter continued in Britain, with particular concern to improve mobility, and every effort was made to keep the rest of the army interested. Ballooning courses were held, particularly for artillery officers, and artillery fire-control from balloons was practised at the Gunner practice camps.

Uncertainty still existed, however, as to the likely effectiveness of the balloons in war. They were used by both sides in the Russo-Japanese War (1904-05). The British Official History comments on several occasions on the location from Russian balloons of Japanese positions and movements; it also comments on the breaking adrift of one of the Russian balloons, its unmanned 1,500-mile flight, the alarm and despondency caused by it in the Lake Baikal area and the rejoicing among Russian staff officers thus relieved from the duty of ascending in it.

The Royal Artillery historian of the period writes that this war intensified experiments in artillery balloon observation,[12] that a method of fire was worked out and embodied in the manual, that the captive balloon or its rough-weather substitute, the kite, could always be depended upon and that their direct communication with the ground was invaluable. A pessimistic article by Colonel F. D. B. Wing in the Journal of the Royal Artillery of August 1906, however, while accepting the value of balloons for watching enemy movement, doubted very much whether they would be available for artillery observation, whether gunner observers could avoid air-sickness and whether observers of any other arm could be trusted to observe fire. Two months later Major C. B. Levita, writing at the conclusion of a practice camp where he had controlled his battery's movement and fire from a balloon, disputed vigorously all the colonel's conclusions, made a number of helpful proposals for the future and ended with a long extract of a letter he had received from Colonel Capper. The latter had written, among other things: 'I have no doubt that improved methods may be suggested and tried and that ultimately we shall find the Gunners running their own balloons, looking on them just as much as integral parts of their batteries as are their own observation instruments.' Reports from the Rhayader artillery practice camp, incidentally, in that same year, noted the advantage gained when the balloon observer was a trained artillery man.

As a result of the interim report of the Committee on Military Ballooning, sanction was given for the construction of a small dirigible and experiments were initiated in aero-engine design and construction. An airship-shed was constructed on the site at Farnborough to which it was agreed that the Balloon Factory should move; it became part of the present Royal Aircraft Establishment. The move took place in 1905-6, that of the Balloon Companies to a neighbouring site at the same time. Work was started on the first British dirigible – to be called *Nulli Secundus*. Many problems had to be solved, not least that of the fire risk arising from the engine's exhaust gases and their contiguity to the airship's hydrogen, and the first flight (with a French engine) did not take place until the autumn of 1907.

In April 1906 Colonel Capper's command became known as the Balloon School, absorbing the balloon companies. In the following month Capper relieved Colonel Templer as Superintendent of the Balloon Factory. Templer retired at the age of sixty years, of which the last twenty-seven had been devoted to British military aeronautics. Indeed he had presided at its creation. He served on for a further year as Consultant Engineer, mainly concerned with dirigibles and particularly with *Nulli Secundus*.

Nulli Secundus made her first flight on 10th September, 1907, the crew consisting of Colonel Capper, Cody (in charge of the engine) and Captain W. A. de C. King, Royal Engineers, the chief instructor of ballooning. In her fourth flight Capper and Cody flew her from Farnborough to London, over Buckingham Palace and the War Office and around St. Paul's Cathedral. Unable to make headway on the return journey against a strong wind, she was landed in the grounds of the Crystal Palace. Great public enthusiasm was aroused by this flight although, five days earlier, a German rigid airship had covered two hundred miles in a flight of over nine hours. For *Nulli Secundus* there was anticlimax and disaster; before the weather had become suitable for the return trip from Crystal Palace to Farnborough a strong wind caused some of the anchoring pickets to pull out, the airship lashed about and – to prevent it breaking loose altogether – the Corporal in charge of the ground party slit open the nose of the envelope. The airship was dismantled and returned to Farnborough by road, where she was radically redesigned and reconstructed. She flew again between 24th July and 15th August, experiencing both control and engine troubles, after which she was deflated and flew no more.

In May 1909 a second airship – very small and thus popularly called

Baby – was launched. She proved unstable and sometimes uncontrollable; it was decided to lengthen her into what amounted to a fresh aircraft.

More significant than any of these events were the activities of the brothers Wright, of Dayton, Ohio. After experiments with a succession of biplane gliders in which they solved their control problems, they fitted an eight horse-power petrol engine to their latest biplane, which they called *The Flyer*, and on 17th December, 1903, both Orville and Wilbur flew it, in turn, for twelve and fifty-nine seconds respectively. The machine was damaged and the brothers set to work to construct *Flyer II*; this, in November 1904, Wilbur Wright flew for $2\frac{3}{4}$ miles in just over five minutes.

Colonel Capper visited the Wright Brothers in the following month, and returned to England with terms from them for an exclusive contract to the British Government. The latter was, however, as financially cautious as was the American Government, and the moment passed.

In 1905 *Flyer III* made flights of twenty, thirty-three and thirty-eight minutes, after which, almost unbelievably, the brothers put their aircraft away for $2\frac{1}{2}$ years, concentrating on an analysis of their results and the patenting of their inventions. No governmental moves were made in either continent, while the Wrights' price rose with their confidence that they had outstripped the field.

There had, however, been stirrings in Britain, which helped no doubt to postpone any dealings with the Wrights. John William Dunne, a subaltern of the Wiltshire Regiment, was invalided home from the South African War in 1900, preoccupied with the problems of reconnaissance which he had encountered there and seeking to solve them with the aid of some form of mechanical flying apparatus. He studied some of the possibilities of dirigible balloons and rotary wings and then returned to South Africa. Invalided home again in 1903, Dunne designed the 'stable system of aeroplane surfaces' for which he became famous, modelling his aircraft wings on the swept-back wings of sea birds, with angle-of-incidence decreasing progressively to become negative at the wing-tips. Colonel Capper met him in 1905, after seeing and being impressed by some of his glider models and, as a result, Dunne found himself attached to the Balloon Factory and constructing full-scale monoplane and biplane gliders on the same principle. In 1907, to preserve secrecy, these aircraft were transported for trials to the Duke of Atholl's estate at Blair Atholl; the Duke, by ancient statute, had the right to maintain a private army and exercised it to eject those who were too interested.

Capper made the first flight in the monoplane, which crashed on take-off and flew no more. Lieutenant Lancelot Gibbs of the Royal Field Artillery made some short flights in the biplane, control (by the Lilienthal method of swinging the body) being made more difficult by the automatic stability of the design. Back at Blair Atholl in 1908, with Dunne not well enough to fly, Gibbs flew a fresh biplane in a number of hill-soaring flights, but two successive engine-fits proved failures and a forty-yard powered hop was the best achievement. The War Office then withdrew its support and it was left to four noblemen, the Marquess of Tullibardine, Lord Rothschild, the Duke of Westminster and Earl Fitzwilliam, to form the 'Blair Atholl Syndicate' and support financially the continued development of the Dunne machines.

Some success was achieved and manufacturing licenses were sold in America and France. Dunne's claims for the stability of his design were amply proved; he himself flew 'hands off' for considerable periods, while Captain A. D. Carden, Royal Engineers, with only one arm, gained his pilot's certificate in a Dunne biplane. The War Office showed belated interest in 1914, but by this time the ideas of military airmen were turning towards the future problems of fighting other aircraft and the manoeuvres and aerobatics this would require. Superstability militated against aerial fighting and the Dunne designs were not pursued. Had our 1940 ideas of Air Observation Posts developed thirty years earlier, it might have been a different story. Dunne must certainly be recognised as one of the pioneers of British flying; it was later, as a philosopher, the discoverer of serialism and the author, in the nineteen twenties and thirties, of *An Experiment with Time*, *The New Immortality* and other works, that he achieved world fame.

Cody was another pioneer of aeroplane development in Britain. While perfecting his kite systems in 1905 he made a form of 'glider-kite' (the term is Walker's) in which a man could be lifted as part of a kite system, could release himself and descend as in a glider. Cody himself, and probably others, achieved glides of up to eighty yards. Thence he proceeded to a 'motor-kite' (again Walker's term), consisting of a modified kite, with a biplane-tail behind it, an undercarriage, propellor and twelve horsepower engine. This was tested both on the ground and attached to a wire between two posts; despite a certain amount of conflicting evidence, it seems unlikely that it ever flew free with a pilot. During the winter of 1907–08 Cody constructed a 'pusher' biplane with a large front elevator and, on 16th May, 1908, managed a sixty yard hop. He was sharing a fifty horsepower *Antoinette* engine with *Nulli Secundus*, and it now became the dirigible's turn for it. By the end of 1908, however, Cody had regained possession of the engine and flown five hundred yards. As in the case of Dunne, the War Office now withdrew support from Cody's aeroplane; continuing at his own expense, however, he triumphantly achieved a forty-mile flight in September 1909.

In describing the early work on aeroplanes by Dunne and Cody, we have for convenience advanced somewhat beyond 14th May, 1908, when Orville and Wilbur Wright, emerging from their retirement with a modified *Flyer III* biplane, started to fly once again. They were still regarded almost everywhere either as charlatans or hopeless optimists. An American business man, O. Berg, however, advised then strongly to go to France, the leading nation aeronautically, and to demonstrate there the state of their art; Wilbur took his advice and established himself with his aircraft near Le Mans, where a French syndicate agreed to buy his patents and a certain number of machines provided he completed their exacting tests of performance and reliability. Orville remained in America and on 12th September, during United States army trials, flew fifty miles in $1\frac{1}{4}$ hours. The United States Government having been given its opportunity to take the lead in aeroplane development, Wilbur now forged ahead in France. By the end of September he had made flights of thirty and ninety minutes, by mid-October he had completed the syndicate's tests and by the end of the year he had an eighty-mile flight to his credit.

On a hitherto incredulous world the effect of the events of these three autumn months was sensational. Mechanical flight was seen to be achieved; many who had felt themselves on the edge of important discoveries pressed on with growing confidence. In France this was particularly so; Léon Delagrange, Henry Farman and Louis Blériot all made flights in 1908 which, but for the Wrights, would have been significant. For the British, it was Louis Blériot who made the most significant flight of all when, on Sunday, 25th July, 1909, he took off from Calais at 4.30 a.m. in his self designed monoplane and landed by Dover Castle forty minutes later.

The Awakening

---◇---

'Awake, arise, or be forever fall'n!'
MILTON: *Paradise Lost*

The impact upon the British people, usually totally uninterested in matters related to their own defence, of M. Blériot's nonchalant breaching of their insularity, was clearly exceptional. The British Press contrasted with venom Continental enterprise and British lethargy in the development of flying, while the *Daily Graphic* of 26th July, 1909, the morrow of the flight, had this to say on defence:

M. Blériot has guided an aeroplane in a given direction, and under not too favourable conditions, over the strip of water which makes England an island. There is no need to labour the point. The lesson is for all to read. What M. Blériot can do in 1909, a hundred, nay a thousand aeroplanes may be able to do in five years' time. When Mr. Farman flew a mile, it was possible to say that an ingenious toy had been invented. But a machine which can fly from Calais to Dover is not a toy, but an instrument of warfare of which soldiers and statesmen must take account.

If the Press and the people were quick to react, the soldiers and statesmen were somewhat slower. It has been suggested that they were right to be cautious at this early stage, when the influence of aerial vehicles on strategy and tactics was difficult to assess, and the development prospects of lighter-than-air and heavier-than-air vehicles equally so. Many misconceptions were rife, even among the early experts.[1] The government had to balance the needs of aviation against the remaining needs of defence, and their need to know more before committing substantial resources against their estimate of the time available. In the event they ran things somewhat close.

Observation and reconnaissance are valueless without the means to report the results, and the mobility of aeroplanes and the visual command of any aircraft are wasted without quick communications. The message bags by which Coutelle's original aérostiers communicated their observations were by no means slow or unreliable; telephones were even more satisfactory for balloon observers. Dirigibles and aeroplanes posed more difficult problems, the solution of which demanded wireless. Marconi had achieved modest results by 1897; ten years later the War Office

initiated experiments to determine the best form of wireless apparatus to
use in balloons.

Weather conditions and airsickness greatly prejudiced the initial trials
with captive balloons. In May 1908, however, the Trials Officer,
Lieutenant C. J. Aston, Royal Engineers, with the ubiquitous Colonel
Capper, made a free flight in a balloon which carried a wireless receiver
and picked up signals from stations distant twenty and twenty-five miles
respectively. Soon afterwards signals transmitted from a balloon were
picked up by a ground station eight miles away. The trials were then
discontinued by the War Office until the following year, when they were
entrusted to Captain H. P. T. Lefroy, commanding the Wireless
Experimental Section, Royal Engineers – wireless being another child
fathered by that versatile corps. By 1911 good progress had been made.

In 1908 and 1909 air observation, to the Army, still implied balloons
or kites; dirigibles were balloons of a special kind and, anyway, in an
early stage of development. The Royal Engineers raised in 1908 a
Territorial Force Balloon Company of Volunteer soldiers, the 'London
Balloon Company'. *Field Service Regulations, 1909*, the Army's tactical
manual, made favourable references to balloons and kites for observation
(including that of artillery fire), reconnaissance, ascertaining the position
of one's own troops and the nature of the ground. No mention was
made of heavier-than-air aircraft.

Progress with dirigibles was mixed in 1910. *Gamma* appeared in
February for her initial trials and *Beta*, the outcome of lengthening *Baby*,
appeared successfully in May and did a night flight in June. A potential
war-airship, *Delta*, was 'laid-down' at the Balloon Factory. Two suppos-
edly successful airships from France, however, failed conspicuously, the
Clément-Bayard, which never flew again, and the *Lebaudy*, purchased by
the *Morning Post* newspaper, which struck a house and was irretrievably
wrecked on her first trial flight. This was a depressing start for Major
Sir Alexander Bannerman, who relieved Colonel Capper at this point as
Commandant of the Balloon School.

Capper was appointed Commandant of the School of Military Engineering and later became, in turn, the Commander of 24th Division on
the Western Front in France, Director-General of the Tank Corps and
Lieutenant Governor of Jersey. It was fortunate, indeed, for British
military aviation to have had at its head at a crucial period a man of
determination but also of tact, and a wise man, able to see the Wrights'
aeroplanes not as inefficient interlopers in the world of the balloon and
airship but as the first manifestations of a new force in warfare.

At the time of Blériot's Channel flight the British Army possessed one
aeroplane, if we except that of the indomitable Cody flying around at
his own expense. The one Army aeroplane, a Wright biplane, was the
gift of the Hon. C. S. Rolls, together with the offer to experiment with
it on behalf of the military and also to instruct. Sadly, Rolls was killed

in a flying accident a year later. The War Office, with a view to experiment, ordered a *Blériot XII* monoplane and later two other types, a *Henry Farman* pusher biplane and a similar *Paulhan*, each with a fifty horse-power *Gnome* engine. During 1909, however, three army officers, all Gunners, were flying aeroplanes on Salisbury Plain. One of them was Lieutenant Lancelot Gibbs, whom we met in the last chapter as Dunne's pilot and who had acquired a *Henry Farman* aeroplane, the other two were Captains John Duncan Bertie Fulton and Bertram Dickson. Fulton was an inspired amateur engineer; he had recently received an award from the War Office for an artillery invention and he used it to help to buy a *Blériot* monoplane. Dickson had bought a Henry Farman biplane and had learnt to fly it at the Farman school in France.

These three officers did their best to demonstrate to the Army the possibilities of aeroplanes for reconnaissance. Dickson and Gibbs were allowed to make some reconnaissance flights (in their own aeroplanes) during the 1910 Army manoeuvres; Gamble records that they experienced difficulty in persuading commanding officers to make use of their services, that the cavalry feared that the noise of the aeroplanes would frighten their horses and that general scepticism resulted from the postponement of flights in bad weather.[2] Gibbs thereafter disappeared from active aeronautics; it appears that he had hurt his back in a minor accident earlier that year and, as a result, had to discontinue flying. *Beta* took part in the 1910 manoeuvres also, flying a thousand miles and sending many reconnaissance reports. Wireless experiments took place from an aeroplane flown by Mr. Robert Loraine. In their attention to aviation, however, the French manoeuvres of that year far outshone the British; each of the two Army Corps were supported by four aeroplanes, while the four airships taking part in the exercise, with three further aeroplanes, formed a separate unit.

The British and Colonial Aeroplane Company, later to be called the Bristol Company, established a flying school at Larkhill at the end of 1910 and Dickson retired from the army and joined them. Not long afterwards he was involved in an air collision at an aviation meeting at Milan and was badly injured. His death in 1913 was probably an outcome of the accident.

The *Blériot XII* monoplane appeared at the end of the year, with Lieutenant R. A. Cammell, Royal Engineers, in charge; he had learnt to fly it at the Blériot works. Its trials at Larkhill, where it acquired the name 'Man-killer', were unsatisfactory and ended with engine-failure and a forced landing while en route to Farnborough. Some time later there emerged from the Balloon Factory a 'tail-first' experimental biplane known as the *SE1* and later destined to come to grief. Geoffrey de Havilland was employed at the factory and designed an experimental biplane of the *Farman* type against the anticipated increase in flying instruction. A start had been made.

Various changes took place, during 1909 and 1910, in the organisation of British military aviation. In May, 1910 there was set up a scientific committee, the Advisory Committee for Aeronautics, to advise the Admiralty and War Office, while a civilian, Mervyn O'Gorman, was appointed head of the Balloon Factory (soon to become the Royal Aircraft Factory) with direct responsibility to the Army Council. Finally it was decided to organise British military aviation into a special unit, the Air Battalion, Royal Engineers, to include therein officers of all arms of the service, an Airship Company (embracing balloons and kites) under Captain E. M. Maitland of the Essex Regiment, an Aeroplane Company under Captain Fulton and an Air Battalion Reserve. This battalion formed in April, 1911, but its resources were at first quite insufficient for the scheme of expansion and training which it had been set.

This is, perhaps, an appropriate juncture at which to discuss the situation of the British artillery, as regards air observation. We have seen that the South African War had demonstrated the need for artillery to be able to occupy covered positions behind crest-lines and to fire 'indirectly', controlled by an observer at an 'observation post'. It had also demonstrated the possibility, anyway, of observing artillery fire, if not controlling it, from a balloon. The art had been regularly practised at artillery firing camps, together with kite-observation when winds were too strong for balloons. The Russo-Japanese war seemed to have confirmed the necessity for concealed battery positions and thus, sometimes, for air observation posts. If no very enthusiastic reports had been received on the efficiency of the rival balloonists, no alternative had emerged for an air O.P. The possibility of direct, or re-transmitted, telephone communication between balloon and guns was important to gunners and balloons had been shown to be comparatively invulnerable to weapons of the day. Their main disadvantage was the airsickness they induced in many observers and resulting difficulty in using binoculars; the German elongated *Drachen* balloon gave increased stability but, so far as the British were concerned, the development of elongated balloons seems to have been swallowed up by dirigible development.

It is apparent that, from about 1910 onwards, a shortage of balloons began to be felt. They were mentioned less and less in reports on training and there is positive reference to the reduced support available to the 1911 artillery practice camp at Lydd due to 'the many demands on the small establishment of the Air Battalion'.[3] The same author writes that 'the eventual inability of balloons to keep the air in face of hostile aeroplanes and improved artillery was anticipated'.

It is far from certain that the gunners of 1910 and 1911 protested vigorously at the disappearance of their O.P.s – it is probable that they did not, since the Royal Artillery historian makes no mention of it. Few gunners had yet recognised the air O.P. as a real necessity; most gunners realised, on the other hand, that there were many other burning artillery problems which had to be solved before this imminent war should burst upon them. Some of the more air-minded may have supposed that the dirigible – which started from the simple concept of a positively mobile, rather than captive or drifting, balloon – would become the future air O.P. Already, however, it was becoming clear that the expense and vulnerability of such an airship put it outside the realms of possibility for such a role. The fact was that – in Britain – the spherical balloon was drifting into obsolescence without anything comparable replacing it. We shall see that the aeroplane was pressed into service for artillery obser-vation and overcame its initial difficulties quite well, while wartime necessity brought back the balloon – in kite-balloon form. The complete artillery air O.P., however, was still thirty years away.

Strategical and tactical reconnaissance was at that time regarded, no doubt correctly, as the principal role of the aeroplane and, in 1910, there was little thought of any other role. In December of that year the British and Colonial Aeroplane Company sent out to India three Bristol biplanes, with a small team of pilots and mechanics, to show the Army what the aeroplane could do. At Calcutta at that time was an air-minded Royal Field Artillery officer, Captain William Sefton Brancker; officially or unofficially he became the liaison link between the Bristol team and the Army in India. Those familiar with India and its climate will not be surprised to learn that considerable troubles were experienced with the wood and fabric of the aircraft, low grade petrol and so on. Brancker, however, arranged for one of the aircraft to take part in manoeuvres in the Hyderabad state, some three infantry brigades being involved.

Like Lieutenant Ward, with his dusk balloon sortie in the summer manoeuvres of 1889, Captain Brancker had an immediate success within a few minutes of the start of the manoeuvres. Flying with one of the Bristol pilots, a Frenchman Jullerot, he found part of the enemy force for which they had been briefed to search, perceived in time that his own airfield had been captured by hostile cavalry and landed elsewhere. Brancker's report reached the commander of the force an hour and a half after take-off. This was probably the highlight of the team's visit although, in spite of accidents and ill-health, further flying took place; the Army seems to have been impressed and efforts were made (without success) to start a military flying school in India. Brancker, however, had a big part still to play in the development of military flying.

Not much had hitherto been written about naval aviation, partly because the Royal Navy was distinctly late in the field and partly because, as mentioned in the introduction, it is only intended to describe naval aviation developments when they have a relevance to the main subject of this book. By 1909 the Admiralty had become interested in their need for aviation and, impressed by the Germans, commissioned an experimental rigid airship, the *Mayfly*. First launched in May 1911, and promptly returned to her hangar for modification, she broke her back and became a total loss as she re-emerged in September. In

November, however, the Navy started training aeroplane pilots at Eastchurch, on the Isle of Sheppey. By the end of 1911 a seaplane had achieved its first successful landing (if that is the word) and Mr. T. O. M. Sopwith was well advanced with a flying boat.

Aircraft shortage and unserviceability were playing havoc with the training of the Aeroplane Company at this time; they were hard-pressed to keep their pilots in flying practice and could do little combined training with other arms. When the 1911 autumn manoeuvres were cancelled the company attempted a cross-country flight from Larkhill to Hardwick, near Cambridge – an expensive fiasco in which four aircraft crashed and only two pilots arrived safely.

In contrast to the state of military aviation in Britain, visitors to France, and particularly to the French manoeuvres, continued to report a far more advanced and professional organisation, with over two hundred aeroplanes and a high standard of pilot training. Good co-operation was also achieved, both with cavalry and artillery, and they had had success with air photography. Two French pilots – the naval Lieutenant Conneau (who called himself Beaumont) and Jules Védrines – won first and second prize in the Circuit of Britain race in July 1911. The *Aero Magazine* of the following month wrote of them: '(They) are men who go about their flying in a very businesslike and thorough way. They avoided accidents, and they took the requisite amount of risk; they flew well-tested machines, both of which are quite beyond the experimental stage; and by exercising their knowledge of the aerial navigation which they have picked up in Continental competitions, they overcame all difficulties, and won so easily that no-one else had a right to be considered in the race at all'. Later in the same year military trials were held in France to attract aircraft of suitable designs for the roles. And M. Paul Cornu, an engineer of Lisieux, became in 1907 the first man to rise from the ground in a helicopter; unfortunately, like many after him, he found out what an expensive business helicopter development was, and was forced to discontinue it.

In Germany the emphasis had been on rigid airships; Count Zeppelin's name had already passed into our general vocabulary and the Royal Navy, in particular, were wondering how to deal with his products in war. Where aeroplanes were concerned, Germany's progress was not so marked but a young Dutchman, Fokker, had started to design for the Germans aeroplanes of great promise. The Germans were ahead of others in specialised anti-aircraft gun design, appreciating that to expect other sorts of gun to be successfully adapted to engage aircraft was over-optimistic.

Reports on the progress made in aviation beyond our shores reached the War Office and British Government from many sources, but often from quite junior officers – captains and lieutenants – who, as trained aeroplane pilots, were attached for periods to the French Air Corps.

One of the healthy features of those times, as it seems to the modern British officer, was the attention paid by their seniors to the reports and views of the young men who were recognised and accepted as the only experts of this new military art.

The government must also have been aware of the growth of national and military anxiety at our unpreparedness in the air. Several organisations or (as we should term them now) pressure-groups existed to provide the megaphone, as it were, to the public's mutterings – the Aeronautical Society of Great Britain, which was founded in 1866 with the timeless aim of increasing our knowledge of aeronautics,[4] the Royal Aero Club, whose predecessors had splintered-off from the Aeronautical Society in 1901 with the less scientific aim of 'encouraging aeronautics', and the Aerial League of the British Empire (now simply the Air League) who formed in 1909 with aims which could be summarised as 'making the British people air-minded'. Less objectively, the many private aircraft companies which sprang up at this time were, naturally enough, very ready to urge the need to expand military aviation and the press were very ready to support them. Finally the international situation was full of menace.

By these various means the deficiencies in the British aeronautical situation came to the government's attention and a sub-committee of the Committee of Imperial Defence, under Lord Haldane, was charged with the task of considering 'the future development of aerial navigation for naval and military purposes, and the measures which might be taken to secure to this country an efficient aerial service'. At the same time the War Office announced the conditions of a military competition to be held in the following summer (1912), with prizes for constructors of aeroplanes most suitable for military use.

Considering that Lord Haldane's sub-committee delegated their duties to a 'technical sub-committee', under the Rt-Hon. Colonel J. E. B. Seely, and considering the technical committees relied on an inner committee of four (still under Seely) for the detailed plans, it is remarkable that the Committee of Imperial Defence were able to approve their sub-committee's report before the end of April 1912. This report, in effect, created the Royal Flying Corps. Raleigh seems to suggest that the committee's intention was to form 'a new and independent service, taking rank with the Army and Navy',[5] but the small size of the new service, the comparatively junior ranks of its officers and the limited knowledge of everyone concerning future roles and methods surely precludes such a possibility. It is very clear, however, that the Royal Flying Corps was intended to be a single organisation, incorporating a naval and a military wing (each wing constituting, when needed, a reserve for the other) and that a Central Flying School should assume responsibility for all elementary flying training.

For the Military Wing, an organisation was envisaged which would comprise seven aeroplane squadrons, each of twelve aircraft, an airship squadron (probably incorporating two flights of kites, but as to balloons, no indication given), and a workshop. Officer-pilots were to be drawn from all regiments and corps of the Army and also by direct recruitment of qualified civilians. Ground crews, including many skilled tradesmen, were to be found by direct recruitment and, of course, many of the sappers of the Air Battalion were expected to transfer to the new Corps.

For the Naval Wing the prescription was not nearly so detailed; it was thought that forty pilots a year would need to be trained and that, when the Central Flying School had assumed this burden, the Naval Flying School – at, presumably, Eastchurch – would give specialised training to naval personnel and carry out experiments in naval aspects of aviation. The Advisory Committee for Aeronautics would continue its work, and a permanent consultative committee, representative of Army and Navy and other departments which might become concerned, would be set up with the title of 'The Air Committee'.

And so the Royal Engineers laid down their responsibility for army aviation. The considerable expansion in aviation envisaged by the most cautious of prophets, and the importance of the tactical part to be played by it, made it certain that it could no longer remain a limited portion of one corps of the Army. Nevertheless the Army had good cause to be grateful to the Corps of Royal Engineers which, with Abel and Templer, had started military ballooning, had nursed it into manhood and had absorbed in turn kites, dirigibles and aeroplanes – all with the very minimum of encouragement from the authorities.

The Airship Company of the Air Battalion remained at Farnborough, becoming No.1 Squadron, R.F.C. They had the airships *Beta* and *Gamma*, and later *Delta* and *Eta*, the kites and a few spherical balloons which seem to have been used mostly for the reconnaissance training of aeroplane pilots when aeroplanes were in short supply. Major Maitland remained in command. The Aeroplane Company at Larkhill became No.3 Squadron, R.F.C., under Major H. R. M. Brooke-Popham. His predecessor, Captain Fulton, became an Instructor at the Central Flying School at Upavon and later the Chief Inspector of the Aeronautical Inspection Department, set up to examine the aircraft in service with the squadrons and the aircraft and engines in course of construction by contractors. Notable among the early army pilots, he died prematurely in November 1915. No.2 Squadron was formed around a nucleus of aeroplane pilots at Farnborough, under Captain C. J. Burke. No.4 Squadron began to form at Netheravon in September 1912, under Major G. H. Raleigh.

The first commander of the Military Wing of the Royal Flying Corps was Major Frederick Sykes, 15th Hussars. A new War Office branch was formed to co-ordinate with the Admiralty all mutual affairs of the R.F.C. and to issue to the Military Wing and Central Flying School the instructions of the 'Director of Military Training'. In July 1912 Major Sefton Brancker took over this branch and Brigadier-General David

Henderson became his Director. Fourteen months later the branch expanded into a 'Directorate of Military Aeronautics', with Henderson the Director and three branches responsible for, respectively, administration and training, equipment and contracts.

One of the main problems for the Royal Flying Corps was the provision of aircraft, the more so since there was as yet no agreement as to what kinds of aircraft were wanted. The War Office's Military Aeroplane Competition at Larkhill from 1st–25th August, 1912, seemed therefore most relevant. The 'conditions to be fulfilled by a military aeroplane' formed the basis of the marking system and incorporated many forward-looking requirements, for example:

350 lb. payload.

Three hours' endurance.

Glide angle one in six or better.

Take-off, with the above payload, from long grass, clover or harrowed land, in still air, in one hundred yards.

Land without damage on rough plough. After landing on smooth turf, in still air, pull up within seventy-five yards.

Mobility in road movement.

Dual-control.

Good field of view for pilot and observer.

Engine able to be started by the pilot alone.

All parts of the aeroplane strictly interchangeable.

Twenty-four aeroplanes took part, of which the French provided five monoplanes and a triplane, the British nine monoplanes and nine biplanes. The Royal Aircraft Factory was ineligible for entry but several of their aircraft flew during the competition. There was one fatal accident, to a British pilot, and three British aircraft had landing accidents and four engine trouble. One French aircraft had engine trouble.

Everyone was pleased for Cody when he was awarded both the 'All-comers' and 'British National' prizes for his personally designed, built and piloted aeroplane – a climax to his achievements with kites, airships and aeroplanes. Just a year later he was, sad to relate, killed in an aeroplane accident at Farnborough when flying a machine designed to use, alternatively, floats or wheeled undercarriage. No aviator so captured the affection of the British public as did Cody. They saw in him a man of unique courage and determination and a man also of warm human qualities; his fellow aviators knew him to be a natural engineer of genius.

After Cody, in the War Office competition, came five French aircraft, with two Bristol aircraft equal seventh; nor was Cody's aeroplane really what was required for the R.F.C. To relieve the disappointment, however, the Royal Aircraft Factory's *B.E.2* Biplane scored a considerable success with its flying at Larkhill and, with Geoffrey de Havilland at the controls, created a British altitude record.

In the next two years the Factory designed and built many effective aeroplanes in the *B.E.*, *F.E.*, *S.E.* and *R.E.* series, and certainly played the greatest part in the struggle to equip the R.F.C. before the outbreak of war. The significance of the respective lettering had already disappeared by 1914; the *F.E.s* had pusher-propellors, resulting in clear vision in front, useful for night observation and thought at first to be equally suitable for aerial fighting. The *R.E.* series were exceptionally stable and therefore considered suitable for reconnaissance but, like Dunne's aeroplanes, they suffered from the disadvantages of stability when abrupt manoeuvrability was required in air fighting and in evasion of hostile attack.

In the second half of the summer of 1912 there were three successive fatal accidents to British army pilots and their passengers, the aircraft in each case being a monoplane. The War Office 'grounded' monoplanes and ordered an investigation – which in due course absolved the monoplane from blame. The dog had been given its bad name, however, and no more monoplanes were ordered for the R.F.C. – a matter which adversely affected future British aircraft development.

Early in 1913 a fresh wave of Press agitation occurred, sparked off by an actual or rumoured German airship cruise near the British coast. In reply to questions in Parliament about military aircraft deficiencies, Colonel Seely quoted figures which were widely disbelieved or, at best, regarded as misleading. One outcome was the authority to purchase a number of additional aeroplanes, of several assorted types. It was War Office policy to diversify in this manner, to spread orders throughout the trade and thus preserve national skills of design and construction. This has been adversely criticised and, from the point of view of the wartime squadron commander, it was hardly a convenient arrangement. But what was the alternative? No one could yet foretell how the tactics of the military aeroplane, or its construction and performance, would develop; standardisation could have led to triumph, but much more probably to disaster.

In the autumn of 1912 No. 3 Squadron, R.F.C. took part in the training of the Cavalry Division. It was not, apparently, much of a success and both Gamble and Raleigh suggest that the Cavalry treated the aeroplanes with some suspicion – and not only on this occasion. The aeroplane was such a new adjunct of war that, naturally enough, some fairly wild prophecies were made about it. One of these was that aerial reconnaissance might make cavalry obsolete; this could well have been an irritant although, in fact, horsed cavalry was soon to be made obsolete by other factors. The War Office helped to improve relations by making it clear, in a memorandum issued before the 1912 Army manoeuvres and in future issues of *Field Service Regulations*, that cavalry and the air service were complementary to one another, not in competition. Monoplanes were of course banned from the manoeuvres but seven biplanes supported each side and the airships *Beta*, *Gamma* and *Delta* were split between them also. These were successful days for the reconnaissance pilots and observers; much useful information reached the commanders, mostly in good time, and the airships made good use of their wireless. Soldiers and their commanders finished these manoeuvres somewhat sobered by their obvious vulnerability to aerial reconnaissance and concerned to find both passive and active ways of reducing it.

In 1912 and 1913 lessons started to filter through from the Italo-Turkish war in Libya and from the Balkan war. The Italians had a monopoly of air power, including aeroplanes, airships and a kite-balloon. The latter two were used mainly for observation of artillery fire and were successful. The aeroplanes were used for reconnaissance, photography (for map-correction), bombing and leaflet-dropping; the Italians regarded the moral effect of the bombing as significant. In the Balkan War it was the Bulgarians who had the aircraft. A spherical observation balloon was used at the siege of Adrianople and aeroplanes were used for reconnaissance, bombing (which was ineffective) and leaflet dropping. Anti-aircraft fire was encountered and was effective at least to 4,000 feet, at which height an observer was killed.

A lesson was learned in the Balkan War which has had to be relearned in many wars and lesser conflicts, namely that observation is not a natural human gift but an art to be acquired by training and assiduous practice. It was being discovered by the Royal Flying Corps at this same period – witness statements by Major Brooke-Popham, during a lecture to the Staff College on 26th October, 1912, that 'an untrained observer is a useless encumbrance' and that 'it will probably take as long to train an observer as it does a pilot'.[6]

In 1913 the R.F.C. aeroplanes took part in exercises in Scotland and Ireland and in larger-scale manoeuvres in the English Midlands. The lessons of the previous year were confirmed, the need for better air-ground and ground-air communications was recognised and there was a significant improvement in aircraft serviceability.

While reconnaissance was undoubtedly regarded as the principal, almost the sole, object of the aeroplane in war, there had been increasing thought on the relationship between the rival air forces of rival armies at war. In the editorial column of the *Aero* magazine of August 1911 the editor described a conversation with a theorist who argued that armies would no longer be able to conceal their manoeuvres and that their opponents would thus always be able to counter them or, if they were too weak, surrender to avoid the inevitable slaughter; in other words, aeroplanes would make battle impossible. The editor disagreed, but he accepted the power of air reconnaissance and expected armies to find ways and means to counter it, partly perhaps by the use of their own aircraft to intercept, destroy or drive back the enemy reconnaissance aeroplanes. This view was expressed more and more during the next three years; Major H. T. Hawkins, in an article in the *Journal of the*

Royal Artillery of October 1912, while emphasising that 'scouting' was the chief duty of any aerial force, wrote nevertheless: 'The first clash will no longer be between the cavalries, but between the opposing air fleets, striving for mastery of the air'. Major Sykes, commander of the R.F.C's military wing, told the Royal Aeronautical Society on 26th February, 1913, that command of the air had to be won in order to obtain information ourselves and to prevent enemy air reconnaissance from doing so.[7] General Sir James Grierson had said, after the 1912 manoeuvres: 'Personally, I think there is no doubt that, before land fighting takes place, we shall have to fight and destroy the enemy's aircraft. It seems to me impossible for troops to fight while the hostile aircraft are able to keep up their observation. That is to say, warfare will be impossible unless we have the mastery of the air.'

In October 1913 the Secretary of State for War gave his opinion that we should concentrate our efforts on obtaining the mastery of the air in any theatre of war in which we may be engaged, by means of the fighting aeroplane, and thus secure for ourselves the monopoly of reconnaissance with the overwhelming advantages that this would bring.[8] In the next month tests began with the American Lewis Gun, and subsequently No.3 Squadron and the Royal Aircraft Factory collaborated. No R.F.C. aircraft were, however, equipped with guns at the outbreak of war.

We have noticed in these pages the not altogether explainable shortage of balloons in the era of the air battalion and its adverse effect on the British artillery. Throughout 1912 and 1913 efforts were made to establish an 'artillery co-operation' role for the aeroplane. No.3 Squadron was made particularly responsible for this and carried out trials with the field artillery at Larkhill and at the siege artillery practice camps at Rhayader and Lydd. Major Bannerman warned the Gunners that the aeroplane was unlikely to be as effective as the balloon in this role[9] and so, indeed, they found it. Two difficulties were hard to overcome – the lack (except by chance) of trained artillery observer and the lack of effective communications between observer and guns. The former difficulty precluded the *control* of artillery fire from the air; it was possible only to *report* observations of fall-of-shot, leaving the Gun Position Officer to calculate corrections and control the fire. The latter difficulty could only be satisfactorily solved by means of wireless, but the equipment of R.F.C. aeroplanes with wireless transmitters had hardly begun when the war broke out. Meanwhile air-to-ground communication was by message dropped to the guns or by lamp, Very light or smoke-puff signals, and ground-to-air communication was by code-letters fashioned out of large white ground-strips. Gamble comments that none of these methods showed any real advance over those employed by the Compagnie d'Aérostiers in 1794.[10]

By the beginning of 1914, however, a procedure had been agreed between artillery and flying corps, which incorporated methods of indicating the target to the guns and of reporting fall of shot. It was necessarily very slow and – realistically – was not regarded as suitable for engaging targets of opportunity. Details of the procedure appeared in both artillery and R.F.C. manuals of 1914; both of these manuals contained information about kites in the air observation post role, neither mentioned balloons at all. Both manuals were based on the 1914 *Field Service Regulations*, which had the same inclusions and omission except that balloons were mentioned (once) as a possible means of signalling. The principal duties of aircraft were stated to be reconnaissance and the prevention of hostile aerial reconnaissance; it was also stated – surprisingly – that aircraft were capable of offensive action against troops on the ground by means of machine guns and bombs. It was envisaged that the whole of the flying corps in a given theatre of war would normally work under the orders of General Headquarters, but provision was made for decentralisation of R.F.C. units when desirable.

The Committee of Imperial Defence, as we have seen, envisaged a Royal Flying Corps which incorporated both Naval and Military Wings. The Royal Navy thought otherwise and, without arguing the matter, pursued their separate course. In Winston Churchill they had a First Lord of the Admiralty enthusiastically of their opinion. Their flying school at Eastchurch never handed over its functions to the Central Flying School, even though the latter's commandant was a sailor. They looked upon flying as an art to be devoted to the winning of the Navy's battles, not as an overriding function to be controlled centrally. They were sure that the naval pilots should be sailors first and pilots second, and they saw to it that their elementary flying took place at Eastchurch surrounded by naval ideas and atmosphere. The command structure of the Naval Wing climbed directly to the Lords of the Admiralty. Even the name 'Naval Wing' was soon abandoned, to be replaced unofficially by 'Royal Naval Air Service'. Whatever one thinks of the ethics of the Royal Navy's quiet rejection of a Cabinet decision, one must surely understand and agree with them on the detailed issue. It is sound philosophy that boundary-lines between services can be efficiently drawn only on the basis of their respective operational functions, rather than of the element in which they mostly travel or of the vehicles in which various parts of them happen to move into action. Only very serious considerations should be allowed to overturn this philosophy, and such considerations were not present in 1912.

The Navy, as has already been mentioned, had a particular interest in airships, due partly, no doubt, to the potential threat to the Grand Fleet posed by the German Zeppelins. Captain Murray Sueter, with Mervyn O'Gorman of the Royal Aircraft Factory, visited France, Austria and Germany in June 1912 to report on airship progress in those countries. He returned from Germany particularly impressed by German achievement and conveyed his feelings to the Admiralty, who promptly recreated the Naval Airship Section (abolished after the *Mayfly* disaster) and ordered the production of a number of airships in the next two years. A sudden decision was made in October 1913, without much preliminary debate, to transfer all the Army's airships to the Naval Wing. Major Maitland joined that Wing, with a great part of the personnel and equipment of No.1 Squadron, detaching to the Military Wing headquarters only the Kite Section. The few remaining spherical balloons joined the Navy while No.1 Squadron reorganised itself rapidly as an 'aircraft park' for the British Expeditionary Force.

It only remained for the independence and title of the Royal Naval Air Service to be officially recognised. This took place on 1st July, 1914, not by order of the Cabinet but of the Admiralty!

August 1914 was drawing near. No.5 Squadron completed formation that summer at Gosport, under Major J. F. A. Higgins. In June the whole of the Military Wing of the R.F.C. concentrated at Netheravon, Wiltshire, for a trial mobilisation and a month's corps training, under Sykes, which was to pay dividends in August and September. Major Brancker slipped across to the Continent for a reconnaissance of the probable operational area of the R.F.C. near the Belgian frontier.

The Military Wing, or the whole of the Royal Flying Corps as it had now become, went to war with its Headquarters (without the Kite Section), Nos.2, 3, 4 and 5 Squadrons and the Aircraft Park, the latter under Major Carden. Major J. M. Salmond now commanded No.3 Squadron. Nos.2 and 4 Squadrons had *B.E.2* aircraft, No.3 *Blériot XIIs* and *Henry Farmans* and No.5 Squadron a mixture of *Henry Farmans, Avros* and *B.E.8s;* the Aircraft Park held an assortment of some twelve aircraft, including four *Sopwith Tabloids* in cases.

Brigadier-General Sir David Henderson assumed command of the Royal Flying Corps in the field. It was, of course, inevitable that his experience of flying should be no greater than many of his officers – he had qualified as a pilot just three years previously – but he had not held any military command since December 1897, when he had been a captain. He was faced with something of a challenge.

Between 12th and 15th August the squadrons had concentrated their pilots and aircraft at Dover and flown to France.

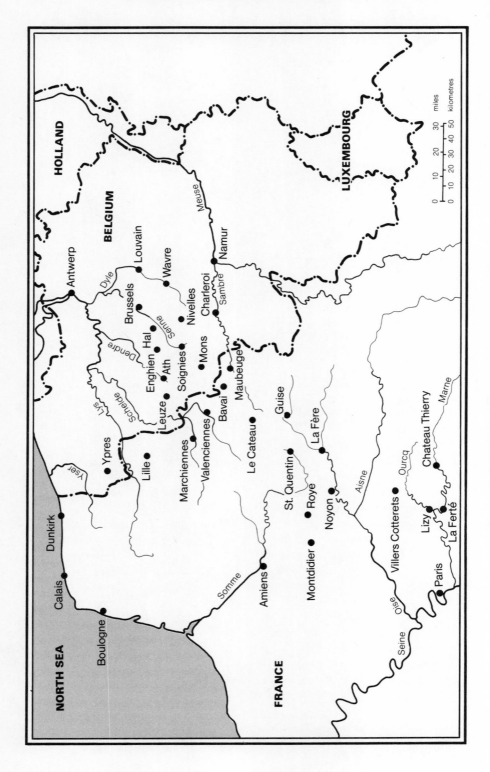

The Aeroplane Goes to War

◇

'The Kestrel hovering by day,
And the little owls that call by night,
Bid him be swift and keen as they,
As keen of ear, as swift of sight.'
JULIAN GRENFELL: *Into Battle*

We have not found it easy, hitherto, to assess the true effectiveness of air observation and reconnaissance in the comparatively minor wars in which they were used. In the Great War of 1914–1918, perhaps nowadays more frequently termed the First World War, the fighting devastated a continent and spilt over into two others: half or more of the peoples of the world were involved in it and five millions lost their lives. The necessity for aircraft for observation and reconnaissance was established beyond doubt and aircraft were used in a number of other roles. For the British the main fighting took place, of course, on the Western Front, mostly on French and Belgian soil, and can be divided into three phases: first, the open warfare of August and September, 1914, culminating in the German stand on the Aisne, the extension of the trench lines to the Channel coast and the development of siege warfare: secondly, the siege warfare which lasted until March 1918, with the efforts of both armies (but principally the Allies) to break out or alternatively to wear down their opponents by a war of attrition: thirdly, the German break-out and final defeat. We shall follow the fortunes of the British air forces, particularly in the army roles of observation and reconnaissance, through each of these three phases, and also look at some of the supplementary theatres of war, the so-called 'side-shows'.

General von Schlieffen, Chief of the German General Staff from 1890 to 1905, was the main architect of the German plan for 1914, which had been somewhat modified by his successor, von Moltke. In its essentials, however, the plan remained a wide sweep round the northern flank of the French armies – which were expected to include a small British expeditionary force – around and to the west of Paris, eventually surrounding and hammering the French between the Upper Seine and the Moselle. To make the sweep as wide as possible it was resolved that the German right wing should advance through Belgium with, or as it turned out without, the latter's permission. The British Expeditionary Force under Sir John French was deployed on the left of the French Fifth Army (General de Lanrezac) initially on the extreme left flank of the Allied armies. The B.E.F. was to move forward, in conformance with the Fifth Army, along the route Maubeuge – Mons – Soignies – Brussels.

The Royal Flying Corps headquarters and Nos.2, 3, and 5 Squadrons concentrated at Amiens on 13th August, being joined there two days later by No.4 Squadron; they then moved to Maubeuge, leaving the aircraft park at Amiens. They had two fatal flying accidents and were also fired upon by British columns on the march; at Maubeuge they painted Union Jacks on the underside of the aircraft wings.[1] At 9.30 a.m. on 19th August the first reconnaissances began, two pilots, without observers, briefed to fly in company for the first part of the flight. They quickly discovered some of the difficulties of aerial navigation over entirely strange country with some portion of concentration distracted, perhaps, by the identification of possible warlike objects on the ground and a look-out for similar objects in the air. The two pilots lost each other and then lost themselves; both wandered around for long periods. Both landed to ask the way – one of them twice; one got back to Maubeuge at noon, the other at 5.30 p.m. It is fair to say that the lessons of these two flights were assimilated; observers were carried in future and accurate information, positive and negative, began to come in. Few aircraft carried wireless transmitters and the range of these was very short: it was not feasible to report the result of a reconnaissance except on return.

On the 20th German columns of all arms were spotted moving from Louvain in the directions of Brussels and Wavre and, that evening, Brussels was entered. Another R.F.C. reconnaissance reported the area Nivelles – Hal – Enghien apparently clear ('No enemy seen') but on the 21st, a day of poor visibility, the same team as on the previous day reported a large body of cavalry, with guns, and some infantry a mile south of Nivelles and more infantry further south on the Charleroi road. On the 21st, also, the French Fifth Army, whose leading elements had crossed the River Sambre between Namur and Charleroi, was attacked by von Bulow's Second German Army and, by nightfall, was forced back to the south of the river. German and French cavalry were in contact at this time on the Charleroi – Mons road, and the B.E.F. could be seen, therefore, to be advancing, unsupported and with at least one flank exposed, against the whole of von Kluck's First Army at the northern end of the German 'sweep'.

On the 22nd, as the B.E.F. moved into position at Mons, Sir John French agreed to hold this position for twenty-four hours to cover the left of the French Fifth Army. The R.F.C. carried out twelve reconnaissances that day, from the reports of which emerged a clear picture of von Kluck's Army closing up on Mons. At the same time, and most significantly, a long column was seen moving due west from Brussels and a pilot and observer who landed some fifteen miles north of Mons received intelligence of German cyclists and cavalry close at hand. Frequent rifle fire was encountered on these reconnaissances; one observer was hit in the leg and Lieutenants V. Waterfall and C.G.G. Bayly of No. 5 Squadron were probably shot down. The crashed aircraft in which they died was first found by Belgians, who removed the incomplete reconnaissance report and started it on a course which ended some time later at the British War Office.

Edmonds, the official British historian, states that it was through afternoon reconnaissances by the R.F.C. that General French first learnt of the defeat and withdrawal of the French Fifth Army to positions well to the right-rear of the B.E.F.;[2] Raleigh, the Air Force historian, is less specific. French certainly had this information by nightfall and undoubtedly felt he had been let down by de Lanrezac. This was perhaps the main occurrence which bedevilled the relationship between these two commanders and induced in Sir John, indeed, a suspicion of his allies which detracted from the full part which the B.E.F. might otherwise have played in the operations of the next three weeks. It led him also to use the R.F.C. to a considerable extent to keep an eye on the movements of adjoining French armies.

On the following day, the 23rd, the British at Mons were attacked by a German force of about double their strength and held them back effectively, mainly by the formidable accuracy of their rifle fire. The R.F.C's activities that day seem to have continued to be strategic rather than tactical, although one reconnaissance report gave the location of an active German battery. Elements of the German Third Army (von Hausen) now appeared on de Lanrezac's right flank and the imminent fall of the fortress of Namur was also reported; de Lanrezac decided to withdraw at once and Sir John French wisely did likewise. On the 23rd, also, the R.F.C. started to move back, by elements, from Maubeuge to Le Cateau, the first of nine such moves which conveyed them to Mélun, fifty miles south of Paris, by 4th September.

As the B.E.F. withdrew, their air reconnaissance was directed upon von Kluck's movements to the north. In the early hours of the 24th, movement was seen in the Ath – Leuze area and south-westward from Leuze, and on the following day a southward movement as far west as Marchiennes. Later, however, this movement became a south-eastward one, apparently aimed at the envelopment of a British position on the line Maubeuge – Bavai – Valenciennes which von Kluck's air reports had erroneously caused him to expect.

On 25th August General Smith-Dorrien, Commander of the British II Corps, decided that his corps faced disintegration and that this could best be avoided by taking up position at Le Cateau, resting an hour or two during the night and holding off the Germans on the 26th. This decision is now generally accepted as correct, and may have done much to save the B.E.F., but it was against French's wishes and for long a matter of controversy. As a result of it, anyway, something less than three British divisions faced something more than three German corps. For the British artillery and infantry the battle was a remarkable success. Soon after midday, with his positions still intact, Smith-Dorrien made the bold decision to order withdrawal. The order took time to reach the

forward units; some indeed it never reached. The stubborn and prolonged resistance of the infantry, and the close co-operation of their
artillery, resulted in one of the most skilful and successful fighting
withdrawals of all time.

The R.F.C. were flying over this battlefield all day, but there are
indications that the troops on the ground were more aware of enemy air
activity. Soldiers under enemy artillery fire, who also saw enemy aircraft
overhead, were inclined to connect the two events – almost certainly
without justification. The fierceness of the fighting, the later confusion
of the battlefield and the absence of effective air-to-ground communication must have made if difficult for the British pilots to intervene
effectively, particularly as they were, of course, under B.E.F. Headquarters and not under Corps control. Captain L. E. O. Charlton of
No.4 Squadron, however, flew at least two sorties for Smith-Dorrien to
assess and report the tactical situation on the left, and subsequently the
right, flank.[3] This use for reconnaissance aircraft – subsequently to be
known as the 'contact sortie' – became (and, one suggests, will always
remain) one of the most important of battle roles. The Official History
gives warm praise to the air reconnaissances of the 26th,[4] incidentally,
stating that they were valuable both positively and negatively and, in
conjunction with other intelligence, should have given G.H.Q. a fairly
clear picture of the situation.

The British II Corps withdrew in a southerly rather than south-
westerly direction, not much molested by the enemy. General Haig's I
Corps fought two rearguard actions, against von Kluck's and von
Bulow's formations respectively, but by the evening of 28th August the
B.E.F. was a single entity again, still on the left of the French Fifth
Army, between the Forêt de St. Gobain, south of La Fère, and Noyon.
Von Kluck, ill-informed by his sources of intelligence, lost touch with
the B.E.F. and came to the conclusion that he had destroyed it. His axis
of advance was nearer west than south-west and brought him into
contact first with a force of French Territorial and Reserve divisions
which was building up under General d'Amade and then with General
Manoury's Sixth Army. This too was in process of forming, as part of
the General Reserve of the Commander-in-Chief General Joffre, who
was for that purpose withdrawing formations from his right wing. As
von Kluck's pressure increased, Manoury and d'Amade withdrew to the
west and south, to an area outside the northern defences of Paris.

On the 29th the French Fifth Army attacked the German Second
Army at Guise. This was intended as little more than a diversion and on
the following day the French were again withdrawing. The consequences
of this short engagement proved, however, catastrophic for the Germans.
Von Bulow believed that he had won a major victory and that the
French Fifth Army was ripe for destruction. The German High Command was struggling with inadequate communications and starting to
lose its grip, and it was direct to von Kluck that von Bulow proposed on
the 30th that the German First Army should now descend upon the

French Fifth Army and help to destroy and disperse it as a preliminary to rolling up the entire French Army from its left. Von Kluck agreed and on the 31st wheeled the bulk of his Army to the south-east. In doing so, he abandoned the Schlieffen plan, with its wide sweep west of Paris, and started to set up the situation for the Battle of the Marne.

On the 31st the R.F.C. was moving its base for the fifth time, to Juilly, twenty miles north-east of Paris. The B.E.F. were withdrawing across the River Aisne between Soissons and Compiègne. Meanwhile air reconnaissance and other reports, from quite early on that day, were of movements of German cavalry, artillery and infantry in the quadrilateral Roye – Noyon – Verberie – Montdidier, mostly in a south-easterly or easterly direction. Some of these movements were in close proximity to the B.E.F's left wing and during the early morning of 1st September there resulted largely accidental encounters at Verberie, Néry (four miles south-east) and Villers-Cotterets. Von Kluck seems to have made a half-move to deal with the menace of the B.E.F., rediscovered on the right flank of his new advance, but the British slipped away and von Kluck quickly resumed his south-easterly movement. R.F.C. reconnaissance reports of that afternoon were particularly important for the Fifth Army. Preliminary indications were conveyed to Joffre and de Lanrezac but at about 8.30 p.m. the following was telephoned to the Fifth Army (and to General Galliéni, the Military Governor of Paris) by Colonel Huguet of the French Mission with the B.E.F:

> It results from very reliable reports from British airmen, all of which agree, that the whole of the German First Army except the IV Reserve Corps are moving south-east to cross the Marne between Chateau Thierry and La Ferté sous Jouarre, and attack the left of the Fifth Army. The heads of the columns will without doubt reach the Marne this evening.[5]

By 4th September Joffre had managed to form yet another French Army, the Ninth, under General Foch, and this he inserted on the right of the Fifth Army, allowing the latter to close up somewhat on the B.E.F. A bag had been formed; to the west was Manoury's Sixth French Army, to the east Foch's Ninth Army and the bottom of the bag was formed by the B.E.F. and the French Fifth Army, the latter now commanded by General Franchet d'Espèrey. Into this bag von Kluck was confidently advancing.

Joffre's counter-offensive and the Battle of the Marne started on 6th September, Manoury's Sixth Army attacking the rear of von Kluck's army from the west and the B.E.F. and Fifth Army advancing north from the foot of the bag. The Schlieffen plan having disappeared into thin air, the Germans were left with virtually only one winning alternative – to break through the French centre. Von Kluck was directed to get his army, somehow, facing that of Manoury, while von Bulow, and the German Third Army (von Hausen) on his left, launched themselves against Foch's Ninth Army and General Langle de Cary's Fourth Army.

By the 8th these attacks had made some, but not decisive, progress. Von Kluck had withdrawn much of his strength from the French Fifth Army and the B.E.F. sectors and redeployed it opposite Manoury, whom he was able to check. In doing so he created a virtual gap opposite the B.E.F. and Franchet d'Espèrey; they were advancing into it. The German High Command was at Luxembourg, with wretched communications to its armies; in the last two days it had received little worthwhile information. In desperation von Moltke sent forward by car his personal representative, Lieutenant-Colonel Hentsch, with powers to co-ordinate any retreat which might be ordered. Hentsch visited the Fifth, Fourth and Third German armies without spectacular result and spent the night of the 8th at von Bulow's headquarters. Here he formed the opinion that an early retreat was probable. On the 9th, soon after Hentsch had left, von Bulow learnt that British infantry and French cavalry were approaching the Marne between Château-Thierry and Lizy, and by 11 a.m. he had ordered withdrawal. Hentsch reached von Kluck at midday and either found that withdrawal orders had already been given or else promptly gave them himself.

For this battle, Nos.3 and 5 Squadrons, R.F.C. were placed for reconnaissance under II and I Corps respectively, No.4 Squadron providing a wireless aeroplane for each. The aircraft returned to their headquarters at night. This system worked well and was continued. Sir John French and his corps commanders were given a very good picture of the movements of von Kluck's forces, of the progress made by the French Fifth and Sixth Armies and of progress made by the leading British troops. On the 8th large numbers of the enemy were seen to be crossing the Marne at La Ferté sous Jouarre and many more queueing up to do so. By evening the bridges east of La Ferté were observed to be still intact (somewhat of a nonsense having been made by von Kluck's rearguard in that area) and the 11th Hussars were able to seize and secure one of them. On the 9th air reports of a large body of enemy north of Château Thierry caused the ever-suspicious Sir John French to halt the advance until afternoon reconnaissance showed clearly that the German First Army was abandoning the battlefield to the north and north-east.

Thus had passed the first critical phase of the Great War. As everyone had expected, reconnaissance and observation had proved the main – indeed as yet the only – role of the air forces; the success of the Royal Flying Corps must surely have exceeded their Army's expectations. After the disappointments of the first reconnaissances, the pilots and observers quickly attained high professional standards. By their reconnaissances before Mons, and by their detection of von Kluck's first 'right-hook' immediately afterwards, they earned and received the confidence of their Commander-in-Chief and were employed in roles of more and more responsibility. The early detection of von Kluck's swing south on 31st August was a further triumph for the R.F.C., followed by their close shadowing of his formations up to and throughout the Battle of the Marne. Their achievement, and its contribution to their Commander's knowledge, was in sharp contrast to the performance of the German air force. Von Kluck, in particular, was seriously deceived by his intelligence on several occasions and particularly out of touch with the movements of the B.E.F.

Sir John French, in his dispatch of the 7th September, paid particular tribute to the R.F.C. As study of the full text confirms, this was no routine compliment paid to the R.F.C. as to others. 'I wish particularly', he wrote, 'to bring to your Lordship's notice the admirable work done by the Royal Flying Corps under Sir David Henderson. Their skill, energy and perseverence have been beyond all praise. They have furnished me with the most complete and accurate information, which has been of incalculable value in the conduct of the operations. Fired at constantly both by friend and foe, and not hesitating to fly in every kind of weather, they have remained undaunted throughout'.

Sir John went on to congratulate them on their 'fighting in the air' and destruction of five enemy machines. Raleigh mentions only three of these 'fights', in which the German pilots, after being engaged by small arms fire in two cases and nothing worse than hostile manoeuvre in the third, decided to land and either escape on foot or be captured.[6] It must not be assumed that armed enemy pilots or observers presented more than the most minor of risks to the reconnaissance crews, nor that the bombs which the latter occasionally carried and dropped held much risk for their targets. As to reconnaissance, however, it is clear from the repeated and favourable references in the Official History that Sir John's opinion of the R.F.C. was also that of his army.[7]

In assessing the performance of the young pilots and observers, one must remember the special problems with which they had to contend. It was but five years since Blériot's channel flight. Though the subsequent development of aeroplanes had been appreciable they were still flimsy and light affairs, susceptible to small wind variations and gusts and to thermal movements of air – the latter at their peak on the continent in August. Their engines set up continuous vibration. All this provided anything but a stable platform for observation, and certainly inhibited the use of telescopes or binoculars. If their pilots came lower, turbulence increased and they were shot at by anyone who had a gun, not very accurately but it was disturbing. The engines were not of high reliability and this fact tended to sap pilot concentration. Finally the speed attained by these early aeroplanes, against the wind, was often horrifyingly low, resulting in embarrassing situations for those who ventured too far down-wind in pursuit of interesting information. The British Expeditionary Force of 1914 has sometimes been described as the best-trained force ever to have gone to war; it was fortunate to have been supported in the air by men who, in the short time available and within the limitations of their remarkable transport, had correctly anticipated their role and trained themselves very adequately to carry it out. This might not have been enough, however, if they had not possessed great character and enterprise.

Nor must one forget the 'ground crew' who, in these unfamiliar conditions, managed to keep the temperamental aircraft serviceable and, simultaneously, to take part in a rapid withdrawal.

The exhausted allied armies followed up – they cannot have been said to have pursued – the retreating Germans. On the 13th the River Aisne was crossed but the Germans held fast to the high ground beyond it, and, with good observation, used their artillery effectively. From 17th September onwards Joffre made a series of moves to outflank the enemy to the north and the latter did likewise. The great port and fortress of Antwerp held out until 10th October; the British Army moved north in the Allied line of battle and held off the strongest of the German thrusts at Ypres; the hard-pressed Belgian Army held on to their vital territory by flooding the land in front of it. By November 1914 rival trench systems extended from the mouth of the Yser to the Swiss frontier, reinforced more and more by barbed wire, machine-guns and masses of artillery of ever-increasing calibres.

The siege had begun.

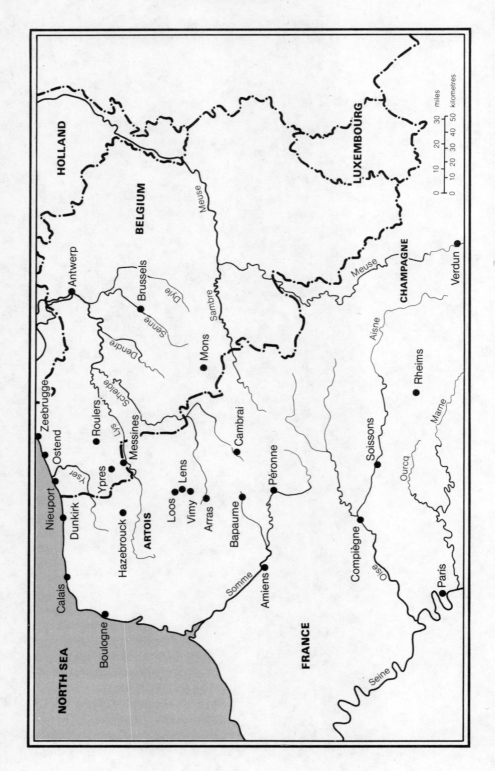

The Siege

◆

'In the great, grim siege that was the Western Front the R.F.C.
was an ancillary of great and increasing importance – but an ancillary. Its primary
job remained reconnaissance and observation for the guns and that it did,
on the whole, extremely well, undeterred by heavy loss.'
Marshal of the Royal Air Force SIR JOHN SLESSOR, foreword to
The Royal Flying Corps.: A History, by Geoffrey Norris.

Although we must not pursue too closely the analogy between the trench warfare in Europe between 1915 and 1918 and the siege of a fortress, we can, for the purpose of this account, consider German-held territory as a fortress with formidable defences, besieged by the British, French and Russian armies. We are not, of course, concerned here with one of the main features of the sieges of history – the starvation of the civilian inhabitants. – but rather with the attempts of the besiegers to break into and storm the fortress, and of the garrison to break out as a preliminary to engaging their enemies in the open.

We can rationalise these attempts into the following:

Early 1915: British, German and French attacks in Artois.

Mid-1915: German and Austrian offensive against the Russians, with the occupation of Poland and Galicia.

Autumn, 1915: French offensive in Champagne and associated British and French attack in Artois – the battle of Loos.

Early 1916: The German Verdun offensive.

Mid-1916: The Russian 'Brusilov' offensive against Austria.

July to November, 1916: The Battle of the Somme.

Early 1917: The Russian Revolution, the German withdrawal to the Hindenburg Line and the accession to the Allies of the United States.

April, 1917: The Battle of Arras and the 'Nivelle' offensive in Champagne.

Autumn, 1917: The third Battle of Ypres, or Passchendaele.

November, 1917: The battle of Cambrai.

December, 1917: The defeat of Russia.

Spring, 1918: The German break-out in the West.

The defences on the Eastern Front, which extended almost twice the distance of those in the West, were never so highly developed. Supply difficulties brought offensives to a halt more certainly than an enemy's defences. The Russian armies showed themselves aware of this and also displayed remarkable resilience. The Revolution of March, 1917, however, and the successive governments which led Russia to Communism, made surrender inevitable and allowed massive movements of German armies to the Western Front.

In the West, all offensives failed to break the deadlock – until March 1918 – though the battle of Cambrai saw the testing of the weapons and tactics which were to give each side in turn the opportunity of victory. Until then machine-guns, barbed wire and artillery reigned supreme, the fire of the attacker's artillery being applied in turn to the wire, to the machine-guns, to the defender's artillery (assembled to engage the assaulting infantry) and to the defender's reserves (as they strove to recapture lost positions). As artillery attained this unprecedented dominance on the battlefield, its problem of observation, ironically, became more difficult than ever before; no one believed any longer that 'direct fire' was feasible but observation posts were an essential to accurate 'indirect' fire and observation posts were hard to come by. The Germans, withdrawing into their 'siege' positions on the Western Front, had selected them on the commanding ground. Artificial vantage points, such as the roofs of buildings, church towers and the like, were engaged and brought low by the German artillery. From our front-line trenches an observer would rarely see farther than the enemy's front line. The artillery needed its air O.Ps.

Information of all kinds was, of course, as necessary to commanders as ever before, but it was much harder to get. Cavalry could not penetrate the barrier of barbed wire and multiple-trench systems, nor could infantry patrols, without extensive measures to get them through the enemy wire and back again. The enemy's infantry, like the allied infantry, lived below ground level, in a vast and ever-changing web of first-line, support and reserve trenches, and communication trenches stretching both laterally and from rear to front. Decisive changes could occur in the number, character and weapons of the inhabitants of these trenches without the watchers from the opposing trenches knowing much about them. An aerial view was required, not only of these forward trenches but of the roads and railways behind them, to enable intelligence staffs to build up pictures of enemy strengths and weaknesses, reinforcements, withdrawals of troops or movements from one part of the front to another. So far as the trench areas were concerned casual observation was unlikely to reveal much of importance; for more detailed examination air photography soon provided the key.

The combination of mud, trenches, barbed wire and prolonged artillery fire by massed artillery, often accompanied by smoke and poison gas, added immeasurably to the 'fog of war'. Normal communications would not often survive an hour's assault. It was very necessary, however, for commanders to be informed of the situation and position of their own troops, if only to prevent their own artillery from firing upon them. Here again the services of an airborne observer were required – an observer provided with effective communications.

Observation for the artillery, visual reconnaissance, air-photography and the 'contact-sortie' became, therefore, the principal tasks of the Royal Flying Corps on the Western Front, all very necessary and positive and often dangerous, if routine and unexciting. Two other tasks emerged – 'negative' in nature – the prevention of the enemy's air reconnaissances from performing for their commanders and their artillery the services we have just described, and the prevention of the crews of armed enemy aircraft from interfering with our aircraft as they performed their roles. These two tasks were often both dangerous and exciting and they caught the imagination of the British public and of writers. As a result the vital importance of the four positive tasks of the R.F.C. has often been forgotten or devalued.

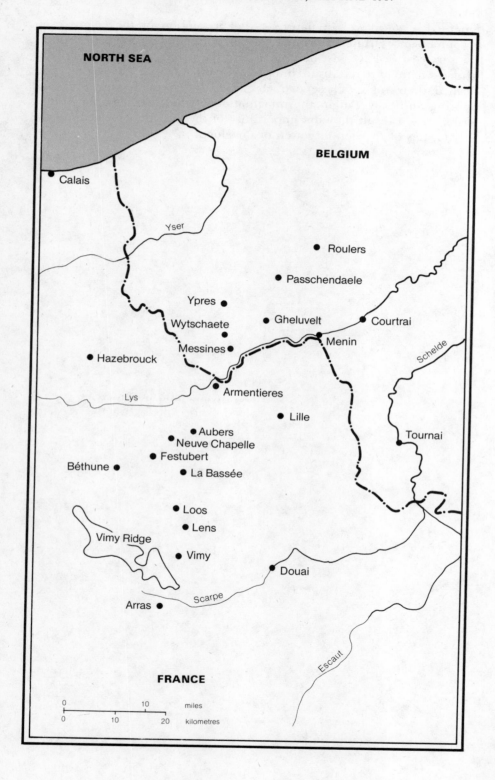

NORTH SEA

BELGIUM

● Calais

Yser

● Roulers

● Passchendaele

Ypres ●

Wytschaete ●   ● Gheluvelt   ● Courtrai

Messines ●   ● Menin

● Hazebrouck

Lys

Armentieres ●

Schelde

● Lille

● Tournai

● Aubers
Neuve Chapelle

● Festubert

Béthune ●   ● La Bassée

● Loos

● Lens

Vimy Ridge   ● Vimy

● Douai

Scarpe

Arras ●

FRANCE

Escaut

| 0 | | 10 | | miles |
| 0 | 10 | | 20 | kilometres |

The Siege
1915
A Year of Education

<>

'Experience is the name every one gives to their mistakes.'
OSCAR WILDE: *Lady Windermere's Fan*, III

In the battles of the spring and autumn of 1915 the Allied armies, as they increased in size, learnt many things and readjusted many ideas. The chief thing they learnt was, perhaps, the inability of the infantryman to make his way unsupported through the network of barbed wire, trenches and machine-guns without massive support, particularly from his artillery, and the enormous quantity of ammunition the artillery required to make the smallest impression on the enemy's trench system and wire and to neutralise the enemy's artillery. They should have learnt also with what a vast problem they were faced in hoping for a total break through the trench system into open country beyond.

The British battles of the spring, fought in Artois and Belgium alongside the French, have usually been identified by the names Neuve-Chapelle, Second Ypres, Aubers Ridge and Festubert.

The first of these – the first planned British attack on the Western wall – took place on 10th March to the north of the junction point with the main French armies. The plan was, in many ways, inspired. The artillery directed a short (thirty-five minute) intense bombardment against about a mile of the enemy's front-line trenches, then lifted their fire to prevent enemy reserves from intervening; the British infantry quickly reached their first objectives. The attack then 'hung up' from two causes – first, communication failures and reluctance of formations to push on with flanks exposed and, second, the shortage of artillery ammunition and thus of adequate support for the infantry in their further efforts to advance. The great achievement of this battle which was overlooked, however, was the attainment of surprise by (*inter alia*) the shortness and sharpness of the artillery bombardment. It took more than two years to re-learn this lesson.

The battle called 'Second Ypres' started on 22nd April with the now famous German chlorine gas attack on French divisions at the north end of the Ypres salient. The effect of the gas was devastating; a huge gap appeared in the Allied line and, had the Germans really had faith in their own weapon, a major break-out could certainly have taken place. Exploitation was cautious, however, and British, Canadian and Indian troops filled the breach. Indecisive, but expensive, attacks and counter-attacks extended this battle until the end of April, leaving the salient reduced but still intact.

On 9th May a French offensive was launched, and quickly destroyed, between Arras and Lens. A simultaneous attack was made by General Haig (whose corps had now expanded into the First British Army) against the dominating Aubers Ridge to the north-east of Neuve-Chapelle. This attack, for which a comprehensive air support plan had been made, failed, once again, for want of artillery ammunition.

As the Germans were seen to be transferring troops south to help oppose the French offensive, Haig mounted fresh attacks in the Festubert area, south of Neuve-Chapelle. These began late on 15th May and continued until the 25th, gaining very little in terms of territory or tactical advantage but, perhaps, taking some of the weight off the French.

In the early days of trench warfare the main role of the Royal Flying Corps remained strategic reconnaissance. In the new environment this implied observation of railway and road traffic, as indicators of enemy build-up in particular sectors. The Germans were often able, however, to evade such reconnaissance by moving by night and lying-up by day. Bad weather thwarted both strategic reconnaissance and tactical reconnaissance over the trench lines; low flying was vulnerable to small-arms fire while, observing from height, it was difficult to see detail within the trenches or to distinguish friend from foe.

Air photography had taken place during the Aisne battle, using an observer's private camera; soon afterwards Major W. G. H. Salmond was sent to liaise with the French air service and thereafter progress in air photography was quick. An experimental photographic section was formed in January 1915 and in the following month the 'A-type', a robust hand-held camera, was first used. In February, too, the photographic section was pronounced a success and established in the R.F.C. on the scale of one per army. Before the battle of Neuve-Chapelle the German trench system was comprehensively photographed and trench maps, derived from the photographs, lavishly distributed; thereafter, this became normal practice. By mid-year the 'C-type' camera was available, fixed to the aircraft and simpler to use. Photographic interpretation was becoming a specialised skill.

The first artillery co-operation sortie of the Great War, like the first air photography, took place on the Aisne.[1] It was no more than a flight with an artillery officer as passenger, the latter noting down on his map the positions of observed hostile batteries. Air observation of fire quickly followed, the observer's reports being dropped by message bag. Brigadier Anstey, whose unpublished research is the best authority on Royal Artillery operations in France and Belgium in the Great War, records that the first engagement in which the airborne observer's reports were sent by wireless was on 13th September, 1914[2]. Pre-war artillery and Flying Corps manuals, as we have seen, had included an agreed system for observing and reporting upon artillery fire – slow, and requiring for success much combined training. This art advanced in step with the science of wireless telegraphy and the two R.F.C. officers who perhaps did most to foster both were Lieutenants Donald Lewis and Baron James. They served together in the Headquarter wireless unit formed in France in September 1914 and developed both equipment and procedures in active artillery-observation sorties over the enemy. Both, sadly, were in the end shot down and killed by anti-aircraft fire – James while observing for artillery.

On the day before the battle of Neuve-Chapelle some registration of targets seems to have been permitted; R.F.C. wireless aircraft, pilots and observers were made available for this, and the same pilots or observers observed and corrected fire when the battle started. There was some more artillery co-operation at the south end of the Ypres salient before the main Ypres battle started, but little afterwards; German artillery observers were active, however, not only in aeroplanes but also in *Drachen* 'sausage-balloons'. The R.F.C. was mostly employed in tactical and strategical reconnaissance; on the day after the gas attack a close watch was kept on the area of penetration and on its flanks. During the confusion of this battle the need was strongly felt for our aircraft to be able to report battle locations and progress and therefore to be able to identify our infantry and to receive and retransmit simple messages.

During the Neuve-Chapelle battle some bombing attacks had been made against railway targets, virtually the first departure by the R.F.C. from the reconnaissance role in one form or another. On 26th April further such attacks were made, without much success. Second-Lieutenant W. B. Rhodes-Moorhouse, however, who hit the railway at Courtrai and, though mortally wounded, brought his aircraft back to base, became posthumously the first Royal Flying Corps soldier to be awarded the Victoria Cross.

For the attack on Aubers Ridge a comprehensive air plan was devised in which every effort seems to have been made to profit from lessons recently learnt. Wireless aeroplanes were attached to the heavy artillery groups, with the role of locating hostile batteries and helping our artillery to engage them. Wireless aeroplanes were also allotted for local reconnaissance and a 'contact patrol' was to be maintained all day, infantry reporting on successive lines by means of white ground-strips. Bombing raids were to take place on railway targets and on certain villages where the forward movement of enemy supplies might easily be interrupted. Of special significance was the local loan of a French *Caquot* artillery observation balloon, manned by the 40ᵉ Compagnie d'Aérostiers. Captain Caquot,[3] a French civil engineer, had performed his national service in such a unit in 1901; mobilised in 1914 he found himself responsible for equipping French units with *Drachen*-type kite-balloons. Finding these ineffective except in calm conditions, he immediately designed modifications in which inflated vertical fins above and below the tail were supplemented by horizontal surfaces, his final design having a triple inflated tail. It was universally adopted by the Allies.

The attack on Aubers Ridge, on 9th May, was a failure, however.

Shortage of artillery ammunition was again the main trouble, inaccuracy of artillery fire another. The artillery co-operation pilots reported on the 10th that the registrations of the previous day were out of date, due to changed atmospheric conditions. Air-observed engagements were slow and it was desirable, but not yet possible, to engage targets of opportunity as well as prearranged ones. Tactical reconnaissance aircraft were able to report the movement forward of enemy reinforcements, but contact patrols remained untried, since the infantry never reached the first of their report lines. Before the battle the R.F.C. had been tasked to prevent enemy from overflying the British part of the battlefield; whether they succeeded is not certain – the enemy did not, however, seem surprised by the British attack.

During the Festubert battle the R.F.C. was bedevilled by bad weather which made, or helped to make, bombing attacks ineffective. Reconnaissance was intermittent and artillery co-operation similar. The official historian mentions particularly the failure to neutralise the enemy's located artillery.[4]

The French kite-balloon performed well, however. Demands had already been placed for allocations of kite-balloons on a large scale; for the short term the Royal Navy lent one balloon, and later several more. By the autumn, four naval kite-balloons were in action with the British Army.

German air activity over British-held territory had increased during this battle, including artillery observation. We were beginning to pay the penalty for failing to design any effective anti-aircraft gun. By the middle of 1915 some 13-pounder guns had been mounted on special anti-aircraft carriages, but for safety reasons were restricted to the use of unsuitable ammunition. This restriction was eventually lifted but by the middle of 1916 there were little more than a hundred anti-aircraft guns with the British armies in France.

The Allies' autumn offensive consisted of attacks in Champagne and Artois against the southern and northern sectors of a wide German salient; the French made the Champagne attack, the Artois attack was a combined Franco-British operation. The British part in this operation fell to the lot of Haig's First Army and is known as the Battle of Loos. Haig attacked first, after twenty-four hours of not very intense artillery preparation, commencing early on 22nd September with a gas attack under far from ideal conditions. On the 25th, however, there was a moment when a break-through on a narrow front seemed possible if the G.H.Q. Reserve could quickly be committed. Whether such a narrow penetration could have achieved any decision is most doubtful but, anyway, it did not take place, the Reserves being held too far back. The attacks foundered on the 26th, and two days of German counter-attack followed. The French attacks in Artois and Champagne had similarly failed. The British suffered sixty thousand casualties at Loos, the

Germans, outnumbered three to one, had twenty thousand.

When, late in 1914, the B.E.F. had built up two separate Armies, the R.F.C. in France was reorganised into Wings – one for each Army; I Wing was in First Army and its commander at Loos was Lieutenant-Colonel E. B. Ashmore, destined to become most famous as the commander and architect of the London defences against the Gotha attacks of 1917 and 1918. This Wing had four squadrons, each basically allocated to a corps, but with individual flights under the direct control of First Army headquarters for reconnaissance. The corps squadrons were almost entirely employed in artillery co-operation, as were two kite-balloon sections (each having one balloon) which were also part of I Wing.

For the first three days of the battle the weather permitted the artillery co-operation programme to go ahead; this included the registration of hostile batteries and targets in the enemy's first and second-line trenches. Bad weather thereafter curtailed flying, though on most days some observation was possible.[5] The use of air photographs to assist in the identification of targets and of gridded maps for their indication, the introduction of a 'clock-code' procedure for reporting fall-of-shot and the introduction of the light-weight Sterling wireless transmitter had all done much to improve the speed and efficiency of artillery shoots with air observation;[6] nevertheless the Official History, while recording that the most difficult pioneer work had been done, also states that methods had not yet been sufficiently standardised.[7]

In the arrangements made for the battle, provision had once again been made for contact sorties to get early and vital information of the progress of our attacks. Once again this failed. There is no evidence that any signals were made, with three exceptions, to the R.F.C. contact patrols; perhaps it was expecting a lot from troops engaged in the savagery of an assault on a trench system, suffering heavy casualties and often resulting confusion, to be aware of the proximity of friendly aeroplanes and to communicate with them with special equipment carried across 'no-man's-land'. There was also, perhaps, an instinctive reluctance to disclose their position – to anyone. The three exceptions were three messages sent by signal lamp to contact patrol aircraft by an officer and sergeant of No.3 Squadron, R.F.C., who accompanied the infantry advance until wounded and evacuated.

The Battle of Loos marks perhaps. though such matters are never well defined, the real beginning of aerial fighting. It was not an end in itself. 'Reconnaissance, or observation,' wrote Raleigh, 'can never be superseded; knowledge comes before power; and the air is first of all a place to see from.'[8] To observe, however, one needs to survive; very soon the rifle and revolver of 1914 gave place to, or were reinforced by, automatic weapons – the Lewis gun in the case of the R.F.C. From April, 1915, the standard British work-horse reconnaissance and observation aircraft became the *B.E.2c* biplane. The observer manned the Lewis gun – normally in the front cockpit – and had the problem of shooting the enemy aircraft rather than his own propellor, wings or rigging; he was usually provided with alternative mountings for the gun on either side of the cockpit. With these facilities he was expected to defend his aircraft in addition to assisting the pilot to carry out the artillery, photographic or reconnaissance task. In addition, since no one was keen to give the German airmen a free run at their identical tasks, *B.E.2c* aircrews were not discouraged from 'having a go' at German aircraft encountered in the normal run of business.

Early in 1915 a small number of Vickers *F.B.5* Fighter biplanes reached France. These were 'pusher' aeroplanes, with propellor behind the pilot and a large cockpit for the observer in front, with unimpeded field of fire. They had an unimpressive climbing performance, which made interception of the normally high-flying German reconnaissance aircraft rather difficult; escort duty to the more vulnerable of our own observation sorties was a more promising role, and the decision to distribute these fighters around the squadrons was probably correct. The most vulnerable to attack by hostile aircraft were, almost certainly, the photographic aeroplanes (which needed to be flown straight and level over each camera-run) and the artillery aeroplanes (which necessarily spent long periods in one area). Contemporaneously with the British *F.B.5*, the German *Fokker E2* monoplane appeared which, in itself, would have caused no sensation but which incorporated a synchronisation of machine-gun and propellor which allowed the former to be fired through the latter. The tactics developed for this aircraft was to dive steeply upon its target, preferably with the sun behind the dive and aiming the whole aircraft while firing the fixed gun. German attacks upon our observation aircraft were, by autumn, becoming determined and frequent, necessitating fighter patrols to protect them and also to screen our ground movement from increasingly bold enemy air reconnaissance. The appearance of our fighter patrols led the Germans to organise their *Fokkers* into special fighter formations under such leaders as Boelcke and Immelmann, to intervene decisively in different parts of the front. The R.F.C. were ill-equipped to combat this first bid (historically speaking) for air superiority, which for the time passed to the Germans. Militarily speaking, the result was less effective reconnaissance and artillery fire for the British and an improvement in the enemy's possession of those commodities. It was fortunate for the Allies that winter was on its way and that the strategic initiative on the Western Front lay, on the whole, with them.

By the start of the Battle of Loos the Royal Flying Corps contingent with the B.E.F. had expanded to a force of twelve squadrons, 161 aeroplanes and, of course, the four naval kite-balloons. Just before the battle the commander of this force, Major-General Sir David Henderson, returned to his former War Office appointment – altered now almost beyond recognition – of Director-General of Aeronautics. Perhaps the most significant event of 1915 for the Royal Flying Corps, and thus for the history of aerial observation, was the appointment in his place of Colonel H.M. Trenchard, formerly commanding the First Wing – significant because the future development of Royal Flying Corps, and later Royal Air Force, tactical philosophy was increasingly a reflection of Trenchard's own opinions.

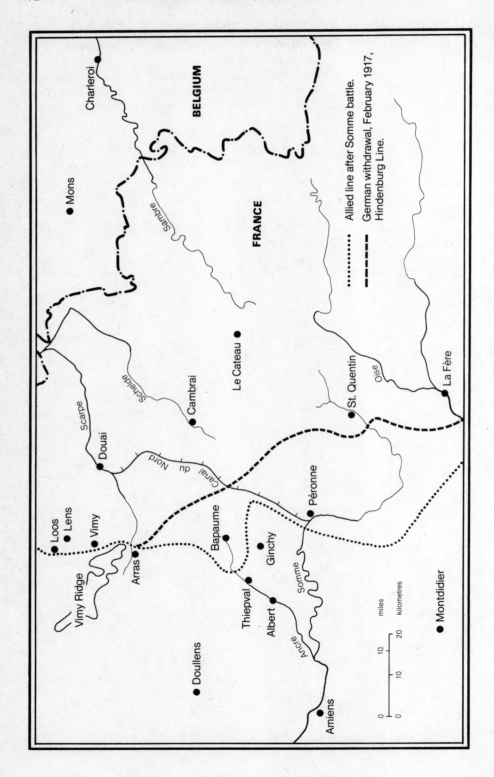

The Siege
1916
The Somme

❖

'We few, we happy few, we band of brothers.'
WILLIAM SHAKESPEARE: *Henry V*, IV, iii

In January 1916 two events important to the British Army took place.
Sir Douglas Haig, possibly the only leader with the particular tempera-
ment to stand up to the strains of the next three years, became
Commander-in-Chief of the British Army in France and the Conscription
Bill became law in the British Parliament. Meanwhile, since early in the
previous month, Allied plans for 1916 had been discussed. These plans
envisaged simultaneous offensives by France and Britain in the West, by
Russia in the East and by Italy against Austria. The front selected for
the British and French offensives, north and south of the Somme river
near Péronne, contained on the German side some of the strongest
defensive positions in the West. Haig would infinitely have preferred the
British effort to have been made in the north, with the support of
maritime operations against the Belgian coast.

On 21st February the Germans anticipated these Allied attacks by an
all-out offensive against the French in the Verdun sector, designed to
attract and destroy there a large mass of French reserves. The crisis for
the French could not be said to be over until the beginning of July.
Their allies gave what help they could, the British taking over the Arras
front and thus holding a line virtually from the North Sea to the Somme.
The Russians and the Italians made hurried and generally ineffective
attacks. In the first week of June, however, the southern half of the
projected Russian offensive, under General Brusilov, erupted with a
force and unexpectedness which found the Austrians totally unprepared,
and they collapsed. German troops were transferred from the Western
front and Falkenhayn, who had relieved von Moltke as Commander-
in-Chief in September 1914, gave place to the Hindenburg – Ludendorff
partnership. Brusilov, in a series of offensives on a broad front, advanced
distances of fifty to a hundred miles to the barrier of the Carpathians;
from his brother generals to the north he received no help at all.
Subsequent advances, which continued until September, were slow and
costly. The Battle of the Somme, in which the British had the greatest
share, finally placed Verdun out of danger.

On 1st July, after a week's preliminary bombardment, General
Rawlinson's Fourth Army attacked on a fourteen-mile front; south of

the Somme the French, against less developed defences, attacked on an eight-mile front with less than half the British strength. German air reconnaissances had, since early in the year, detected many signs of a coming offensive in the areas behind this Allied front – fresh hutments as far back as February;[1] an increase in anti-aircraft fire against reconnaissance aircraft in the sensitive sector, from March onward; an increase in Allied aerodromes and in aircraft thereon, from April; new training areas in the neighbourhood, from May and, in June, the appearance of new communication trenches and new batteries in photographic cover of the Allied positions. All the Germans needed to know was 'When?' and this they learnt from the Allies' extended artillery preparation programme. They sat this out in their deep dug-outs or in the cellars of the villages while the fire of 1500 British guns, and a like number of French, demolished their trenches but produced alternative cover in the shape of 'shell-holes'. On 1st July, when the barrage lifted, the Germans climbed out of their deep shelters with their machine-guns, occupied the shell-holes and engaged the British infantry as they advanced across no-man's-land at a slow walk. Somehow, and in some places, the British got a footing in the German first line, extended it and established a situation when their enemy deemed it wiser to withdraw to their second line. On this day the British lost close on 60,000 dead or wounded.

The French, meanwhile, had been more successful. They had even gained a measure of surprise from staggering their times of attack, from ground mist in the sector nearest to the Somme and from the German belief that the Verdun battle would have drained from them the ability to produce anything more than a demonstration. As a result they stormed the German first line without great loss and captured four thousand prisoners.

On 14th July Rawlinson overran the German second line in a brilliant operation, in which the infantry of four divisions made a night approach of some one thousand yards and, after an intense artillery bombardment of only a few minutes, attacked at dawn. In the late afternoon it even seemed possible that a break through might occur on the left flank, and horsed cavalry rode forward for the first time for two years. But it was not to be.

For the next two months a series of costly but minor engagements took the British by degrees to a jumping-off position, at the summit of the ridge between Ginchy and Thiepval, for the assault on the original German third line. This assault took place on 15th September after three days of artillery preparation; it saw the first appearance on a battlefield of the tank, prematurely exposed to enemy view. Of forty-nine tanks which set off, thirty-two reached their start-line. Of these, only nine managed to accompany the infantry and a further nine to clear-up captured ground. These surviving eighteen tanks, however, caused some alarm and despondency among the enemy.

Further small advances were made and Combles and Thiepval were captured on the two flanks. Finally, on 13th November, General Gough's Fifth Army attacked the enemy salient north of the River Ancre and had some success until rain and mud brought the Battle of the Somme to an end five days later. It had cost the participants, in round figures, casualties as follows: Britain 450,000, France 340,000, Germany 530,000.

To the British Army of today the Somme is nothing more than a reminder of the age of the military bludgeon and of dreadful casualty lists. To the Royal Air Force, successors of the Royal Flying Corps, it is a prominent landmark, the first large-scale air battle fought and won by air forces acting as a cohesive body. To the British Army as a whole, the Somme was a battle which started at the height of summer and continued until the onset of winter. For the Royal Flying Corps it started in the closing weeks of 1915, with air superiority in the hands of their enemies and with their own ability to support the artillery and communicate with the infantry both seriously in doubt; it ended in a victory achieved, a reputation enhanced and a position in the army unchallenged although, as we shall see, their possession of air superiority was once again in question. During the first six months of 1916 there was, of course, constant activity all along the British section of the front; the Germans made two determined attacks on the Ypres salient and another on Vimy ridge. The R.F.C. naturally played their full part both in the routine activities and in the repulse of the three attacks. In retrospect, however, one must regard their most important activity to have been their preparation for the Battle of the Somme.

Both sides, as we have seen, had by now concluded that in artillery power and accuracy lay the best hope of achieving a break-through. The final accuracy of artillery, on which rested the lives of the infantry and their success in attack, depended on the observation and correction of the 'fall of shot' – during preliminary registration and during last-minute adjustment to counter the effects of meteorological changes. The infantry needed the protection of their artillery not only from the rifles and machine-guns in the positions they were assaulting but equally from the enemy's artillery. A constant campaign was conducted, therefore, to locate hostile batteries, record their locations and plan their destruction or 'neutralisation' at a suitable juncture. The location of hostile batteries depended on observation. Ground observation posts with a view of the enemy batteries were virtually an impossibility. Air observation was thus an essential and the R.F.C.'s most important task continued to be, in Frank Courtney's words, the 'unglamorous and hazardous' one of artillery observation[2] Quite an elaborate 'counter-battery' organisation was being built up by the Royal Artillery, with counter-battery (C.B.) groups responsible for engagement of targets in specific zones; a 'zone-call' procedure had been designed to enable an R.F.C. pilot or observer to call for fire on a located target without any pre-arrangement with, or even knowledge of, the battery which would engage. An emergency procedure had been instituted, whereby the instruction 'General artillery action' or 'Corps artillery action', sent out by wireless and other means, resulted in the immediate reversion to artillery tasks of designated squadrons temporarily employed in other tasks. Wireless communication was greatly improved by a device called the clapper-break which enabled the pitch of the Morse-code signal to be varied, thus enabling signals from two aircraft on neighbouring wireless frequencies to be distinguished from each other – and consequently enabling a greater number of artillery observers to operate on a given front. Kite-balloons appeared in every army sector. The ability of the observer to speak by telephone direct to artillery commanders and staffs was most valuable: the balloons were, however, vulnerable to anti-aircraft artillery attack and had to be sited somewhat in rear, whence their observation over the enemy's battery areas was limited – the aeroplanes therefore remained paramount in the counter-battery field. A pamphlet was produced on the art of co-operation of aircraft with artillery; in it artillery and flying corps officers were urged to get together to discuss and improve their co-operation, and particularly to discuss their failures.

Continuous and detailed reconnaissance of the enemy's trench systems was always necessary, culminating on the eve of an attack in searches for newly dug defences and a thorough inspection of the effect of the wire-cutting programme of the gunners. From a great height not much could be seen; lower down enemy A.A. fire and the pilot's consequent evasive action counter-balanced any improvement in observation. Air photographs, however, could be studied at length and in comparative comfort, making use of such aids as stereoscopic viewers and magnifiers; the demand for air photography increased steadily and rose to a crescendo before and during the Somme battle. Due to delays in Wing photographic sections, processing and interpretation were transferred, together with the necessary technicians, to the appropriate squadrons.

Further efforts were made to solve the problem of the contact patrol – the vital channel of communication which everyone wanted but no one had been able to produce 'on the day'. The French encountered similar problems in the Verdun battles and experiences were exchanged. Joffre issued an instruction and the British Fourth Army, with its R.F.C. squadrons, carried out experiments and training west of Albert. Infantry were instructed to signal their positions, on the initiative of junior commanders, when distinctively marked British aircraft posed the question 'Where are you?' by light signal or by klaxon horn; the position was to be indicated by lighting flares or displaying ground-strips, and a proportion of the attacking troops would carry metal mirrors on their backs to make them more easily seen by air observers. Battalion and Brigade headquarters could send messages to observers, for onward transmission, by lamp or by louvred shutters exposing a white background to send morse signals.

To perform these roles efficiently, the R.F.C. had first to gain air superiority. In January 1916, however, they were so far from doing so that Trenchard ordered that all reconnaissance aircraft should be escorted by at least three other fighting machines in close formation and that, if any part of the escort became detached, the reconnaissance should be abandoned. Two months earlier, in response to warning signals from France, air fighting had been placed on the syllabus of pilots' and observers' training in England, and aerobatics began to be taught as an aid to fighting.

Nor were the Home authorities slow in producing fighting aircraft to meet the 'Fokker menace'. In January 1916, the *F.E.2b* started to arrive and in March the *D.H.2*, both were pusher machines designed by Geoffrey de Havilland. The *F.E.2b* was a two-seater, in the large forward-cockpit of which the observer had a wide view and room to wield his Lewis gun. The *D.H.2* was a single-seater, with the gun firing forward. Both were faster, and climbed faster, than their predecessors. In March also the R.F.C. in France started to receive a few of the French single-seater *Nieuport* scouts, tractor biplanes with the gun mounted, pointing forward, on the top wing and fired by cable. These were the three aircraft with which the R.F.C. beat the *Fokker E2 and E3*; before the Somme battle, however, a few *Sopwith 1½-strutter* tractor two-seaters were received, with a forward-firing Vickers machine-gun firing through, and synchronised with, the propellor and some of them carrying in the rear cockpit the *Scarff* ring which enabled the observer's gun to be switched rapidly from side to side. For those Lewis guns which were not replaced by Vickers guns, improved ammunition was provided, making 'jams' less frequent. 'Tracer' ammunition made its appearance, in every sense, assisting correction of aim by enabling the track of the bullet to be seen. By the end of May the 'Fokker menace' was over and the R.F.C. had air superiority over the area of the forthcoming battle.

Hermann, one of the writers in Neumann's book on the German air force, remarks that 'the principal work of fighting machines consisted in destroying the enemy's powers of observation, whether carried out by aeroplanes or balloons, particularly when the artillery on either side was called into action.'[3] In furtherance of this principle periodic fighter attacks were mounted against the German kite-balloons, particularly in the week preceding the start of the battle, and plans were made to deal with both the German artillery and reconnaissance aeroplanes and also German fighters which might be expected to harass our artillery, photographic and contact patrol aeroplanes. Trenchard, who had from April onwards begun to organise his fighting aircraft into separate scout squadrons, believed strongly that their policy should be aggressive, aimed at meeting and engaging enemy aircraft and aircraft formations considerably to the east of the battle lines, rather than above the latter.[4] This policy is a good one for an air force to follow when in superior numbers, and it was successful in parts of the Battle of the Somme, but many will say that it should not be elevated to a cast-iron principle but rather considered in conjunction with a given tactical situation. Trenchard departed from it in this very battle by ordering small scale continuous cover over the battlefield and was forced to modify it further in the adverse conditions of the Battle of Arras.

Bombing is not, of course, within the subject of this book but, since it diverted effort from observation and reconnaissance, it needs to be mentioned. By the end of 1915 day-bombing, for the British, had become an expensive pastime only to be indulged in formations of twelve aircraft or more, including escorts; in the early part of 1916 such raids were mostly limited to objectives within a few miles of the front lines. Small night raids took place, principally to ensure that the R.F.C.'s night flying capability matched that of the German air force, which had started the practice. Generally speaking, each side claimed that their own raids were devastating and their opponents' ineffective. Except in rare cases, such as the Naval Air Service attacks on Zeppelin sheds, where a large, stationary, vulnerable target of concentrated importance presented itself, it is difficult to believe that the bombing of the Great War was worth the cost. As Courtney writes, 'It seems always to have been the instinct of the warrior to try to get somewhere over the top of his foe, so that he could drop something nasty on him', and, again, 'So when war came, we took to bombing with enthusiasm, although we may now wonder what good we thought we were doing.'[5]

At the end of the Battle of Loos the Royal Flying Corps in France contained twelve squadrons each of twelve aircraft. On 1st July, 1916 there were twenty-seven squadrons, in about half of which there were now eighteen aircraft. The R.F.C. had been reorganised into 'brigades' on the basis of one brigade per army. General Rawlinson's Fourth Army, for example, contained IV Brigade, R.F.C., commanded by Brigadier-General E. B. Ashmore, who as a Lieutenant-Colonel had commanded I Wing at Loos. R.F.C. Brigades contained two wings, the 'Corps' Wing of theoretically one squadron per corps in the army and the 'Army' Wing. The Corps squadrons looked after close reconnaissance for corps and divisions, including artillery observation, contact patrols and photography, while the Army Wing, under direct army headquarters control, was responsible for more distant reconnaissance and photography and for fighter protection.

IV Brigade's III (Corps) Wing (Lieutenant-Colonel E. R. Ludlow-Hewitt) started the battle with 16 *Moranes* (4 biplanes, 12 *Parasols*) and 52 *B.E.2cs*.[6] These sixty-eight aeroplanes were intially allotted as follows: 30 to counter-battery, 16 to 'trench flights' (close reconnaissance and destructive bombardment), 13 to contact patrols and 9 to special missions (including photography and the attack of enemy balloons). It will be seen that two-thirds of these aeroplanes were to be employed on predominantly artillery tasks. A varying number of kite-balloon sections were allotted to each army, organised into a kite-balloon squadron under each corps wing. Ludlow-Hewitt was allotted No.1 Kite-Balloon Squadron (under Major C. Bovill) of five balloons for artillery observation and an extra three attached for 'tactical' (as opposed to artillery) duties. IV Brigade's XIV (Army) Wing (Lieutenant-Colonel C. G. Hoare) had a squadron of eighteen *F.E.2bs* and a squadron of nineteen *D.H.2s.*

The headquarters of the R.F.C. had under its direct control IX (Headquarter) Wing – commanded, it is of interest to note, by Lieutenant-Colonel H.C.T. Dowding, destined to command Royal Air Force Fighter Command in the Battle of Britain almost a quarter of a century later. This wing had, on 1st July, 1916, four squadrons of miscellaneous aircraft types designed for long-range reconnaissance and fighting; these were committed to the battle, as were (in the bombing role) squadrons of I, II and III Brigades.

Altogether the R.F.C. had on the front of the attack something over two hundred aeroplanes and the Germans about a hundred. The German air force had, moreover, been driven temporarily east of the battle zone, with their aircraft outclassed and their morale low. In the words of General Fritz von Below, commander of the German Army facing Rawlinson: 'Our own aeroplanes only succeeded in quite exceptional cases in breaking through the hostile patrol barrage and carrying out distant reconnaissances; our artillery machines were driven off whenever they attempted to carry out registration for their own batteries. Photographic reconnaissance could not fulfill the demands made upon it.'[7]

During the week of preliminary bombardment the main role of the R.F.C. was, of course, artillery observation and the adjustment of fire at each stage of the elaborate programme. This task was carried out with little interference by enemy aircraft but rather more by the weather. As the programme developed the German artillery retaliated, revealing fresh battery positions to R.F.C. observers, to be added to the programme of destruction or neutralisation. Short pauses were made in the bombardment to allow air photography and assessment of the effectiveness of fire on trenches and wire; unfortunately such photographs could not reveal the depth of the shelters and the comparative safety of the defenders therein and tended to be optimistically interpreted regarding the state of the wire.

On the 1st July (D-day) R.F.C. pilots flew for a total of 408 hours. The fighter patrols prevented enemy air interference with our corps aircraft and prevented enemy reconnaissance from discovering much; it was a disappointing day for the remainder. The intense and widespread British artillery bombardment defeated efforts to distinguish and correct the fire of individual batteries; the German artillery was not silenced and was able appreciably to add to the horrors of the day for our infantry. Our contact patrol and tactical reconnaissance pilots were often blinded by the battle smoke although they had some successes. Mention is made in the Air Force history of a 600-feet reconnaissance of enemy

positions at Thiepval by Captain C.A.A. Hiatt of No.4 Squadron.[8] The
balloon observers did useful work within their range of observation and
were, to some degree, able to relate enemy artillery fire on our troops to
observed enemy batteries, and to engage the latter.

In the next two days, as the infantry mopped up and consolidated and
the never-ending task of locating and destroying hostile batteries continued, as fresh photographs were taken and as strategic air reconnaissance saw and counted the trains that brought in the German reinforcements to rail-head, the air support machinery started to work more
smoothly. Haig and Rawlinson both sent the R.F.C. appreciative and
encouraging messages. The Gunners and the Flying Corps met on 10th
July to smooth out some of their difficulties; two days later, at 8 p.m.,
an observer of No.9 Squadron saw what appeared to be the start of
covering fire for a German counter-attack, identified and located the
hostile batteries involved and called for retaliatory fire which proved
effective.[9] Kite-balloon observers continued to do well and became useful
retransmitters of messages flashed to them by lamp by our forward
infantry. On occasions they were able to pass information of strategic
interest such as the quite distant movement of trains.

During the day which followed the successful dawn attack of 14th July
the contact aircraft did well. The signalling systems seemed at last to be
working and a particularly useful role was that of reporting to the
artillery when the infantry were ahead of schedule. Low cloud forced the
pilots to fly low but no enemy fighters appeared and they seemed to
enjoy surprising immunity from ground fire. Siegert, who writes of the
Somme battle in Neumann's book, paints a clear picture of the breakdown in relations between the German infantry and air force at this
time; the former saw only Allied aircraft and, says Siegert, lacked the
skill and confidence to shoot them down.[10] On this same 14th July, it
will be remembered, the British dream of the 'cavalry going through'
reached the stage of horsed cavalry, of the 7th Dragoon Guards and
20th Deccan Horse, appearing in the front area. The crew of a contact
aeroplane saw hostile infantry and a machine-gun concealed in crops
and indicated their presence by a Lewis gun attack; the cavalry charged
with the lance, killed a few and captured thirty-two – an incongruous
little episode naturally irrelevant to the battle.

Two months of trench warfare preceded the next major attack. Bad
weather at the end of July restricted both visual and photographic
reconnaissance of hostile battery positions and, when the weather
improved, necessitated urgent and intensive efforts to redraw the
counter-battery map. Close tactical reconnaissance and contact patrols
were unceasing and seem to have been of ever-increasing efficiency and
worth. The modern military reader of the official accounts of the Somme
battles cannot fail to be impressed by the ability of the usually quite
young pilots and observers to observe and think, as it were, at divisional,
corps and army level and to discern – often outside the narrow field of
their particular mission – features of the dreadful panorama likely to

reveal unexpected and important information for the commanders. An unusual degree of reliance was placed in these junior officers; an example, mentioned in the Official History, was the change of a divisional objective only a few hours before a night attack, and the consequential alteration in the 'zero-hour' for the main Army attack, as a direct result of a reconnaissance by Captain C. H. B. Blount and Second-Lieutenant T. S. Pearson of No.34 Squadron.[11] Our kite-balloons, besides continuing their routine artillery and tactical duties, did their bit, evidently, to depress enemy morale. General von Below paid them a tribute, in a memorandum written after the battle, which takes us right back to the action on the river Ourthe in September 1794. 'The innumerable balloons, hanging like grapes in clusters over the enemy's lines, produced a similar (moral) effect, for the troops thought that individual men and machine-guns could be picked up and watched by them and subjected to fire with observation.'[12] While on the subject of lighter-than-air vehicles, mention might be made of the experimental night reconnaissance on 28th August by the naval airship *S.S. 40*; because of her vulnerability in the battle zone she flew at 8000 feet and above and little could be seen.

From the middle of July onwards the Germans had been bringing air, as well as land, reinforcements into the battle area and in August began to form independent fighter squadrons with which to wrest command of the air from the R.F.C. On the 31st of that month there appeared for the first time the formidable *Albatros D 1* scout, with two machine-guns synchronised to fire through the propellor.[13] German air activity increased but, by the next phase of the battle (the attack on the German third line on 15th September), photographic and contact aircraft were still well protected from interference by enemy fighters.

The 15th September, 1916, is claimed by Jones to have been the most active day so far for the R.F.C.[14] Many hostile batteries were engaged, including those withdrawing to fresh positions, and many other targets of opportunity were engaged by the zone-call procedure. The contact aircraft were embarrassed by smoke and morning mist early on, but afterwards had an active day, many crews spending up to eight hours in the air. They used their Lewis-guns freely on enemy infantry and in some cases on enemy artillery. On that day and on the 16th our fighter patrols were heavily engaged with the German air forces, both sides suffering material losses. On the following day R.F.C. losses were heavier still, largely due to the arrival of a new 'commando' fighter unit with the two 'aces' Boelcke and Richthofen.

The Battle of the Somme dragged on for a further two months, General Gough's Fifth Army and his V Brigade, R.F.C., coming increasingly into the picture. So did the German air force, penetrating further and further into and beyond the battle area and attacking the artillery aircraft in particular. Trenchard replied with offensive patrols and bombing attacks on the German aerodromes; the latter were of no significant value while both were expensive in casualties. The enemy's artillery aircraft became active again. Till the end of the battle, however, our artillery, photographic and contact pilots and observers continued to perform their tasks, a tribute to them and to the fighter crews. Twice in September the V Brigade artillery aircraft crews received special commendation from Gough while, on the 26th September, there took place a superlative little operation to capture an important section of a trench known as the 'Gird Trench'. The Guards Division were established on one flank of the German position, the 7th Leicesters on the other. The Leicesters started to bomb their way down the trench and a tank was called for. A contact aircraft (Second-Lieutenant L. G. Wood, pilot, and Lieutenant H. J. L. Cappel) flew out to report, assessed the situation and called for artillery fire on the enemy portion of the trench. As the tank arrived this fire was suspended and the tank and the aircraft then raked the trench in turn. White handkerchiefs indicated surrender, the aircraft dropping a message to this effect to the infantry who collected 370 prisoners.

By the end of September, however, it was clear to Trenchard that he no longer possessed air superiority. Urgent calls went home for reinforcement with aircraft and crews; three more squadrons arrived in October and the Royal Naval Air Service sent another. To offset this advantage, however, the *B.E.12* single-seater tractor fighter, which had appeared during the battle, proved unsuitable for fighting. During October, in spite of poor weather for much of the time, the German air force penetrated the battlefield to a greater and greater extent. Attempts to take the war to the enemy's rear areas by bombing raids led to further losses. In the final battles of the Fifth Army north of the Ancre in mid-November, however, the British corps-squadrons were still able to perform their roles.

The air statistics of the Somme are not very easy to interpret.[15] The artillery registered 8612 targets with the aid of the R.F.C.; the artillery were sometimes disappointed with results and so, one must admit, were the infantry. The enemy, on the other hand, found our artillery devastating and our artillery aircraft very bad for their morale. 19,000 photographs were taken, completely indispensable in trench warfare where key features do not appear on normal maps. The contact patrols, when the thorny problems of communication could be solved, gave moral support to the British infantry. Aircraft and aircrew losses both lay, in all probability, between 350 and 400, those of the Germans a little lower; the greater part of these were incurred outside the area of the ground battle. It is often said that the high casualty rate was due to the insufficiency of pilot-training in the United Kingdom; this was certainly true – from March 1916, fifteen hours was considered a reasonable minimum of solo flying prior to an operational posting. The fault was not so easy to correct, however, given that there were always strident demands for pilot reinforcements, expansions of the Corps and production of new and better types of aircraft. Sadly, but inevitably, it is the greenest pilot (like the greenest soldier) who falls the first victim. We have admired the reconnaissance crews; we need not to be too sorry for them. Their expectation of life, at this period of the war, was still higher than that of the infantrymen and the quality of that life immeasurably higher.

Another common criticism is that 'the people at home', and specifically the Royal Aircraft Factory, provided low-performance, unsafe or unreliable aircraft as coffins for the R.F.C. pilots. One of the most outspoken critics has been Frank Courtney and, since he was a test pilot at the Royal Aircraft Factory for most of 1916, he ought to know. He had left France, however, shot down by Max Immelmann, just as the *Fokker* had gained mastery, and returned at the end of the Somme battle when the *Albatros D1*, Boelcke and Richthofen had gained it again; perhaps he did not really believe that the Germans had lost it in between. Christopher Cole, in his introduction to Royal Flying Corps, 1915–1916, an edited collection of operational summaries, emphasises the infancy of the flying art in 1914 and the necessity to base development and manufacture on the best ideas in the country at that time. 'This resulted', he writes, 'in a natural tendency to concentrate on developing a good, all-round and reliable aeroplane that flew well. It was generally assumed that the aircraft must be a two-seater, and the Royal Aircraft Factory *B.E.2* series met these requirements admirably. The Farnborough designers placed great stress on stability, and the superbly stable *B.E.2c* development of May 1914 was selected for large-scale production. In later service the *B.E.2c's* stability was a disadvantage in combat and inadequate provision for armament rendered it very vulnerable. The heavy losses stimulated violent criticism of the whole Farnborough organisation, and many of the critics chose to ignore other excellent Farnborough designs which helped to give the R.F.C. a definite superiority as they appeared.'

Sefton Brancker, whom we last noticed as a major as he slipped off from the War Office to Belgium in the summer of 1914 to reconnoitre the probable deployment area of the B.E.F., was for the next year responsible for the whole equipment, organisation and expansion of the Flying Corps. Between August and December, 1915 he commanded III Wing, R.F.C. at Loos. By March 1916, as Brigadier-General, he was back in the War Office as Director of Air Organisation. Clearly any criticism of the expansion of the R.F.C. in the first two years of the war must arrive at his door. Christopher Cole's remarks seem fair, however. The Royal Flying Corps, four squadrons strong, was launched into battle, after little more than two years of life, against an enemy who had long planned for this war; at once the R.F.C. proved superior in battle. The combatants were then plunged into quite a different kind of war, which neither side had expected; it was the German airmen who next gained the advantage through the *Fokker* machine-gun and its interruptor gear. Within six months the machines had arrived from Britain which, in time for the Battle of the Somme, gave air superiority once again to the R.F.C. Only in the closing stages of this battle had the Germans drawn ahead again with, among other things, a new winning fighter. Surely Brancker did not need to be ashamed of this record – or his share of it?

1917
The Last Year of
The Siege

—◇—

'Once more unto the breach, dear friends, once more'
WILLIAM SHAKESPEARE: *Henry V,* III, i.
(MAPS pp. 64, 72)

In March 1917 the Russian Revolution broke out. Although nine further months were to pass before Russia finally withdrew from the war, it was already clear to the Germans that their army need no longer be feared, and they started to transfer troops to the Western Front. In April the United States of America came into the war on the Allied side – this implied a huge accession of armed strength but not effectively for fifteen months or more. The Germans aimed therefore to achieve victory by then.

Allied plans for 1917 were made before these events in Russia and America. On the Western Front, where the relatively junior General Nivelle had replaced Joffre, the Allied plan was for an early Franco-British offensive south and north, respectively, of the Somme battlefield, with the object of pinching out the German salient between Soissons and Arras. The Germans anticipated this in February by withdrawing voluntarily from this salient to the strong, prepared 'Hindenburg Line', west of Cambrai and St. Quentin, laying waste the surrendered territory. The planned Allied attacks took place in April, however. The British attack near Arras on 9th April was once again preceded by a long artillery bombardment which surrendered surprise; gas shell and well-planned 'creeping barrages', however, brought greater tactical success than usual on the first day but thereafter the momentum of advance could not be maintained. By 14th April progress had ceased; thereafter there was only the mounting casualty list. Nivelle's Champagne offensive was a disaster – morally rather than materially. No less progress was made than by the British, but Nivelle had been lavish in his promises of a rapid breakthrough and, when these were unfulfilled, morale slumped and mutinies occurred. It was the end of Nivelle; Pétain relieved him and started to nurse the French Army back to health.

It was very necessary for the British Army to take the strain from the French. The British Admiralty had, for some time, been advocating the recapture of the Belgian coast, with its submarine bases, and Haig was attracted to the idea of an offensive in the north. As a preliminary, a long-planned operation was carried out by General Plumer's Second Army to capture the Messines ridge, south of the Ypres salient from which the projected offensive would jump-off. The Battle of Messines was a perfect operation of siege warfare. The artillery concentration was there, as usual – 2,338 guns on a front of about nine miles – and preparation began seventeen days before the attack. Surprise, however, was achieved at 3.10 a.m. on 7th June with the simultaneous explosion of nineteen huge mines beneath the German front-line trenches, followed by the descent of the artillery barrage and the advance of the infantry. Within twenty-four hours the final objectives had been captured. No exploitation took place in this essentially limited operation.

Almost two months later the Third Battle of Ypres began. Gough, whose Fifth Army was mainly involved, was given as his first objective the capture of the Passchendaele – Staden ridge and the railway from Roulers to Thourout, ten miles to the north; in the event the village of Passchendaele was at length captured on 6th November, after which the battle stopped. Before the initial attack there were ten days of preliminary bombardment by three thousand guns after which, on 31st July, the German first and second lines were overrun; heavy and continuous rain prevented exploitation. Gough had not succeeded in capturing the Gheluvelt ridge on his right flank and this was now an essential to further advance; Plumer's Second Army captured the greater part of the ridge in two attacks of 20th and 26th September. On 4th October further advances were made towards the Passchendaele ridge but heavy rain reduced the terrain to a quagmire; attainment of the ridge thus became more necessary than ever but needed a further month's fighting. The British lost 240,000 casualties in the Third Ypres battle, an appalling cost for not much obvious gain but still little more than half those of the Somme; the Germans lost 400,000 and suffered comparable horrors to those of the British.[1]

There remained one engagement to be fought before the Siege was broken – the interesting Battle of Cambrai. General Byng's Third Army was given the task of breaking through a twelve-mile sector of the Hindenburg Line using new tactics in which nearly four hundred tanks were used, mostly in front of the infantry, without preliminary artillery bombardment, to flatten the wire and reduce the fortified defences. New methods of survey and sound-ranging enabled the artillery to bring down a barrage on the enemy's forward and reserve positions and on his batteries without prior 'registration'. This operation was in many ways an experiment and a large-scale raid might have been the occasion for it. In Byng's hands it became, however, an attempt at a breakthrough – but without sufficient reserves. The initial attack, on 20th November, was brilliantly successful; a five-mile penetration was made and the resulting wedge was quickly made into a defensible salient, but there it had to rest. The Germans quickly and efficiently prepared their counterstroke, against the south end of the salient. They too employed fresh tactics; a short but intense artillery bombardment with gas and smoke shell preceded an infantry attack before dawn on 30th November. The infantry advanced in small groups, by-passing resistance, infiltrating at weakly-held points and concentrating into larger parties to attack objectives beyond, including the gun areas. The success of the 30th was as spectacular as that of the 20th; when the lines were stabilised neither side, on balance, had gained much territory. But each had learnt something.

The Royal Flying Corps almost doubled its strength between 1st July, 1916, and 9th April, 1917, the opening of the Battle of Arras.[2] Apart from the new Corps squadrons formed for the Fifth Army during the Somme battle, the increases were entirely in the Army and Headquarter squadrons, reflecting no doubt the necessary increase in the protective element, as compared with the 'working' element of the R.F.C., as air superiority passed to the enemy. The Corps squadrons were mostly equipped with the *B.E.2c* or later *B.E.* derivatives, but four squadrons now had the *R.E.8*.[3] The kite-balloon squadrons had been removed from the Corps wings and concentrated, for command and administration but not of course for deployment and battle duties, in a separate kite-balloon wing in each R.F.C. Brigade. In the army squadrons significant fighting aircraft were appearing or were soon to appear, particularly the famous two-seater *Bristol Fighter*, the *Sopwith Pup* and *Sopwith Triplane*, the French-designed *Spad*, the *S.E.5* and *S.E.5a* and the unstable but superbly manoeuvrable *Sopwith Camel*. At the start of the battle of Arras, however, only the *Pup*, the *Triplane* and the two *S.E.5s* were a match for the latest *Halberstadt* and *Albatros*. The German air force, it would seem, was well provided with experienced pilots and, in Richthofen, possessed an astute tactician and leader.

The British air plan for the Arras battle relied, as at the Somme, on offensive patrols well to the east of the battle area to protect the Corps aircraft but, in addition, 'line patrols' were provided to give some protection in the immediate vicinity of the battle. Every reconnaissance, and particularly every photographic reconnaissance, required a heavy escort.

On the opening day of the battle, 9th April, the counter-battery programme was unusually effective, the German artillery fire being described in many reports as feeble. By the 11th the German air force had intervened seriously in the battle; seven Corps aircraft were shot down and there were fighter casualties also.

Throughout April the losses mounted of aircraft, pilots and observers.[4] The R.F.C. had recourse to infantry volunteers, many of whom had never previously flown, to man the Lewis guns. Photographic sorties were most vulnerable but German fighters penetrated frequently into the battle area to attack artillery and contact patrol aircraft and began to 'strafe' the British trenches. German artillery aircraft became more active. Richthofen, meanwhile, developed an organisation whereby several groups of fighters could quickly concentrate for operation in mass, assisted by forward ground observers to warn them of special R.F.C. activity.

Long-range reconnaissance attempts by the R.F.C. were almost always abortive; their offensive patrols had to be drawn back closer to the battle area and the line patrols strengthened. On the 29th, Richthofen claimed his fiftieth victim and, two days later, returned to Germany on leave.

Simultaneously the situation of the R.F.C. started to improve. On 2nd May, and again on the 7th, well planned and executed attacks were made on enemy kite-balloons, which had normally been hauled down too quickly for our fighters. Apart from these successes, however, the R.F.C. aircrews began to enjoy increased freedom of action, for reasons not easy to analyse. They had been getting used to the new aircraft and were having less engine and gun trouble than formerly; the growing concentration in mass of the German air formations left large areas of sky, and periods of the day, relatively free of their attention and allowed British patrols to be increased in size during the most active periods. It only needed a small relief, a small success or two, a small reduction in the casualty rate, to allow the new British pilots to acquire more combat experience and confidence. It seems that the skilled and experienced German air crews nevertheless allowed their opponents just this small breathing space. Perhaps the Germans were getting a little battle-weary, and had not at this juncture the leader to lift them above it and to keep a watchful eye on the need to adjust their tactics? Perhaps Richthofen's leave was not altogether irrelevant?

At Messines the initial British success was principally due to the great mines, but the subsequent momentum of the advance, the consolidation and the repulse of the German counter-attacks were won by the British artillery – especially by its suppression of the enemy's batteries. Almost half of the German heavy guns and a quarter of the lighter ones were lost between 5th and 7th June, and, among German reasons for their loss of the battle, pride of place is given to the overwhelming domination of the British artillery.[5] Air observation was particularly important because nothing east of the ridge could be seen from ground observation posts; the whole emphasis of the Corps squadrons' work was on artillery co-operation and, in the preparatory stages, virtually the whole of the Corps aircraft were so employed, two-thirds on counter-battery tasks and a third on the observation of trench and wire bombardment. The aircraft assigned to the latter role became contact patrol aircraft when the infantry attacked on 7th June.

A few more matters of artillery interest may be mentioned. First, during the preparatory period, the German wire and trench systems were photographed daily and the enemy gun areas every other day. Secondly, six artillery kite-balloons were deployed within five thousand yards of the front line and, during the night before the infantry assault, two more balloons were deployed within three thousand yards of the front to give depth to observation – one of these for artillery, the other for general tactical observation.

A third point of interest is that 'dress rehearsals' of the 'D-day' barrage were carried out on both 3rd and 5th June, with the object of assessing the enemy's reaction and locating his reinforcing batteries. As a result of air observation of these, a very full counter-battery programme was prepared for the 7th. And, fourthly, one ought to mention the three-hour disruption of the counter-battery programme of the 6th by the German bombing of an ammunition train, with subsequent inter-mittent explosions alongside an aerodrome where four R.F.C. squadrons were based.

Because of the success of the counter-battery programme the reaction of the enemy artillery was weak. Buried British telephone cables mostly remained uncut. The advancing infantry were also able to signal back by lamp from the west face of the ridge, sometimes by way of our kite-balloon observers. A new feature was the institution of 'counter-attack patrols' – wireless aircraft watching particularly for enemy forming-up for such attacks and calling for artillery fire upon them, using the zone-call procedure. A counter-attack on II Anzac Corps on the 7th was anticipated by warnings from these patrols and also from a kite-balloon observer and, on the evening of the 8th, a larger-scale concentration opposite the same corps was spotted and broken up by an artillery barrage.

As has already been said, Messines was a perfect operation of siege warfare. It was so because General Plumer and his excellent staff understood better than most the meticulous preparation required, and because there happened to be time for it. The Royal Flying Corps benefited, with the rest of the Second Army, from this happy situation and were enabled to show themselves to their best advantage.[6] The II Brigade, Royal Flying Corps, (Brigadier-General T. I. Webb-Bowen) operated with the smooth efficiency characteristic of Second Army as a whole. II (Corps) Wing was commanded by Lieutenant-Colonel C. F. de S. Murphy. Its squadrons mainly engaged in this battle, equipped with a mixture of *R.E.8s* and *B.E.2cs*, were Nos. 6 (Major A. S. Barratt, destined to command the Royal Air Force in France in 1940), 42 (Major J. L. Kinnear) and 53 (Major C. S. Wynne-Eyton). II Balloon Wing was commanded by Lieutenant-Colonel W. F. MacNeece.

The Corps aircraft were protected from enemy air interference by continuous fighter cover by day, with the general aim of preventing enemy aircraft from penetrating west of their own 'balloon-line', some six miles behind the front. A 'compass station' network had been devised to locate enemy aircraft which used their wireless transmitters, and to report to R.F.C. units and to forward posts which displayed appropriate ground panels to pass the information to friendly aircraft.[7] Between 15th May and 9th June the II Brigade's Corps Wing lost only four aeroplanes, their Army Wing twenty-nine; the latter (XI Wing, Lieutenant-Colonel G. B. Stopford) must be said, therefore, to have done an excellent protective job.

In the Third battle of Ypres the disparity in numbers between the air forces was less than formerly – on the main (Fifth and Second Army) fronts, in fact, numbers were almost equal. In the period leading up to the first (31st July) assault, an intensive air offensive was initiated under Trenchard's orders, with the objects of curbing enemy air and artillery operations and with their interference with our Corps aircraft. Detailed implementation of the plan was left to R.F.C. brigade commanders and their army commanders and staffs – in the central sector the general aim was to force enemy fighters, bombers and artillery aircraft to the east of their 'balloon line', about five miles behind their front. For most of July fierce air battles were fought, on a larger scale than previously, and at the end of it the R.F.C. had clearly won local air superiority over the German air force.

The weather became the main enemy; the low-clouds and rain which created swamps for the infantrymen hampered reconnaissance and observation and made flying conditions perilous. German attacks on 10th July, which eliminated a small British bridgehead north of the Yser, covering Nieuport, achieved surprise because no signs of their concentration had been detected by the British air reconnaissances in the bad visibility of the previous two days. The comprehensive air plans for 31st July, the day of the main assault, had mostly to be cancelled because of morning mist and thick, low clouds; the R.F.C.'s failure, both on 31st July and 16th August, to observe the concentrations of enemy for counter-attacks was blamed on similar weather conditions. In the last month of the battle, except for the Corps aircraft which laboured on, the rival air forces were virtually grounded except on rare days of fine weather.

Up to 30th July the Corps aircraft were used entirely for artillery co-operation and for tactical photography, after which a proportion were diverted to contact-patrolling and machine-gunning of enemy infantry – this latter role now entering the field of official policy. As at Messines, there was a false opening barrage on 28th July to encourage the enemy to disclose his retaliation plan and expose his hitherto 'silent' batteries.

On the 31st the R.F.C. support given to the assault was not of a high order and the weather could not entirely be blamed. There was failure in communication both between infantry and contact patrol crews and between the latter and the formation headquarters.[8] The army squadron pilots, cheated by the weather of their offensive patrols, were sent into the German rear areas to machine-gun what targets they could find. Troops on the march, in woods or in villages, horse and motor convoys, staff-cars, machine-gun emplacements, aerodromes and battery positions are mentioned by the air force historian, who complains bitterly of the failure of the army in general to appreciate what the R.F.C. was thus doing for them.[9] Well, this is what the Official Historian of the Great War wrote, some years after the event:

> Corps squadrons had confined their action to reporting the progress of the infantry, whilst the Army squadrons roved over the German

back areas machine-gunning and bombing ground targets, such as troops on the move, transport and airfields, at the pilots' discretion. Although this work was done in a most courageous and effective manner, as the German regimental histories admit, the messages sent back gave no clue to the probable relation to the battle of the enemy formations encountered and no advantage was taken of the clear period of visibility before midday to search the back area for the expected advance of the counter-attack divisions. The need for a closer co-operation between the squadrons of the R.F.C. and the ground operations was emphasised by Major-General Trenchard in a circular letter after the battle.[10]

The air force historian,[11] and perhaps Trenchard also, may have interpreted adverse criticism of the Army squadrons' activities as a plea for air support to take place in view of the supported infantry. In fact the lesson to be learnt was quite different – that one piece of valuable information about the enemy is worth any number of individual harassments unrelated to the main battle.

In the operations of 16th to 18th August, which followed the failure of Fifth Army to capture the Gheluvelt ridge, special counter-attack patrols were instituted, as at Messines, but evidently in insufficient numbers since they missed counter-attacks building up against XIX Corps. There was adverse criticism by the same Corps of the standard of R.F.C. artillery co-operation[12] and, once again, an impression is given of random 'ground-strafing'.[13]

The Second Army's battles of the 20th and 26th for the Gheluvelt ridge bore the stamp of the men of Messines. Specific instructions were issued on the necessity for close watch for, and reports of, enemy movements which might presage a counter-attack, and maps were issued to the R.F.C. to indicate likely assembly areas and approach routes for possible counter-attack formations. The II Brigade's patrol area, extending east to the Roulers – Menin railway, was to be patrolled continuously at low level (500 feet or less), to watch for counter-attack evidence and to intercept enemy low-flying aircraft. The Corps squadrons (the same ones as at Messines but with Major A. W. H. James now commanding No.6 Squadron) were also to provide counter-attack patrols. The result of this, and much more, efficient planning was very evident in the battles which followed. Of 20th September, the Official History states that the Royal Flying Corps 'played a vital part in the preparation,[14] particularly as the location of targets relied mainly on air reconnaissance and photographic reports'[15] and that co-operation between air observers and artillery, 'due to better weather conditions and to an improved technique', showed a marked advance.[16] The contact patrols did well, after early mist had cleared, and the counter-attack patrols played a prominent part in the detection and destruction of eight separate attacks on the Second and Fifth armies. Again, on 26th, the Corps aeroplanes did well in all their roles. Numerous counter-attacks were spotted at an early stage by the air-observers and broken up by artillery fire.

The Second Army demonstrated in these two battles how the German tactics of 'elastic defence' – a thinly-held forward zone coupled with provision for heavy and rapid counter-attack – could be defeated. They demonstrated also the power of good teamwork, and how the operators of aircraft could be part of the team. They were such only because they owed to the team their first loyalty; this is true of every army unit and formation and is, very nearly, a tactical essential.

The Third Army's battle of Cambrai, the last episode of 1917 on the Western Front, did not further the arts of aerial observation and reconnaissance. A combination of November fog and military secrecy reduced flying, before the battle, to the minimum. The artillery, as we have seen, was to open fire without prior registration by shooting; as a result, ranging with air observation was not allowed, nor had enemy batteries been located by the R.F.C., but rather (when they fired) by 'flash-spotting' and 'sound-ranging' methods. It was hoped, however, that, once the battle had started, the Corps aircraft would be able to notify the locations of active German batteries, to give general observations of fire sufficient to enable neutralisation of such batteries and to report promptly all concentrations of enemy troops. Four fighter squadrons had been earmarked for the direct attack of hostile batteries, machine-gun emplacements and infantry. The attacks on the batteries were not to be by haphazard selection of the pilots but were planned as part of the counter-battery operations.

The 20th November, date of the spectacular British assaults, was dull and misty; flying was possible but dangerous. Air observation was impossible at first, dangerous later and always unreliable. Artillery co-operation seems to have failed entirely, while contact patrols failed on important occasions when other means of communication had broken down and fog of war was obstructing progress. The army squadrons, meanwhile, carried out early and expensive attacks on German airfields and attacked enemy batteries and infantry. The air force historian distinguishes rather illogically between these two classes of target, arguing that guns are difficult to destroy but that the moral effect of low-level air attacks on infantry is high.[17] Guns, however, needed soldiers to fire them and those soldiers were no less susceptible than the infantry to 'moral effects'. This was a new form of attack for the soldiers – of both sides – to experience and no doubt bad for morale initially. As soldiers became accustomed to it, however, they discovered that its bark was worse than its bite.

By the 23rd British air reconnaissance patrols were reporting substantial rail movements from the north and north-west and road movements around Cambrai. By the same date the German air force had substantially reinforced their hitherto outnumbered units in this sector, notably with Richthofen and his 'circus'. German artillery pilots started to locate and register the British batteries and in the next six days their reconnaissance aircraft became increasingly active, particularly on the front of the British VII Corps at the south end of the salient created by the recent attack. Additional artillery activity, and troop movements observed, persuaded the Corps commander that he was about to be attacked, and he foretold, for good measure, the time and place of the initial attack. He was not believed; indeed some of his own artillery remained detached further north in a counter-battery role, while the I Brigade and IX Wing squadrons which had been under command of Third Army were returned to their normal duties.

As the German infantry formed up for their attack on the British VII Corps in the early hours of the 30th, and as their artillery preparation began, British reconnaissance aircraft were overhead – but their crews saw nothing except the flashes of the German guns, some of which they were able to locate. The German infantry attacks were preceded by low-level air attacks – presumably to distract the British from the infiltrating assault groups; other aircraft accompanied the assault in a combined contact-patrol and close-support role. The Germans attacked simultaneously at several points on the salient and it was not clear for some time which was the main effort; the R.F.C. fighter squadrons were mostly involved at the north-east corner of the salient. In the south, where the battle had to be saved, the decision lay with the infantry soldiers.

The air force historian emphasises three special features of this battle, from the air view-point – the development of low-flying air attacks on the infantry, the rapid reaction of the German air force, and the serious penalties resulting from deficiencies in air observation.[18] No one, surely, would dispute these; but there is something more to say about each of them.

Something has already been written, above, about the moral effect on troops of a new form of attack; in the long run, if a weapon or means of attack is to be feared, it must be seen to be dangerous. The aeroplane of 1917 was not, in practice, an efficient means of delivering a light explosive projectile or a bullet, especially if the human target was in a trench. Artillery was much more efficient and the pilot of an aeroplane was normally better employed in helping the artillery, from his superior viewpoint, to achieve an accurate delivery of their shells. Sometimes artillery could not be brought to bear upon the target; then the aeroplane could take its place and its lesser accuracy and weight of fire had to be accepted. What have these arguments to do with the 'Eye in the Air'? Simply that for every eye at the sighting-device of an airborne weapon there was one less eye brooding over the enemy scene and the enemy's movements, watching the trials and successes of our own side – collecting information vital to the commander and his battle-machine.

The German air force did indeed react superbly to this quite unexpected crisis. In two days they had converted R.F.C. air supremacy into at most air parity – had the weather cleared they might have gone further. Not only did they *arrive* – these reinforcements – but in less than

a week they integrated themselves effectively into the battle organisation
of an army with which they had not been operating or training. They
set about routine tasks such as artillery registration but they were also
ready by 30th November to come forward with the assaulting infantry
and give them the closest possible support.

The air force historian, in his remarks on the consequence of failure
of observation, seemed to be concerned with one particular failure on
the first day of this battle, where success, he thought, might have led to
spectacular results. One must differ from him on this latter point, while
noting a much wider failure of air observation by the British in this
battle, in which the Corps squadron functions were hardly carried out
at all. This was no doubt attributable to the mist. Mist is a common
feature during November in Europe and the probability of its interference
with air reconnaissance on the vital day must surely have been anticipated. Some limited, no doubt dangerous, reconnaissance should have
been possible during the battle, since bombing and low strafing took
place. One is not convinced that contingency plans were made for such
limited reconnaissance nor, indeed, that the general planning of the
Cambrai offensive was carried down to sufficient detail. It is remarkable
to discover, for example, that the cavalry corps, riding forwards towards
the long hoped-for break out into the open country, had not been
provided with air photographs of the relevant crossings of the Canal du
Nord.[19]

The situation, as 1917 drew to its close, was full of foreboding for the
Allies. In the east, the garrison of the German fortress had swarmed out
and overwhelmed the besiegers; in the west the British and French,
exhausted by repeated battering at the walls, watched uneasily as the
enemy's reinforcements thronged the battlements and wondered whether
the Americans would arrive in time. In fact, as we know, the siege was
coming to its end; we are therefore at a good point to take stock, within
the scope of this narrative, of the developments of the last three years.
It might be useful to start by considering the German air force, which
seems unjustly to have acquired in British eyes a reputation for lack of
enterprise.[20]

It must be remembered, in the first place, that the Germans were,
almost from the beginning, outnumbered in aircraft and aircrew. For
that reason alone they had to be more careful. The prevailing wind was
from the west; this meant quite a lot in the early days of low-powered
aeroplanes; a two-way trip might occupy the same time for both German
and British pilot, but the former had the greater chance of being attacked
before he reached his target. The Germans needed, of course, to range
their artillery and to protect the aerial observers who were doing it; if
they managed to do this effectively from within their own territory,
protected by their excellent anti-aircraft guns, they were sensible to do
so. If, furthermore, by so doing they enticed British aircraft well over

German-held territory, there was a good prospect of damaged aircraft being forced down on the German side of the front. The German air force, therefore, tended to confine themselves in the early days to the immediate battle area and to the function and protection of observation. They were well-prepared, however, to send reconnaissance aeroplanes through the British air defences when they needed to do so, usually at a great height; the amount of good intelligence they compiled before the Somme battle is proof of this.

Shortcomings in this philosophy were revealed in the Somme fighting, as we have seen; the German infantry did not like to be harassed by the R.F.C. and to see no German aircraft, while the German air force felt it would disrupt their operations less if their infantry tried to shoot down the offending British aircraft themselves. This failure in confidence had to be corrected and the Germans adopted the contact patrol concept, establishing a close relationship with infantry and kite-balloon observers, forming specialised flights and later developing special armoured battle aeroplanes. At Arras, and again at Cambrai, these methods were well demonstrated. The Germans encountered, as one would expect, all the same communication and other difficulties which beset the R.F.C. and attempted to solve them in a similar manner.

Returning now to a consideration of the developments of the last three years from the British viewpoint, we must reiterate what has been said before – that artillery co-operation was by far the most important and aircraft-consuming role. The path of such co-operation had not always run smoothly, however, and by the end of 1917 there was some concern, both in artillery and flying corps circles. Inadequate communications, lack of continuity among the experts (both of the Royal Artillery and the Royal Flying Corps), lack of standardisation of procedures and bad observation – all were quoted as reasons for inaccuracies and errors for which the British infantry ultimately had to pay. In the next chapter this matter will be discussed more fully.

Next in importance was air photography, an area in which problems were perhaps less acute than elsewhere but where aircraft were very vulnerable and needed special protection. Third in line were the contact and counter-attack patrols, not to be confused one with the other. The former were concerned with the position and progress of friendly troops, the latter with those of the enemy. Both demanded of the aircrews courageous flying, skilled observation and discrimination. Contact patrols required of our troops on the ground good aircraft recognition and an appreciation of the real importance of the aircraft's role. Both on the ground and in the air there was needed a determination that the system should work; it must be accepted that the system had not worked well enough, often enough, and early in 1918 an excellent training pamphlet was published to standardise and improve procedures.[21]

Before leaving the subjects of photography and contact patrols it should be mentioned that long-range cameras were developed with which useful pictures were taken from balloons, and that the latter sometimes played a useful part in relaying messages sent from the infantry by signal lamp and passed on by telephone.

Aerial fighting developed quite naturally from the need to protect the 'working aeroplanes' – and the 'working balloons' also. As the enemy threat increased it became necessary to concentrate fighters into groups and, at the time of the Somme battle, the Trenchard doctrine was propounded that these groups should carry the battle into the enemy's territory in order to attract the enemy's air forces to the protection of vulnerable points in that territory and away, therefore, from our own working aeroplanes. One danger of this policy was that the enemy, by locating his vulnerable points farther and farther back might draw the British fighter and bombing forces farther and farther away from those they were supposed to be protecting, allowing the latter to be harassed by quite small numbers of enemy fighters which had eluded the attentions of the deep-penetrating British fighters. Another was that the main protective object of the fighter force might be forgotten and that aerial fighting might become an end in itself instead of a means to an end, or that an ambitious search for air 'supremacy' might involve the bombing of aerodromes and aircraft factories by fleets of bombers protected by fighters, all provided and manned at the expense of the army's supply of reconnaissance and observation aircraft. Trenchard had, as yet, fallen into none of these traps. He had very sensibly contrived that the main fighting took place on the enemy's side of the army's battlefield but he left sufficient protection over that battlefield to give freedom of action to the working aeroplanes. He had carried out regular bombing raids on railway targets, aerodromes and billets – and one cannot suppose that they were very effective – but he had not done so to an extent which seriously starved the corps squadrons of aircraft or crews.

The famous paper of 22nd September, 1916, in which Trenchard expounded his doctrine, really said little more than that offensive action was a good principle of war, but it included two axioms of the kind which new organisations tend to feed to laymen before the latter are knowledgeable enough to question them.[22] They were: 'An aeroplane is an offensive and not a defensive weapon' and 'The aeroplane is not a defence against the aeroplane'. In reply to the former statement, one could say that the aeroplane is not a weapon at all, but a vehicle; whether you use any weapon which you may carry in the vehicle offensively or defensively must depend on the tactical situation – the guns in the aeroplanes which cruised about London in the dark, looking for Zeppelins, were certainly ready for defensive use; so were those of the fighters which intercepted the German formations en route to attack our corps aircraft. As to the principle of the aeroplane (or presumably the weapons of the aeroplane) 'not being a defence against the aeroplane', Basil Collier, in his *History of Air Power*, comprehensively demolishes its validity.[23] Like so many home-made axioms it died hard, only just in time for the Battle of Britain finally to illustrate its absurdity.

During this long siege the men of the Royal Flying Corps did not undergo the horrors and privations of the soldiers in the trenches: pilots and observers had, however, flown long hours, sometimes in dangerous weather. They had found themselves, for two extended periods, out-classed by the aircraft and weapons of their opponents but compelled by the situation of their armies to fly and fight on against considerable odds. They suffered heavy casualties but continued to ensure that their army formation received, usually, the support which they expected. Their ground crews, spared likewise the trenches but unable to share with the aircrew the inspiration of their exciting roles, fought a real and dedicated battle to maintain the aircraft strength.

1   General John Money, pioneer of British Air Observation, from a photograph of a portrait by Sir Nathaniel Dance.

2   Jean-Marie-Joseph Coutelle – chemist, aeronaut, soldier – from a sketch by Dutertie in Tissandier's 'Histoire des Ballons et des Aéronauts célèbres, 1783–1800'.

3   George Edward Grover – pressure for air reconnaissance in the 1860s.

4   James Lethbridge Templer, best known of the pioneers.

5   Captive Balloon, 1893, Lieutenant H. B. Jones, Royal Engineers, in the 'car'.

overleaf ▶

| 2 | 3 |
| 4 | 5 |

COUTELLE

8 [TOP] Louis Blériot, Madame Blériot, and others, with the aeroplane which M. Blériot had just flown across the Channel, 25 July 1909.

9 [ABOVE] *Blériot XI,* Oran, Algeria, 1910.

◀ overleaf

6	7

6   Man-carrying kite taking-off, *c.* 1906. The figure in the cowboy hat is probably Cody.

7   James William Dunne, *c.* 1912, designer of stable aircraft.

10 [TOP] *Beta,* successful British airship.

11 [ABOVE] 'The indomitable Cody' with a biplane of his own design which he flew in the 1911 Circuit-of-Britain race.

12   Three pioneers of aeroplane reconnaissance in Britain.
     Captain John Duncan Bertie Fulton, with Louis Paulhan (right),
     St. Cyr, 1911.

13   Lancelot Gibbs, *c.* 1914.

14   Captain Bertram Dickson, *c.* 1911.

overleaf ▶

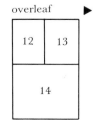

◀ overleaf

15
16

15 Henry Farman biplane, used in the first demonstrations to the Army of aeroplane reconnaissance.

16 Geoffrey de Havilland and the BE2.

17 [TOP LEFT] Major Frederick Sykes, first commander of the Military Wing of the Royal Flying Corps.

18 [TOP RIGHT] *BE 2c* flying over trenches.

[ABOVE] Two pioneers of artillery observation from aeroplanes.

19 [LEFT] Lieutenant Donald Lewis.

20 [RIGHT] Lieutenant Baron James.

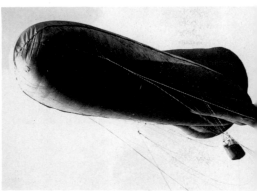

◀

21 [OVERLEAF] Air photograph by III Wing, R.F.C., with hand-held 'A-type' camera, of Fort du Vert Galand, four miles north-west of Lille, 28 April 1915.

22 [LEFT] Belgian troops with a German-designed *Drachen* observation balloon.

23 [BELOW] *Caquot* balloon in half a gale.

24 [BOTTOM] 'The Fokker menace' (*Fokker E 2*).

◀ overleaf

25	
26	27

25   The Somme, Thiepval, 3rd July 1916.

26   Edward Bailey Ashmore, who commanded IV Brigade, R.F.C. Possibly a 1918 photograph.

27   Edward Ludlow-Hewitt – a 1914 photograph of the Commander of II (Corps) Wing.

28 [TOP LEFT] Brigadier-General W. Sefton Brancker who played a big part in the development of military flying.

29 [TOP RIGHT] Major General Hugh Trenchard, 1917, from a painting by Sir William Orpen.

30 [ABOVE] Dismantling a *BE 2c,* forced down on the old Somme battlefield, March 1917.

31 [TOP] *RE 8*, standard RFC reconnaissance
aeroplane 1916–18.

32 [ABOVE] No. 1 Aircraft Depot, St. Omer –
repair and reassembly of an RE 8.

33 [OVERLEAF] Ypres-Menin road, July 1917, ▶
oblique air photograph, looking east.

34 [TOP LEFT] Andrew Walser, noteworthy in the field of artillery reconnaissance.

35 [TOP RIGHT] *RE 8* returns to base at sunset, February 1918.

36 [ABOVE] Gallipoli – the balloon-ship *Manica*.

37   The first VC of air reconnaissance. Captain E. M. F. West.

38   Oblique air photograph, September 1918, looking south-east towards the Bapaume-Cambrai road.

39   King George V inspects 74 Squadron, R.F.C., near Ypres, August 1918 – Plumer extreme left, Webb-Bowen behind the King.

overleaf ▶

37	38
39	

CAMBRAI - BAPAUME Rd.

E 20 d 8.6

MŒUVRES.

The Artillery Problem

◇

'. . . . and but for these vile guns,
He would himself have been a soldier.'
WILLIAM SHAKESPEARE: *Henry IV, Part I*, I, iii

We have seen how, in the second half of the nineteenth century, a revolution in gun design radically increased range and brought therewith a problem of observation;[1] we have seen how the introduction of the military balloon and later the kite helped to solve this problem; we have seen how the spherical balloon slipped silently away from the British army in favour of the aeroplane. Because of the lack of any efficient means of communication between the aeroplane of 1914 and the guns, the former was not ready to assume the full function of the artillery observation balloon, but wireless was being developed and before the battle of the Marne ended British aeroplanes, equipped with wireless, were operating. On 13th September, 1914, air observation and wireless combined, in the fighting on the Aisne, to permit the engagement of a target not visible from the ground.

We have also seen how, while the British artillery's problem of observation was intensified by German choice of ground to defend, its requirement both of guns and observation posts was enlarged fifty times by the siege conditions developing on the Western front, in which artillery was seen as the only means of breaking the deadlock and of preventing the enemy's artillery from so doing. We have seen how these factors combined to make artillery observation the main role of the Royal Flying Corps and aerial photography (for the artillery and for others) the most important of its remaining tasks.

The Germans, as well as the Allies, deployed large masses of artillery, particularly of the heavier natures, in positions hidden from ground observation. The Allies needed to locate these masses and, at an appropriate time, to engage them. An extensive counter-battery organisation grew up to coordinate both the means of location and the plans for engagement, the R.F.C. being deeply involved in both. Besides this counter-battery (C.B.) role, trench-bombardment was, of course, a major artillery commitment, particularly before and during major attacks. Here again the R.F.C. was involved, though less intimately and extensively than in the C.B. role. The British infantry were inclined to favour the heaviest possible artillery bombardment of the targets which immediately faced them, if necessary at the expense of C.B. activity, but quickly changed their mind when the enemy's artillery fire descended

upon them.[2] Even if all the hostile batteries were not to be engaged in
the initial stages, therefore, it was necessary to locate and 'register' them
for engagement at short notice during the battle.

By the end of 1915 it could be said that the R.F.C. role of 'artillery
co-operation' had been established, and a scheme worked out for an
aeroplane observer to initiate artillery fire on important targets of fleeting
opportunity. The balloon, in the elongated shape of the kite-balloon,
had also returned to the British army, primarily for artillery observation.
But air superiority had passed to the enemy, placing the artillery aircraft
in jeopardy and demanding the provision of protective aircraft.

In 1916, prior to the Somme battle, much occurred to the benefit of
air co-operation with the British artillery. The appearance of the Corps
squadrons, with their own photographic processing resources, assisted
close liaison between pilots, observers and artillery officers; wireless
developments increased the number of aircraft which could operate on
a given length of front;[3] the 'zone-call' procedure ensured that selected
batteries would always be ready to answer calls for fire on 'fleeting'
targets; a pamphlet appeared and combined training took place. The
long bombardment which preceded the beginning of the Somme battle
did not, however, 'crush' the enemy artillery and the British infantry
suffered for that;[4] Anstey attributed it to poor artillery-air co-operation
and he blamed both sides of the partnership. Both sides took early steps
to improve matters and co-operation became very good for the rest of
the battle.

The year 1917 started with the worst period of air inferiority that the
R.F.C. were to experience and Arras was fought under these conditions.
Counter-battery measures before and during the opening attack were
very effective, thereafter they deteriorated. The Official History
adversely criticises over-optimistic observation of fire by inexperienced
air observers;[5] this natural tendency was no doubt increased by incursions
by enemy fighters into the British corps' areas. Anstey more generously
writes that 'the Artillery owed a great deal to the excellent photographs
which were obtained with considerable loss by intrepid airmen in the
face of the fast and powerful German fighter planes'[6].

At Messines, with air superiority regained and with all the advantages
of a deliberately planned siege operation, artillery co-operation probably
reached the peak of its efficiency in this war. Anstey writes: 'As for
counter-battery, daily programmes were drawn up by the C.B.S.Os,
(counter-battery staff officers) whose staff had been strengthened for the
battle. Results of air shoots were first telephoned by batteries to the
C.B.S.O., and were then followed by a written report. The C.B.S.O.
compared this with the R.F.C. report on the same shoot, and so judged
the effect, checking his judgement by a study of the photograph of the
target taken after the firing was over. Every evening a conference was
held by the C.B.S.O. with the squadron commander, the O.C. of the
Balloon Section, the C.B. group commanders and officers of the Field
Survey Company and Sound-Ranging Section'.[7] And, he continues:

'The artillery already had the advantage of firing into a salient, and the admirable visibility allowed air and balloon observers, aided by ground observation . . . . . , eventually to smother the German batteries, strong points, and other targets'. Rawlins records that S.O.S. calls from aircraft proved very valuable; these were calls to the artillery to bring down fire in front of their supported infantry in accordance with prearranged plans to deal with enemy attacks upon them.[8]

In the Third Ypres battle the standard of the R.F.C.'s artillery co-operation was variable and the air historian refers to a weakening of the liaison between the artillery squadrons and the gunners themselves.[9] The latter, meanwhile, had been profiting from other methods of locating hostile batteries, 'flash-spotting' and 'sound-ranging' – the former based on the observation of a hostile gun flash from two separate but known locations, the latter based on the different times at which separately located sound-receivers recorded the firing of a particular hostile gun. These developments, together with accurate methods of pin-pointing our own battery positions, enabled the opening Cambrai bombardment to descend without any of the normal preliminaries and without air observation. Air observation should have been useful thereafter but, as we have seen, failed, due perhaps to a combination of bad visibility and lack of practice by gunners and their air observers in the application of their art to conditions more fluid than usual.

During the three years between the battles of Aisne and Cambrai an immense amount of thought, discussion and practice had taken place in the matter of air observation of artillery fire. And yet, at the end of it, the participants themselves were dissatisfied with the standards attained – even in the deliberate tempo of siege warfare. Before discussing the difficulties in more detail it will be useful, perhaps, to describe the system as it existed in 1917. The clear memory of Colonel R. Macleod (who was Artillery Liaison Officer with Fourth Army's Corps Wing in the Somme battles) has been of the greatest help, as have successive contemporary pamphlets on the subject – one drafted by Macleod. A. J. Insall, who was a fighter observer, not an artillery observer, by trade, nevertheless acted in the latter capacity on many occasions and in his book *Observer* wrote expressively on the subject.[10]

A 'Corps squadron' would usually have had three flights, and a normal arrangement would have been for two flights to have been employed in counter-battery tasks and the third in tasks related to the artillery's bombardment of the enemy's forward trenches and other fortifications prior to the main infantry assault. This third flight was responsible, after the assault, for contact patrols. All flights carried out photography over the immediate battle area. Within these two main divisions of artillery task there were two main types of 'shoot' – the *prearranged* and the *impromptu*. A prearranged shoot implied that the engagement of the particular target had been planned beforehand and that a particular observer and battery would conduct it, an impromptu shoot that the air observer had spotted a .target, not on the planned programme but nevertheless important enough to warrant engagement.

Most shoots were prearranged, in accordance with programmes drawn up by C.B. staffs in conjunction with Corps squadrons. they could be aimed at registration, destruction or neutralisation. *Registration* was the process of 'ranging' upon a target, or a point near at hand, so that fire could be opened upon the target later without delay or subsequent 'ranging'. *Destruction* implied serious damage to field works, guns or other equipment, *neutralisation* the causing of casualties, confusion and temporary inactivity. *Ranging* was the process of firing rounds of ammunition at different elevations of the gun or guns, to obtain fall of shot closely short of, and beyond, the target and thus arriving at the most advantageous range to use when engaging the target for 'effect'. This was necessitated by the many variables in the manufacture of guns and ammunition and in the factors affecting a shell in flight, which together gave a 'spread' on the ground to a number of shells which theoretically should have landed on the same spot. *Destruction* demanded a considerable expenditure of time and ammunition; *neutralisation* less. Code letters were allocated to squadrons and batteries to ensure correct communication linkage by wireless and letters and numbers enabled each target to be identified for future engagement if necessary.

Impromptu shoots were initiated by air observers against such targets as hostile batteries engaging our infantry or artillery, active mortars, or anti-aircraft guns engaging our aeroplanes. Different code-signals could be used to offer to range a particular battery at once or later, to offer to range any battery able to accept the task, or to indicate inability to range on that target (because, perhaps, already ranging on a more important one). In the last of these situations the observer would try to observe concentrations of fire upon the target and indicate generally their effect. Description of target locations, and where necessary the allocations of batteries to targets, were facilitated by specially squared and zoned maps or photographs carried by both observers and batteries and by the use of a common reference system.

A special form of impromptu shoot was against the fleeting target – one likely to be in evidence only for a limited time, enemy infantry assaulting, for example, or artillery or transport on the move. The procedures and codes enabled the observer to describe the nature of such target, indicate the degree of importance and give the location, and they prescribed the appropriate artillery response. The 'LL' call, for example, was to be answered by every battery which could bear upon the target; in such a case only a general indication of effect could, of course, be given by the observer.

The observer was provided with a wireless transmitter with which he sent signals in Morse code to an R.F.C. receiving set located at his affiliated battery. (His signals were overheard by another receiver at a 'central wireless station' in each Corps area, whence telephone lines were available to artillery batteries and which was used to resolve communication troubles as between aircraft and battery). The battery could only communicate with the aircraft by means of ground-strip signals or occasionally by lamp – some twenty letter-combinations or symbols were available for this purpose. The observer had his map or photograph and a celluloid sheet bearing upon it the inscribed face of a clock, with lines radiating from the centre to the twelve clock hours and with concentric circles described at radii 50, 100, 200, 300 and thence at hundred yard intervals to 500 yards, each at the scale of the map; these circles were lettered, from the centre, A to F. The pilot was required to imagine two inner circles, letter Y and Z, 10 and 25 yards from the centre. This celluloid sheet was positioned over the map with its centre over the map position of the target to be engaged and with the 12 o'clock radius pointing due north on the map. The position of a shell-burst observed on the ground and spotted on the map could then be described by reference to the letter of the relevant circle and the relevant clock-hour on the celluloid, and some such signal as C4 or B7 transmitted to the battery. There the artillery officer in charge would convert it to a suitable change in line and range for the ranging procedure which he was adopting. This was the famous 'clock-code' system.[11]

The aeroplane flew, usually at between 3,000 and 6,000 feet, between the battery and the target. On the outward journey the observer watched the target area, counting the seconds of 'time of flight of shell' since the battery fired and spotting the shell-burst at the appropriate moment. As the aircraft turned back onto the inward course the observer transmitted the clock-code version of the displacement of the burst from the centre of the target, and watched and timed the flash from the battery as the next round or salvo was fired. The aircraft was turned once again on to the outward course. In the interests of protection from anti-aircraft artillery fire and possible fighter interception, it was advisable not to allow this flying pattern to become too stereotyped and, when the air situation was unfavourable, it might not be possible to extend it far beyond one's own front line. The air observer confined himself to observing and transmitting his observations; it was the battery commander or his representative who decided when to conclude ranging, when and how to fire for effect, when and how to register the target; he kept the aeroplane's crew in the picture with his ground-strip signals.

Some deviousness surrounds the term 'observer', from which the present author has not been altogether free. In this chapter the term has been used to describe the airborne individual who observed artillery fire, but it has been used elsewhere to describe the member of the crew of a two-seater aircraft, other than the pilot. This second crew member had duties other than artillery-spotting, duties which varied with such factors as the seat-positions in the aircraft, the type of armament and mounting and the prescribed fighting and evasion tactics; in all cases he will have been responsible for looking out for enemy fighters in those sectors blind for practical purposes to the pilot. These duties would certainly, if conscientiously carried out, have made it difficult for him to devote adequate attention to artillery observation. The better man for the latter was usually the pilot, who had anyway to position the aircraft appropriately to observe in turn the firing battery and the bursting shell and could readily cope with the key of the wireless transmitter. He might find the large-scale map and the celluloid sheet more or less intolerable, but one questions whether the latter was essential to the conduct of the shoot, except as an initial indication of the 12 o'clock line on the ground. In the Fourth Army on the Somme it was certainly the pilots who did the artillery observation; Macleod confirms this and a letter from Trenchard seems to suggest that the practice was general in the R.F.C.[12] In this Trenchard himself inclined to deviousness, for he must have known well that in many Corps wings (at that time) it was the observer, and not the pilot, who did the artillery observation.[13] Before the end of the war it had become normal, however, for the pilot to do so.

Insall well describes the unglamorous job of the artillery pilots and observers and the special brand of courage they needed to display in a role not calculated to protect them from anti-aircraft fire and trespassing enemy fighters.[14] 'Aces' were not readily produced within their community, but one personality has emerged in Andrew Walser. An officer of the 10th London Regiment of the pre-war Territorial Force, Walser served with the Royal Flying Corps from the beginning of the war. He flew in Gallipoli, and there had his first operational experience of observing gunfire – both of naval vessels and of army artillery. Afterwards, under Ludlow-Hewitt in the Somme battle, he acquired a uniquely high reputation for accurate artillery observation; because he adjusted his flying pattern to reduce the critical time-lag between observation and the next order to fire, he earned also a reputation for speed. Later, still with the Fourth Army, he commanded No. 52 Squadron, R.F.C. and developed therein methods of co-operation between aeroplanes and balloons in the engagement of artillery targets.

The kite-balloons, within the accepted boundaries of their capabilities, did very well. Usually they were deployed, with anti-aircraft artillery protection, some three miles behind the front line, ascending to a height of about 4,500 feet if cloud permitted it. From here their observers obtained only a moderate view, for example, of the enemy gun areas. They could use binoculars, however, acquired a most comprehensive knowledge of their zone of observation and were well placed to spot those small changes of scene which were often the first warning of important events to come. They effectively observed artillery fire upon the enemy's forward trench systems, fire of the 'field' guns in addition to that of heavier artillery, and could often spot and measure the compass-bearing of the flashes of hostile batteries; further, they could sometimes establish a relationship between the gun-flashes and the target those guns were engaging, information of great value to the C.B. staffs. This role they could continue into the night. Their prime advantage over the artillery aeroplanes was accorded by their communications, with telephone connections with and between their own 'chart-rooms', the C.B. staffs, artillery brigades and firing batteries. They reported shell bursts as left or right, over or short, a procedure more in line with normal artillery practice than that of the 'clock code'.

During 1917, Walser's two forms of co-operation between aeroplanes and balloons were developed. In the first, provision was made for an aeroplane observer who had to leave a shoot unfinished to hand over to a balloon observer for the latter to continue. In the second the balloon observer, his excellent communications aiding him to observe his particular shell-bursts and to reduce delays, started the shoot, handing over to the aeroplane observer for better observation of the concluding stages.

Balloon observers – on both sides – needed to possess a high degree of cold-blooded courage. As their success became more and more apparent their balloons became regular targets for cunningly contrived and determined attacks by enemy fighter aeroplanes. Balloon crews, unlike the British aeroplane crews, were provided with parachutes. Time was inevitably short to initiate emergency descents, however; copious rigging lines impeded the jumpers or fouled the parachutes, and the menace of a fiercely burning and falling hydrogen balloon accompanied them. The parachutes of those times were far from infallible. Balloon cables parted often enough, as a result of strong winds, enemy action, or the hazards of their own shells or aeroplanes; the prevailing wind usually ensured that the balloon's subsequent flight was over enemy territory.

Because it has been said that the kite-balloons were successful, the artillery aeroplanes should not be pronounced unsuccessful. From the three year period of the siege the British artillery emerged with credit and, remembering its ground-observation problem, all its air observers must emphatically share that credit. Nevertheless, as we have seen, in spite of much thought and repeated efforts, neither gunners nor airmen believed at the end of 1917 that the system was working well enough. We cannot presume, sixty years later, to solve their problems but we may, perhaps, consider them.

Communication was one of the main difficulties. Late in 1918, after years of endeavour, speech-radio (radio-telephony, or R/T as it was called) reached a few aircraft in an acceptable form. To the end, however, the artillery observers had to communicate by means of one-way morse code signals (wireless-telegraphy, or W/T), with only the most primitive means of receiving replies from the batteries – means which usually involved the pilots in a flight back to the battery area itself. The wireless sets which they used were, if not in their infancy, at least in childhood; interference and background noise, jamming and other manifestations could not always be avoided or corrected during a sortie. Wireless aerials at battery positions, 150 feet or more in length, were very vulnerable to enemy artillery fire. Troubles like this sometimes led to loss of confidence between observers and gunners, who were anyway remote from one another, connected by no familiar, friendly voices nor by common skills and background.

Observing, as we have said before and will say again, is not, as generally assumed, a natural skill of human beings; it needs to be acquired and assiduously practised. Observation from the air is a specialised branch of the skill, involving – for example – appreciation of the effects of light and shade upon colour, knowledge of camouflage and adjustment of eye focus to varying heights and to vertical or oblique views. Until 1917 the initial training of pilots and observers in the United Kingdom had included only the most haphazard efforts to teach the basic art of observation. When training was, like all other war preparations, hurried, and when it had to incorporate such matters as wireless, photography, machine-guns and artillery procedure, to say nothing of flying, it was obviously difficult to spend much time in observation. Pilots and observers had to acquire this skill 'on the job', therefore, and to make many mistakes in the process. As every experienced artilleryman knows, one of the most common faults in the observation of fall-of-shot is optimism; the observer longs to see his rounds straddle the target or actually hit it, and the wish is father to the thought. The success of huge concentrations of artillery fire often depended on the accuracy of one or two observations, during registration, by a recently qualified pilot or observer. The official historian wrote, of the artillery preparations for the battle of Arras:

.The C.B. reports, founded on 'O.Ks' and 'explosions' signalled by young aircraft observers, often with an inadequate view of their targets were absurdly optimistic, and the eagerness with which they were known to be studied by high commanders did not tend to check their exuberance.[15]

Observation, requiring close concentration, was not helped by the *vulnerability* of the artillery aeroplanes to enemy anti-aircraft guns and fighter attacks. Our fighter screens and patrols indeed protected their corps aircraft most admirably, but nothing could prevent occasional enemy fighters from penetrating to the artillery areas, as the Corps aircraft crews well knew. Batteries posted look-outs to watch for such fighters, but they had, of course, no reliable and rapid means of warning artillery pilots. Aeroplanes flying over the zone between the rival artillery areas were also vulnerable to inadvertent destruction by their own or the enemy's shells. Contact patrol aircraft were particularly vulnerable, and it is recorded variously that some were destroyed in this manner, but artillery aeroplanes must also have been in great danger – particularly during the large-scale artillery preparation before the major battles. They flew, as we have seen, at between 3,000 and 6,000 feet; the apexes of the trajectories of the British medium and heavy guns of those days, at maximum range, were at heights varying from 8,000 to 14,000 feet and, at minimum practical range, at 3,000 to 7,000 feet. Short of, or beyond, the highest points of trajectory every height-band from zero upwards was penetrated. It is indeed surprising to find, in the various pamphlets of those times on the art of artillery co-operation, no mention of this danger or advice as to how to minimise it.

The *slowness* of shoots with aeroplane observation was notable, due both to delays imposed by one-way wireless procedure, to the necessity for the aeroplane to be suitably positioned to view both the firing of the gun and the arrival of the shell, and to the conversion of clock-code corrections into gun corrections.[16] Pilots were often airborne for two or three hours to engage two or three targets. In siege warfare a certain deliberation was acceptable, but it was poor preparation for the antici-pated day of the breakthrough. The fleeting-opportunity shoots always demanded speed and, realistically, the prescribed procedures envisaged shooting 'off the map' without ranging. This accepted a reduction in accuracy, which could only be redressed by a greater volume of fire. All too often, however, there seems to have been a clash of priorities at the batteries tasked to answer calls from air observers for fire onto impromptu targets, and a surprising number of the latter did not get answered.

Last, but far from least, was the need for *artillery experience*. Throughout the war, in all the efforts by the various parties to improve artillery co-operation, in all the training pamphlets, tremendous emphasis was placed upon the need for frequent visits of observers to batteries, to see the procedure and problems of a shoot, from the gun end as it were. And yet, writing of the 1917 period, the air historian comments that 'the time was past when pilots could pay frequent visits, for professional discussion, to the batteries with which they worked';[17] this was, according to him, because of the great increase in artillery strength in 1917 and he goes on, as usual, to blame artillery officers for the failures which resulted. In fact, visits to batteries of the sort described, though far better than nothing, were nothing like enough. The observation post had become an essential part (perhaps the most sensitive part) of the battery's organisation for battle – 'part of the weapon system', in modern parlance. Captain K. M. Loch, M.C., wrote in 1920, 'No Battery Commander allows an untrained officer to carry out a shoot unsupervised and as a corollary no observer should require this super-vision'.[18] Indeed no member of the battery would carry out a shoot until he had served an apprenticeship on the guns, in the battery command-post and as a signaller and knew what it was all about – to return again to modern parlance. But the air observer, supplied with inferior com-munications and a number of functions unrelated to observation, was entrusted with this most important link in the battery's battle function without any but the most superficial knowledge of the remaining links. One is left nevertheless with a feeling of admiration for these pilots and observers, often young in years and experience, for taking on such a responsible and daunting job and, by force of character and intellect, very often succeeding in it.

Not surprisingly it occurred to a number of people that a promising solution to these problems would be for the Royal Artillery to assume operational control of the artillery co-operation flights and of the kite-balloons. When the balloons appeared early in 1915, it was proposed that the artillery should take them over. According to the air historian, this proposal was defeated on three grounds, first that the balloons would collect information for others besides the artillery, secondly that their work would be supplementary to that of the aeroplanes and thirdly that the supply and maintenance problems associated with balloons could be solved only through the medium of the stores branch of the R.F.C.[19] The third assertion is remarkable, since the R.F.C. possessed at that time no balloons, no other lighter-than-air craft and no gas; if the B.E.F.'s normal supply machinery could not have coped with the problem, the Royal Navy would have seemed the appropriate source of supply, possessing as they did all three commodities. As to the other two arguments, one can deny neither but they seem to have had little force. Certainly the work of the kite-balloons was supplementary to that of the aeroplane observers; it was also supplementary to that of the artillery observation posts on the ground. The real basis of the R.F.C. case was the feeling that the important thing about the balloon was that it climbed into the air; in truth the important thing, operationally, was that it was an observation post. Operational factors may not invariably be over-riding, but they must always be given first consideration. In 1915 the argument that the balloons would be serving others besides the artillery seemed perhaps convincing. But within a very short time it became generally appreciated that of all arms the artillery needed the best observation, and that it was very much in the interest of infantry, cavalry, tanks and commanders to ensure that they had it. Once this was established it followed quickly that the artillery became the chief observers in the battle area and the chief distributors to commanders and others of the information thus gleaned. It became more natural than ever that they should have the balloons.

In the latter stages of the Somme battle, General Rawlinson of the Fourth, and General Horne of the First Armies proposed independently that 'artillery (aeroplane) squadrons' should be placed, except for purely technical matters, under the direct orders of the Corps artillery commanders.[20] The grounds for this proposal were the need for very high skill in the air observer, the need for enough aircraft and trained observers for this particular artillery task and the need for intimate relations between the artillery units and the air observers, working in combination. Rawlinson made the interesting statement that 'the large percentage of effective shoots carried out with aeroplane observation have been the work of a few men.' Trenchard chimed in with his letter of 1st November, 1916 (already quoted in part in another context),[21] claiming that the pilot, and not the observer, did the artillery observation – this was true, in Fourth Army, but irrelevant to the proposal. He also said that to hand over the artillery machines would necessitate acquiring other such machines to do 'other work' (presumably contact patrols) and that artillery requirements 'such as photography at a distance behind the lines' could only be met by fighter aircraft, that a large part of the work of the artillery aircrew was technical (and he quoted wireless and machine-guns) and that the actual observation of fall-of-shot was the easiest part of the job. He asked for more artillery officers in his squadrons. These arguments sound rather desperate, but they succeeded with Haig, to whom the matter finally came. It was decided, however, that the balloon sections should shortly come within the artillery chain of command and that, as a preliminary, a number of artillery officers should be trained as balloon observers. These officers were duly trained but the balloons never, in fact, came under artillery command; the reason for this has not survived.

Perhaps we may close with a quotation from the enemy of that time:

Unless he [the air observer] possessed an intimate knowledge of the science of gunnery, the artillery would have been robbed of much of its efficiency, even though it were still assisted by some sort of aeroplane observation.[22]

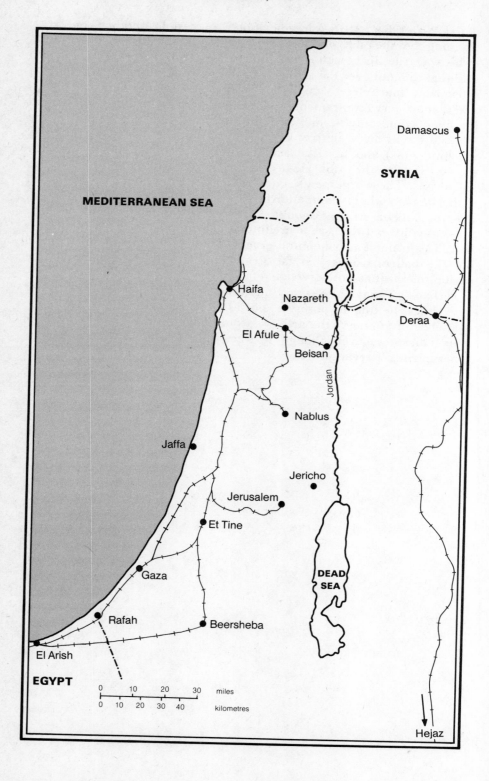

MEDITERRANEAN SEA

SYRIA

Damascus

Deraa

Haifa

Nazareth

El Afule

Beisan

Jordan

Nablus

Jaffa

Jericho

Jerusalem

Et Tine

DEAD
SEA

Gaza

Rafah

Beersheba

El Arish

EGYPT

| 0 | 10 | 20 | 30 | miles |
| 0 | 10 | 20 | 30 | 40 | kilometres |

Hejaz

The Sideshows

---◇---

'As many arrows, loosed several ways,
Fly to one mark'
WILLIAM SHAKESPEARE: Henry V, I, ii

The word 'sideshows', which was commonly used to describe Great War
theatres other than those of the Western and Eastern Fronts in Europe,
had a bitter sound for many of those who served therein, who felt, very
often, that the word typified their neglect by the home authorities. The
war, ultimately, had to be won in Northern Europe, across the frontiers
of Germany, France and Russia; it was appreciation of this fact which
led to the use of the word 'sideshow' and it led also, particularly after
the failure of the Gallipoli operations, to a reluctance to support such
operations to the extent thought necessary by those involved. Those who
fought in the sideshows fought as well as any, often in conditions as
unpleasant in their way as those on the Western Front, and with home
leave far less accessible. All the sideshows had their effect on the war as
a whole, if only to release troops for more sensitive theatres or to tie up
opposing forces away from the decisive fronts. Allied operations against
Austria, Bulgaria and Turkey – because of the comparative proximity
of these countries to Germany's southern flanks – always held a prospect
of decision.

Six of the sideshows are briefly discussed in this chapter – Gallipoli,
German East Africa, Salonika, north-east Italy, Palestine and Mesopotamia. Because the combatants in all these theatres of war had artillery
and machine-guns it was very necessary to dig trenches; sometimes these
entrenchments led to a form of siege warfare, but only in Gallipoli did
the key to mobility prove so hard to turn as on the Western Front. We
are here concerned, of course, with aerial observation and reconnaissance
and how they assisted the armies in very different conditions and
environments.

---◇---

GALLIPOLI

The Gallipoli operations arose initially from a desire to strike quickly at
Turkey, after her first acts of war in October 1914, and to relieve
pressure on the Russians in the Caucasus. Twelve Allied divisions were
eventually involved in costly fighting in and around lodgements on the

south-west tip of the Gallipoli peninsula, before withdrawing in January 1916.

An initial naval attempt to force the passage of the Dardanelles and threaten Constantinople took place in February and March 1915 and came to grief in unlocated minefields. The army's first landings, fifteen miles apart, took place on 25th April but, thanks largely to the quick reaction of Mustapha Kemal, commander of the Turkish reserve, achieved no more than the occupation of two small patches of coast. A fresh landing at Suvla Bay, on 6th August, a few miles north of the previous landings, achieved complete surprise and, with only moderate initiative and determination, might have led to a Turkish débâcle; sadly this was lacking. Eventually the costly operation was called off, skilful and bloodless evacuations taking place on 18th December and 8th January.

The air support of the Gallipoli operation was in the hands of the Royal Naval Air Service and when, in July, Colonel F. H. Sykes (from R.F.C. headquarters in France) came out to command the Allied air forces in the Eastern Mediterranean protocol demanded that he be given the naval rank of Wing Captain.

Six seaplanes (operating from the seaplane-carrier *Ark Royal*) and two aeroplanes (operating from the island of Tenedos, twenty miles away to the south) initially composed the air fleet. They were of assorted types, mostly bedevilled by lack of engine power and reliability; the seaplanes also had trouble in taking off from unduly calm or unduly choppy seas. From April onwards No.3 Squadron, R.N.A.S., reinforced the force with further assorted aircraft types and in the same month there arrived the good ship *Manica*, a converted tramp steamer, bearing a *Drachen* kite-balloon. Aeroplane observers were at first recruited from young naval officers, whose lightness of weight was their chief recommendation and who had neither training nor experience in air observation. Communications were quite inadequate until wireless began to work towards the middle of 1915 and none but improvised photographic equipment existed until August. It is not surprising that the Official History describes the British forces as 'little better than blind'.[1]

Aircraft were used principally for tactical reconnaissance, observation of the fire of naval guns and, after British army artillery got ashore, of their fire also. The Official History claims that the results of observation of naval gunfire had sometimes to be conveyed to the guns through the medium of a written message dropped at Tenedos and conveyed thence by destroyer.[2] Tactical reconnaissance reports were often misleading, because of the inexperience of observers in assessing terrain configuration from the air.

The army and its artillery were particularly in need of air observation. The Turks held the commanding heights, and ground within view of the British was mostly rugged and intersected with deep ravines. Bad maps made air photographs essential. Because of the greatness of the need, shortcomings were gradually overcome. Reconnaissance became more efficient and photography more professional. Diagrams of enemy trench systems were issued from June and thereafter the army may be said to have relied fully on the information their air force provided. The Turkish weakness in the path of our forces landing at Suvla Bay, and the subsequent build-up, were made fully clear by the air reports.

Artillery observation improved. The *Manica's* balloon, with its superior communications, was most successful in observing naval gunfire, and, with the coming of wireless, aeroplanes were used increasingly and more and more effectively to observe for the army's artillery, the latter now providing a large percentage of the air observers.[3]

Turkish aircraft never seriously threatened our reconnaissance aircraft and aerial fighting never developed. During the evacuations, however, our air force had the role of discouraging enemy reconnaissance aircraft from approaching the beach-heads.

The instinct to 'drop something nasty on the foe' led, here as elsewhere, to the start of aerial bombing, but it is hard to find evidence of success. The air force history claims that a bomb, dropped from a *Nieuport* aircraft in September 1915, nearly hit a car containing Mustapha Kemal;[4] had this occurred on 25th April and had the bomb hit the car instead of missing it, there might have been a different tale to tell.

———————◇———————

GERMAN EAST AFRICA

General von Lettow-Vorbeck, commander in 1914 of the German forces in the territory of some 250,000 square miles which is now Tanzania, found himself in the unenviable situation of being surrounded by enemies and without hope of relief except by a complete German victory in Europe. He decided that his task was to occupy as many enemy troops as possible for as long as possible, and admirably he carried out that task. With an original force of about five thousand, he eventually attracted to the area at least twenty times as many of his enemy and, although by the end of 1917 he had lost all hold of German East Africa, he was still able to wage guerilla warfare and did so until the Armistice.

Generals Smuts and Van Deventer, who commanded in turn a mainly South African force, invaded the colony from the north and gradually worked south, easing their opponents out of one position after another. Subsidiary advances were made by Belgian and British forces from the north-west and south-west respectively.

Lettow-Vorbeck had no air force, whereas R.F.C. and R.N.A.S. units were in action from the autumn of 1915.[5] The difficulties of the Allied air force were mainly administrative – the long and difficult lines of communication and the depredations of climate. The bush, and the jungles in the river valleys, gave excellent cover to infantry and pilots could not easily observe them. Topographical and route reconnaissance from the air proved very useful, however, in reducing delay, while contact sorties – to locate and communicate between widely separated

groups – became a regular feature of these operations. Artillery observation took place occasionally, in bush country where ground observation
was difficult and on the coast, using the guns of H.M. Ships.

Bombing took place, on a minor scale, almost throughout. The
Africans were unprepared by education or background for this form of
attack and, early on, the air forces had some success in stampeding
load-carrying porters and thus in immobilising enemy columns. As this
ceased to be a novelty, however, Lettow-Vorbeck and his officers must
certainly have stiffened their followers against it and thus made possible
their long and skilful campaign.

SALONIKA

The joint Anglo-French expedition to southern Macedonia resulted from
the 1915 Austrian offensive against Serbia and the related entry of
Bulgaria into the war on the side of Germany. The Allies were too late
to save Serbia but preserved a bridgehead around, and named after, the
port of Salonika, where for three years, over half a million French,
British, Italian, Serbian, Albanian, Montenegran and eventually Greek
soldiers faced an almost impenetrable mountain barrier along a front of
150 miles, and were prey to every kind of sickness but particularly to
malaria. The Germans, with some truth, called this bridgehead 'the
largest Allied concentration camp.'

The British contribution to the Allied force was of two corps of, at
most, six divisions altogether, commanded by General Milne, and their
operations were destined to be centred on the fifteen miles of front from
Lake Dojran (forty miles north of Salonika) westward to the River
Vardar. They were opposed by high quality Bulgarian troops, well
supplied with artillery, ensconced in natural defensive positions of great
strength and with superb observation over the British positions.

Air reconnaissances, in the early days, were made in British naval
seaplanes or in French aeroplanes. In July 1916 No.17 Squadron,
R.F.C. was transferred from Egypt and in September No.47 Squadron,
No.17 Balloon Section and XVI Wing headquarters (Lieutenant-Colonel
G. W. P. Dawes) arrived from England. These Squadrons had *B.E.2c*
and later *B.E.12* aircraft, both outclassed by the *Halberstadt* and *Albatros*
fighters which the Germans very soon brought into action on the
Salonika front. Reconnaissance remained the principal role of the British
air forces, including photography and artillery observation, but early in
1917 bombing became an enthusiasm of both the opposing air forces.

The Germans had carried out a few bombing raids at the beginning
of 1916, and had had a Zeppelin shot down by a British torpedo-boat,
but now they formed a special bombing force of, mostly, *Rumplers* with
which they harassed Allied aerodromes and camps. The British formed
a composite R.N.A.S.–R.F.C. squadron (*Sopwith 1½-strutters* and
B.E.12s) to retaliate upon the enemy's aerodrome; neither party can be

said to have achieved anything decisive, but the German bombing force was transferred to the Western Front in May.

In April and May, 1917, the British carried out an unsuccessful offensive, ill-co-ordinated with an offensive in the French sector to the west. The air force historian (who was, as it happens, an R.F.C. officer in the Salonika theatre) attributes the failure of the British offensive to their inability to neutralise the well-concealed and protected Bulgarian artillery and, specifically, to the failure of the R.F.C. and others accurately to locate it.[6] XII Corps, which carried out the attacks, had the support of No.47 Squadron; they had also two kite-balloons, which had reinforced the British front since February and seem to have done well in the battle. Both No.47 and No.17 Squadron, however, had had to perform the bombing, fighting and long-range reconnaissance roles which, on the Western Front, fell to the lot of the Army and G.H.Q. wings or squadrons. More important still, perhaps, the multifarious activities of this squadron had prevented the combined training of, and liaison between, R.F.C. artillery and infantry which had in France proved such a prerequisite of co-operation in battle.

As to the failure of the British to locate the Bulgarian artillery, the author is indebted to Dr. Malcolm MacEwan for his information and comment on this matter. Dr. MacEwan was in Salonika in 1917; he was a Gunner officer and a Royal Flying Corps observer.

'Everybody knew,' he writes, 'that the enemy could not possibly have the number of batteries which aerial photographs, sound-ranging and flash-spotting showed them to have. Personally I believed, and still believe, that the effect was given by extremely good camouflage, correct in every detail. The effect of this vast artillery deterrent was enormous.'

He describes how his views received some support.

Suddenly, one morning in the winter of '17–'18, we found that the ground was several feet deep in snow. Infantry battalions rapidly cleared a path for us to take off on, but so slippery was the ground that the aircraft simply embedded themselves in the banked up snow and in many cases wrote themselves off. Three of us decided to rev-up to maximum revs on the top of the snow, and on a signal the aircraft were released by the men who held them back, when we found to our amazement that they took off beautifully. We took photographs of the whole debated enemy gun area and found, in quickly developed film, that only about a third of the enemy batteries were in use, as the tracks of the men from the guns to their dug-outs showed – and nothing else. The muzzle flashes on the ground also showed which guns had fired that morning.

Allied reconnaissance, in the second half of 1917, particularly from balloons, suffered from the attentions of a German fighter pilot 'ace' von Eschwege – whose destruction was eventually engineered by the ingenious use of a decoy balloon with a dummy observer and a basketful of explosive remotely detonated from the ground at the moment of attack.

From December 1917 *S.E.5* fighters and a few *Bristol Monoplanes* arrived;[7] in April 1918 No.150 Fighter Squadron was formed within the theatre, Nos.17 and 47 Squadrons becoming Corps squadrons, but still with some responsibilities for long-range reconnaissance and bombing. By May 1918 No.150 Squadron had received some *Sopwith Camels* and air superiority had passed finally to the British air forces.

ITALY

From May 1915, when Italy entered the war on the Allied side, until October 1917, indecisive fighting between Italians and Austrians took place on the frontier, both in the mountains and in the coastal plains. The German-inspired breakthrough of Caporetto thereupon sent the Italians into headlong retreat almost to the gates of Venice.

British and French armies were sent to the rescue, but the Italians had successfully stabilised their position on the River Piave (north of Venice) and the spring 1918 crises on the Western Front resulted in a reduction of the British force in Italy from six to four divisions. At the same time the British air force in Italy, which had built up to a brigade of two wings, five squadrons and a kite-balloon wing, now reduced to a single wing. This was composed of one Corps squadron of *R.E.8s* and *Bristol Fighters*, three Fighter squadrons of *Camels* and two kite-balloon sections.

The German air force, which had strongly reinforced the Austrians at Caporetto, were confident and aggressive when R.F.C. units first arrived in Italy and were well able to disrupt attempts at reconnaissance. Gradually this situation changed, due partly, it seems, to a policy of bombing of enemy aerodromes but also, no doubt, to the withdrawal of German air units to the Western Front, and for the rest of the war the British had local air superiority.

In March 1918 the British Corps moved to the mountainous Asiago sector in the north. An early Austrian offensive was expected and considerable reconnaissance took place to detect preparations for it; Austrian concealment was good, however, and little was seen. The Austrians increased their own air reconnaissance effort in June and British fighter patrols were increased proportionately. The promised enemy offensive came, both in the Asiago and on the lower Piave. Weather preventing air reconnaissance in the Asiago, British fighters were diverted to the support of the Italians on the Piave, with attacks on pontoon bridges and bridgeheads across the river and with later harassment of the enemy's withdrawal. Later *R.E.8s* were attached to Italian formations, mainly in the artillery role.

In this theatre one can clearly perceive a decline in the reconnaissance and observation roles in favour of the more spectacular roles of bombing and low-level ground-attack.

PALESTINE

The principal task of the British force in Egypt, on the opening of hostilities with Turkey, was the defence of the Suez Canal and for this two Indian divisions and a cavalry brigade were initially available. By mid-November, 1914, there were three *Maurice Farman* and two *Henry Farman* aeroplanes in Egypt, which permitted reconnaissance over the Sinai desert to a depth of some forty-five miles. More valuable were the seven French *Nieuport* seaplanes which operated from two (formerly German) cargo boats and from a cruiser off the Sinai coast. The French pilots and their British observers flew deep over the desert with great skill and courage and were rewarded with much good information about the Turkish forces in the south of Palestine and about their build-up for an advance across the desert to the Canal in February 1915.

The attack on the Canal was easily beaten off, and the enemy withdrew. Soon afterwards, however, serviceability troubles assailed the French seaplanes and in March they were transferred to Gallipoli. The Official History describes the British force in Egypt as 'deprived of its eyes' and it is significant that the dispatch of a column of all arms in pursuit of the Turkish retreat was cancelled owing to lack of information about the enemy.[8]

It was not until November 1915, when V Wing arrived from England under Lieutenant-Colonel W. G. H. Salmond, that things improved. The Wing had two squadrons of *B.E.2cs* and its main duty was photography on behalf of the topographical section for the production of maps of the area east of the Canal. The squadrons also reconnoitred deep over the desert, and found it comparatively free of Turks. Very soon small detachments had to be found to support operations against the Senussi in the Western Desert and against the Sultan of Darfur in Equatorial Africa.

In April 1916 the first German aeroplanes – *Rumplers C 1*, *Aviatiks* and the famous *Fokker* monoplanes firing through their propellors – started to arrive in the theatre, outclassing the *B.E.2cs*. At once the Germans gained a measure of air superiority and retained it until the autumn of 1917. Their pilots, here as elsewhere, were generally outnumbered and unable to obtain by reconnaissance as plentiful information as they would have wished; they were able to hamper, though never entirely to prevent, the R.F.C.'s efforts in the same field. In the circumstances it is surprising that either side should have wasted time, effort and aeroplanes in bombing on a most paltry scale and (in case of the R.F.C.) in low-level machine-gun attacks on enemy troops, transport and aerodromes. The recipients of such favours invariably discounted their effects but perhaps, for the R.F.C., they provided the training which resulted in significant results later in the campaign.

In keeping with the build-up of the British force in Egypt and surrounding territories, a Middle East Brigade, R.F.C., was formed in Egypt on 1st July, 1916, Salmond being promoted to command it. It

consisted of V Wing in the Egyptian theatre, with one British and one
Australian squadron, and squadrons in Salonika (shortly to become a
Wing), East Africa and Mesopotamia; it also had a Reserve Wing in
Egypt, with pilot and technical training functions, and, of course, the
usual aircraft parks.

In the early spring a British force had started to advance slowly east
of the Canal, in phase with the construction of a railway along the Sinai
coast, and, in early August the Turks advanced to attack them some
twenty-five miles from the Canal. The R.F.C. gave good warning of the
Turkish approach and, during the battle which followed, watched for
possible enemy reinforcements. They also ranged the guns of the naval
monitor *M5* on a Turkish camp east of the battlefield. The Turks
retreated and the British followed them up; on 20th December El Arish
was occupied after the R.F.C. had reported it clear of enemy and, on
8th January, 1917, a British column descended on Rafah and captured
and withdrew with its garrison of sixteen hundred. The R.F.C. was
particularly commended for their support of this operation, by reconnaissance before and during the battle and by artillery observation.[9] The
latter art had, it seems, been slow to develop in this theatre of war.

The Arab rebellion against Turkish rule had erupted in the Hejaz in
June 1916 and from November R.F.C. aeroplanes and R.N.A.S.
seaplanes supported the Arab guerilla operations in Hejaz and along the
railway to the north, by reconnaissance, photography and desultory
bombing.

Sir Archibald Murray, Commander-in-Chief Egypt, who was becoming more and more directly committed to the advance into Palestine,
now moved against the next Turkish line of resistance, Beersheba to
Gaza. An attempt was made on 26th March to isolate and seize Gaza.
Early morning fog did not lift until 7.30 a.m. but by 8 Kress, the
German commander of the Turkish force, had received from his air
force a very clear idea of what was happening and he immediately set in
motion a relieving force. This force does not appear to have been
observed from the air until 4.30 p.m; the commander of the Desert
Column, not yet in possession of the ridge commanding the town from
the east and now aware of this new threat from the north-east, decided
to draw back; a general withdrawal resulted. The Turks energetically
fortified their defences, particularly those of Gaza, while the German air
force received reinforcements, particularly a few (the Official History
states 'two') *Halberstadt* fighters. Because of their high performance these
exerted an influence far in excess of their numbers. Murray's job was
not simple.

The Second Battle of Gaza was a siege operation, commencing with
a day's bombardment from land and sea for which the R.F.C. observed
extensively. On 20th April an assault was attempted but, as had so often
been discovered on the Western front, the defenders were still present
and active and could not be displaced. Turkish reserves attempted to
intervene in the battle but were spotted by the R.F.C. and held off. The

air force historian claims that a force of 2,800 infantry and cavalry, concealed in a river bed, were attacked and dispersed by a total of 48 20-lb. bombs dropped from four aircraft.[10] Reports of this kind are very prevalent in accounts of early aerial bombing exploits; it may be remarked that the weight of explosive dropped in this sortie was the equivalent of about 75 seconds' engagement by a single battery of light (18-pounder) field guns, and would indeed have been fortunate to have put 2,800 enemy to flight.

General Sir Edmund Allenby replaced Murray after this battle and requested and received the reinforcements hitherto denied to his predecessor. By the end of December his force had risen to ten divisions. A separate Palestine R.F.C. Brigade had been formed (under Salmond initially, though Sefton Brancker commanded from early November and A. E. Borton from mid-December onwards). This Brigade had a Corps and an Army Wing, the former equipped with a mixture of *B.E.2es* and *R.E.8s* and the latter with both those types and also *D.H.2s*, *Vickers Bullets*,[11] *Bristol Fighters* and a few others. Two kite-balloons belatedly reached the theatre. This combination, and particularly the *Bristol Fighter*, swung air superiority back to the British.

The preservation of secrecy before Allenby's offensive of the autumn of 1917 involved good air-concealment drills and discipline in every unit, troop movements only by night and denial to German aircraft of the skies over the concentration area, particularly during the sensitive periods when the cavalry had perforce to water their horses. From 27th October fighter cover was continuous; it is probable that only one German aircraft penetrated it and took photographs and that this aircraft was forced down on the way back.

On the 27th Allenby demonstrated strongly against Gaza. The two kite-balloons observed for 116 separate shoots, including one for a 6-inch battery engaging the Turkish railhead and twenty-four for guns of naval vessels, using telephone communication to a signal station on the coast. The Corps Wing was similarly engaged, their aircraft having located and recorded 131 hostile batteries before the bombardment opened.

With his right flank covered by the Arabs under Feisal and Lawrence, Allenby struck suddenly at Beersheba on the 31st and captured it at once. The battle swung back to Gaza, while fresh photographic cover of the whole front was prepared and distributed. Then, on the 6th November, three divisions attacked the central sector of the Turkish defences and broke through. This, with an intense artillery and naval bombardment of the Gaza area on the 7th, started a Turkish retreat which became headlong.

A large part of the British air force was now diverted to the direct attack of the retreating Turks and of the German aerodromes. At one of these, Et Tine, where an ammunition depot was also bombed on the 9th, unusual panic broke out, horses and men stampeded, communications were destroyed and for lack of orders units withdrew unnecessarily. Order was not restored until the following day.[12] The bombing of the aerodromes and of transport on the roads immobilised the German air force for virtually two weeks.

The Turkish army eventually stood fast north of Jaffa and south of Jerusalem. The main battle for Jerusalem started on 8th December, 1917, and three days later Allenby entered the city. Efforts to retake it were easily beaten off and in the second half of February, 1918, Jericho was captured. the R.F.C. now enjoyed overwhelming air superiority. In the words of the Official History: 'The work of the Royal Flying Corps was even more valuable than usual. It had completely dominated the enemy and broken up all his formations in the air. From it early information of his dispositions and of his successive retirements had always been obtained.'[13]

It is worthy of note that in the flush of success the Army still felt the need for information and the airmen were able to provide it. The third battle of Gaza, however, may longest be remembered as the first occasion on which offensive air action achieved results commensurate with the cost, whether in terms of casualties or loss of reconnaissance effort.

———————◇———————

MESOPOTAMIA

In November 1914, to safeguard the oilfields on the Persian Gulf, a small force provided by the Indian Government landed near, and captured, the port of Basra, at the south-eastern limit of Mesopotamia, which we should now call Iraq. The British general, Nixon, decided that he must, for security, enlarge his bridgehead and in May 1915 he pushed the two divisions, which his force now contained, some hundred miles up the rivers Tigris and Euphrates. Arguments, militarily less sound perhaps, thereupon encouraged him to push Major-General Townshend's division farther up the Tigris and then to set his sights on the politically attractive target of Baghdad. At Ctesiphon, however, twenty miles short of Baghdad, an indecisive battle was fought on 22nd and 23rd November, after which Townshend withdrew his division to Kut-el-Amara. Here he was invested and, after several relief attempts by inadequate forces had failed, was forced to surrender at the end of April, 1916.

Because the Indian Government had accepted responsibility for the Expeditionary Force to Basra, and because it was beyond its powers to provide an effective air component, air reconnaissance was slow to develop and dependent for its build-up on enterprise and improvisation. Two *Maurice Farman* aeroplanes arrived from England in May 1915, five pilots and fifty mechanics from Australia and New Zealand; later, when the Royal Navy sent out seaplanes, they became effective only when wheels had replaced floats.

Of all theatres of war, however, the regions of the Tigris and Euphrates called most stridently for air reconnaissance and were most suited to it.

... tanding points. **2.40pm.**
3.10pm, 3.40pm Racing: From
Goodwood, featuring **2.45pm** The
Crowson Rated Stakes (7f); **3.15pm**
The Ladbroke Racing Sprint H'cap
(6f); **3.50pm** The Tripleprint Cele-
bration Mile (mile). The commenta-
tors are Jim McGrath, Julian Wilson
and Willie Carson. **4.40pm Final
Score:** The day's news and results,
plus **Swimming:** Hamilton Bland
and Andy Jameson with the latest
news from the European Champi-
onships in Spain. *(All times are subject to change)* (S)   49689472

**5.20pm News;
Weather**   9456694
5.30pm Local News; Weather

5.35pm Dad's Army
Comedy series starring Arthur Lowe
and Clive Dunn. The platoon are
guarding a vital telephone link, but
awake to find a bomb enmeshed in
the wires. (Txt, Rpt)   828149
Followed by
**The Nation's
Favourite Children's Book**

Slint.
goals from the day's other Premier-
ship matches. Introduced by
Desmond Lynam with Alan Hansen
and Mark Lawrenson. Commentary
by John Motson, Jon Champion and
Tony Gubba. (Txt, S)   4429385

**12.00midnight
Top of the Pops**
As yesterday. (Txt, S)   99926

**12.30am FILM
Running Cool**
Action drama. A biker and his gang
help an old friend to fight off a land
developer. (105mins, 1993, Txt)
*Starring: Andrew Divoff, Dedee
Pfeiffer, Tracy Sebastian.*
See Films, page 16   309453

2.15-2.20am Weather

REGIONAL VARIATIONS

WALES
10.45am Grandstand. (S) 48067656
4.55pm Wales on Saturday: Continues
at 5.30pm. 9456694 **5.30-6.05pm**
Wales on Saturday. 570762

6.45pm Summer Dance
The Paris Opera Ballet perform Prokofiev's
Romeo and Juliet. (S)   67420675

**9.15pm Whatever
Happened to the Likely Lads?**
Vintage sitcom starring James Bolam and
Rodney Bewes. (Txt, Rpt)   860694

9.45pm Our Friends in the North
BAFTA-winning drama series set in New-
castle, starring Daniel Craig, Chris Eccleston,
Gina McKee and Mark Strong. It's 1979 –
Nicky stands for Parliament, Tosker meets the
woman of his dreams, and Geordie is dealing
in drugs. (Txt, Rpt, S)   4154694

**11.00pm FILM: The Great Northfield
Minnesota Raid** Western starring Cliff
Robertson and Robert Duvall. (90mins, 1971)
See Films, page 16.   82033
12.30am Cricket Highlights of the third
day's play at The Oval in the sixth Test
between England and Australia. (S) 7611892
**1.10-2.40am FILM: Ringo and His
Golden Pistol** Western starring Mark
Damon. (90mins, 1966) *See Films, page 16;*
Weather View.   166043

tracist cop Bob Hoskins gets a heart transplant and, ironically, the donor is murdered black lawyer Denzel Washington — who then comes back as a ghost. The story couldn't be more contrived, but it comes with a rewarding line in unpredictable details — and the banter between the stars is genuinely funny. (US/1989; Dir. **James D Parriott**). Rating ✓✓✓

Closet Land 18+
BBC2, 11.55pm-1.25am (23.55-01.25)
PREMIERE A powerful political thriller that gets two excellent performances from Madeleine Stowe, as a children's author, and Alan Rickman, as a police interrogator. (US/1990; Dir. **Radha Baradwaj**). Rating ✓✓✓

Tiffany Jones 18+
C5, 12.35am-2.15am (00.35-02.15)
Mindless kitsch, based on a cartoon strip, in which Anouska Hempel gets involved in a dangerous political plot. (GB/1973; Dir. **Peter Walker**). Rating ✓

Island of Terror 15+
BBC1, 12.45am-2.00am (00.45-02.00)
Doctor Peter Cushing is baffled by the discovery of some boneless corpses on a foggy Irish island in this intriguing and atmospheric chiller. (GB/1966; Dir. **Terence Fisher**). Rating ✓✓✓

The Hypnotist F
C4, 1.15am-2.55am (01.15-02.55)
Patricia Roc chooses psychiatrist Roland Culver to cure her fiancé Paul Carpenter's mental problems, and predictably dull criminal goings-on are the result. (GB/1956; Dir. **Montgomery Tully**). Rating ✓✓

Venetian Bird F
BBC2, 1.25am-3.00am (01.25-03.00)
Playing a British private eye who goes to Venice in search of a missing Italian war hero, Richard Todd's inflexible performance is proof that roles in civilian clothes just didn't suit him. (GB/1952; Dir. **Ralph Thomas**). Rating ✓✓

Sin 15+
C5, 2.15am-3.50am (02.15-03.50)
A very tepid attempt at a steamy thriller in which Raquel Welch and Richard Johnson thrash around with a silly rather than sexy script. (Greece/1970; Dir. **George Pan Cosmatos**). Rating ✓

The Clairvoyant F
C4, 2.25am-4.20am (02.55-04.20)
Claude Rains's intense performance (complemented by effectively eerie highlighting of his eyes) is the best thing about this scrappy and sometimes long-winded thriller. (GB/1935; Dir. **Maurice Elvey**). Rating ✓✓

Pearl of the South Pacific F
C5, 3.50am-5.20am (03.50-05.20)
With a wobbly American accent, David Farrar stops over on a South Seas island with Virginia Mayo. (US/1955; Dir. **Allan Dwan**). Rating ✓

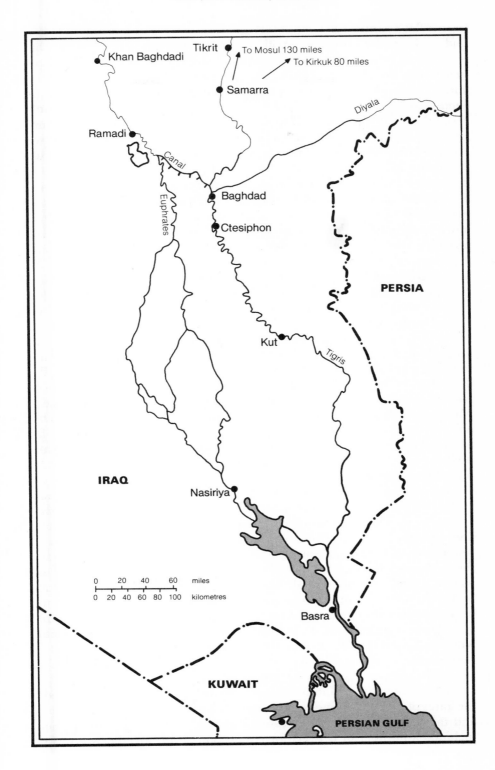

Khan Baghdadi

Tikrit

To Mosul 130 miles

To Kirkuk 80 miles

Samarra

Diyala

Ramadi

Canal

Euphrates

Baghdad

Ctesiphon

PERSIA

Kut

Tigris

IRAQ

Nasiriya

0   20   40   60   miles
0 20 40 60 80 100 kilometres

Basra

KUWAIT

PERSIAN GULF

In this flat country, ground observation posts were almost impossible to find and, in the absence of balloons and aeroplanes, the artillery had recourse to 'observation ladders'. Cavalry movement over the wide open spaces was much restricted in the hot season by the distress of their horses, and, when they discovered something, it was not difficult for the enemy to limit their discovery to a very small segment of the whole. From the air it was very easy to spot, against the featureless background, any form of field defence; it was less easy to judge to what extent it was occupied but, with experience, this problem could be solved. Heat was an enemy to the airman too. It warped his aircraft's wings and caused the engines to overheat; it radically reduced take-off and climb performance. Heat haze and sandstorms often reduced the observed area to a small circle of sand immediately below the aircraft. All these difficulties, however, could be and were overcome, while the two great rivers provided unequalled aids to aerial navigation and convenient sites for floating workshops and stores.

The commanders were blind without air reconnaissance, were quick to appreciate the achievements of the pilots and quick also to tailor their operations to the aeroplane's potentialities. In all the advances and engagements which preceded Townshend's withdrawal into Kut the pilots furnished important information and, ironically, the Kut disaster might have been avoided had not a pilot, returning with information of the build-up of Turkish forces on the Ctesiphon position, been shot down by anti-aircraft fire and captured. Pilot and aircraft reinforcements had by this time enabled No. 30 Squadron, R.F.C., to be organised in Mesopotamia, partly from Egypt and partly by incorporating what had already been improvised on the spot. Incredible to relate, however, five officers of this squadron, the rank and file of two flights and three unserviceable aeroplanes were permitted to be shut up in Kut and, in due course, surrendered.

Only two aircraft remained for the support of the early relief attempts. In February, however, there arrived two steel *Henry Farmans* with *Canton Unis* engines (both airframe and engine standing up well to the climate) and also four *B.E.2cs*. These enabled the R.F.C. to play its part in the remaining, and vain, attempts to save Kut, including in the later stages the dropping of supplies. The strain on the pilots was very great, and was increased by the arrival, and aggressive behaviour, of a German flight. Nor was strain the prerogative of the pilots, for the maintenance of aeroplanes in flying condition demanded tremendous efforts from ground-crew in conditions of great heat and discomfort. The reaction which followed the fall of Kut led to a high sickness rate; this, and the reinforcement of the German flight, gave the enemy a period of air superiority.

General Sir F. S. Maude, the new British commander, remained at the gates of Kut, receiving reinforcements and preparing administratively and tactically for a renewed offensive early in 1917. His reinforcements included a number of *B.E.2cs* for No. 30 Squadron, together with Major

J. E. Tennant as squadron Commander and a number of experienced pilots from other theatres, also a fortunate windfall in the shape of four naval kite-balloons which the army promptly appropriated for the use of its gunners and of the naval river craft on the Tigris whose guns were supporting army operations. No.30 Squadron, thus revived, took the initiative against the German air force detachment both in the air and by bombing their aerodrome, and regained air superiority. Their pilots supported Maude's preparatory operations along the south bank of the Tigris by extensive air photography (for the production of battle maps), by intensified artillery co-operation and by contact sorties. 'Fleeting targets' were regularly engaged and the contact patrols seem to have proved more successful than in many of the battles in France, probably due to the lesser numbers of troops operating over slightly more extensive areas, and thus to less battle confusion.

The Turkish army was not to be trapped, as Maude had hoped, in the Kut position but withdrew rapidly along the north bank of the Tigris – pursued by the British. In the early stages of the pursuit, when our artillery had the river to cross and consequently found the enemy out of range, the R.F.C. carried out some bombing – not nearly heavy enough to be effective. Although the Turks withdrew in good order they could not oppose the British south of Baghdad and this fine political prize was Maude's on 10th March, 1917.

Maude was now committed to advancing north-west up the Tigris and Euphrates to cover Baghdad, and also northwards to link with the Russians in Persia (Iran). The last of these operations, in the hills, ravines and broken ground in and alongside the Diyala valley, posed new and trickier reconnaissance problems to the R.F.C.

In April 1917 Oberleutnant Schüz, commander of the German air force unit supporting the Turks in Mesopotamia, returned from a visit to Germany with a convoy of nine new scout aircraft. We may quote him verbatim.

In order to confound the English by the unexpected appearance of a new type, I covered the 300 odd miles from the railhead of the Baghdad line to the front in one day. But even this rapidity was of no use. On the same day an English machine appeared at a great height and dropped a tin of cigarettes with the following message: 'The British airmen send their compliments to Captain S, and are pleased to welcome him back to Mesopotamia. We shall be pleased to offer him a warm reception in the air. We enclose a tin of English cigarettes and will send him a Baghdad melon when they are in season. Au revoir. Our compliments to the other German airmen. The Royal Flying Corps.'[14]

Schüz's *Halberstadt* scouts, however, swung air superiority to the Germans for a period, British reconnaissance and artillery sorties being disrupted. This situation had been anticipated, and before the autumn campaigning season was far advanced *R.E.8s* had replaced the *B.E.2cs*, with *Spads, Bristol Scouts* and *Martinsyde Scouts* in addition. With these aircraft appeared No.63 Squadron, and its arrival was spectacular. Reaching Mesopotamia at its hottest, unacclimatised, direct from England, they succumbed rapidly to sandfly fever, heatstroke and other ills and very soon two-thirds of their strength were in hospital. It was a month before the first operational sortie took place and, of the two aircraft involved, one crashed and the other forced-landed in enemy territory. By the end of 1917 this squadron had recovered and air superiority had returned to the British.

In September 1917 the British advanced again up Tigris and Euphrates. At Ramadi on the Euphrates General Brooking, with a composite group of about divisional strength, brilliantly trapped and captured a Turkish force of 3,500 men. He was supported by a flight of No.30 Squadron, whose preliminary visual and photographic reconnaissance disclosed the emphasis of the Turkish defence system and determined Brooking's plan. On the Tigris, a timely reconnaissance on the 22nd October indicated a build-up of Turkish forces north of Samarra; Maude attacked first and the Turks withdrew to successive positions covering Tikrit, the first being stormed and the second bombarded – the latter with R.F.C. observation. In the final fighting for Tikrit artillery co-operation was good between No.63 Squadron and the Indian divisions engaged, and the town was captured on 5th November.

Twelve days later General Maude was dead – of cholera. He was succeeded by General Sir W. R. Marshall, one of his Corps Commanders.

On the Euphrates, Brooking moved forward in February 1918 and on 26th March attacked a Turkish force of 4,000 entrenched at Khan Baghdadi, having on the previous night placed his Cavalry brigade across the Turkish line of retreat. As at Ramadi, the surrounded force surrendered. For this battle Brooking had a composite R.F.C. unit of three flights under Major H. de Havilland, one flight allotted to the Cavalry Brigade, one (together with a kite-balloon) to the Gunners of the main attack and the third to the remaining reconnaissance and contact patrol tasks. With characteristic foresight Brooking established his headquarters alongside the best aeroplane landing ground in the district.

The Official History records that 'the excellent work during the 26th March of the British air force had contributed greatly to the success gained' and it goes on to list this work as follows:

Guiding the direction of the cavalry brigade,

Constant information to its commander of enemy movements and of the operations of our infantry,

Co-operation with the artillery of the main attack,

Much useful reconnaissance information,

Harassing enemy infantry with bombs and machine-guns,

Locating Turkish guns on barges in the morning and bombing them in the afternoon.[15]

We cannot do better than conclude the chapter with this tribute to the exponents of the art of air reconnaissance – in a theatre where, from understanding of the facts of life and warfare, that art flourished.

1918
The Break-Out

◇

'There is no other course open to us but to fight it out!'
FIELD MARSHAL SIR DOUGLAS HAIG'S Order of the Day, 11th April, 1918.

(MAP, front end-paper)

On 21st March, 1918, the first of the German offensives which were to break the long siege of the Western Front burst upon the British Third and Fifth Armies in the Somme sector. On that day the Royal Flying Corps was within a fortnight of the end of its short but distinguished life, the decision having been made to merge the R.N.A.S. and the R.F.C. in a new, independent Royal Air Force. This decision was to influence the future development of air observation and reconnaissance for the British Army but had little effect on air operations in the final battles of the War which were, of course, conducted by the same combinations of soldiers and airmen as in the previous three years. Description and discussion of the events, almost entirely political, leading to the establishment of the Royal Air Force will be deferred to a later chapter, with one short exception.

The principal factor which led to the decision to form a separate air force was the birth and growth of the concept of bombing as a means of attacking directly the industries and centres of population of the enemy. This does not appear to have been the brain child of military parents but rather of civilians under the stress of the *Gotha* raids on London; Haig and Trenchard were unimpressed by it. It became, however, 'part of the project' and the Independent Bombing Force was duly created early in June. It was located in France, though the French did not want to be associated with its functions, and the final irony was that Trenchard was appointed to command it, having been replaced as G.O.C., Royal Flying Corps, in January 1918, by Major-General J. M. Salmond. The potentialities of the Independent Bombing Force could hardly be tested in the time available; by the end of the war, however, it had absorbed eleven squadrons – and these we must rate a diversion of the main effort over the final battlefields.

The first stage of the German break-out in the West consisted of two consecutive operations which were given the codenames 'Michael' and 'Georg'. 'Michael' was to be a breakthrough by three armies (with about a five to two superiority in divisions) between La Fère, fifteen miles south of St. Quentin, and Arras, the southern of the three armies then forming a defensive flank while the other two rolled up the British to the north. 'Georg' would follow, two further armies driving south of

Ypres to the Channel ports. Ludendorff, Chief Staff Officer of the German forces in the west and architect of these plans, hoped as a result to have opened up a large gap between British and French and to have Paris at his mercy.

Great pains were taken by the Germans to preserve secrecy; troops and aircraft, for example, were held back from the key sectors until the last moment. That their offensive would occur was, however, inevitable; the Allies had time to anticipate it – by preparing a philosophy of defence against the particular threat, with appropriate procedures to accompany it, and, of course, by air reconnaissance. The latter revealed more than normal road and rail movement in the area behind the planned sector of attack and, as the date approached, networks of light railways and an increase in lights displayed in rear areas by night. What the Allies could not do was to correct the disparity in numbers.

Courses in air co-operation took place during the winter for commanders up to Brigadier-Generals and for staff officers. Among many memoranda issued by the British G.H.Q. was one on 'The employment of the Royal Flying Corps in Defence'. Reconnaissance, artillery co-operation, contact patrols, bombing, low-flying air attacks – all found their place in the overall philosophy, together with the need to gain and maintain ascendancy over the enemy air force to allow the other roles to continue. Schemes were drawn up (with maps to illustrate them and with both schemes and maps kept up to date) to detail squadrons to tasks so that all should be ready when the blow fell, without need for elaborate briefing. The Corps squadrons on the Western Front had mostly *R.E.8* aircraft, the Army squadrons mostly *S.E.5s, Camels* and *Bristol Fighters.*

Most of these preparations were defeated by fog and the German tactics. The latter might have been predicted, for there had been a preview at Cambrai – a short intense period of artillery preparation, including gas shell, followed by infantry infiltration in small highly trained groups deep into the British defences. Nothing could have helped them more than fog. On the Fifth Army's front, in the south, the fog did not clear till midday, by which time their battle zone had been deeply penetrated by the German infantry, their communications uprooted by the German artillery and their own artillery largely neutralised by a combination of both. Somehow the corps squadrons managed to get some aircraft up in the fog, but their pilots could see little. As the fog cleared later in the morning they saw many spectacular targets and called for fire upon them; none of these calls was answered.

On the Third Army front, in the north, the fog cleared earlier, air reconnaissance was wide and deep and calls for artillery fire were sometimes answered.

The failure of the British organisation for artillery-air co-operation proved no transitory affair, though there were some redeeming examples to prove that the system was workable. Responsibility for this disaster must be placed fairly and squarely upon the artillery. The Official History states:

> It must be emphasised that the organisation for co-operation between the artillery and the R.F.C. failed completely from the very first. For long periods, not only in the fog of the first morning but throughout the retreat, there was no communication between the batteries and the aeroplanes, although the zone call system had been introduced primarily to meet the conditions of open warfare. This unfortunate state of affairs was in no way due to the failure of the air officers to understand the importance of this co-operation or to carry out their share of it.[1]

The Official History, which is supported by the Artillery historian,[2] goes on to detail some of the causes of failure – severance of telephone and breakdown of wireless communications, continual movement of batteries, lost equipment, neglect to erect wireless masts, bad siting of wireless sets, failure to keep wireless operators briefed as to the zones covered – in other words a standard of training and interior economy which could not stand up to the very intense strain which was placed upon it.

To rub salt into the Gunners' wounds, the Official History records:

> 'Contact patrol work and close reconnaissances were maintained by the Royal Flying Corps, and its reports often gave the corps staffs the best information which they received as to the movements of their fighting troops and of the enemy's advance.'[3]

The German attack swept on, particularly against the unfortunate Fifth Army which fell back in some confusion. Third Army resisted more successfully (though withdrawing to preserve its contact points with Fifth Army, which were always under threat) and this resistance seems to have caused Ludendorff to change his original plan to an immediate thrust towards Paris instead of a rolling-up of the Allied left wing. By 24th March the Germans had occupied Péronne and crossed the Somme to the south of it. On the same day the junction of British and French armies on the former's right flank began to be threatened both by the German advance and by the obvious intention of the French to withdraw south-west.

This was perhaps the lowest point in the Allied fortunes and it inspired the appointment of General Foch as co-ordinator of the action of Allied armies on the Western Front and soon afterwards as Commander-in-Chief. French reinforcements moved north, German attacks in the Arras sector (the north flank of the offensive) made little impression, the Fifth Army rallied as their pursuers outran their supplies and succumbed to fatigue, and French orders for withdrawal south-west were cancelled. Albert and Montdidier were lost but by 5th April the offensive had come to a halt fifteen miles short of the key-objective, Amiens.

Throughout this battle dependence on air reconnaissance was absolute; virtually no other source of information produced it in time. Air observers monitored and gave early warning of the dangerous gaps opening up on the two flanks of the Fifth Army and, more generally, of the strengths and direction of movement of advancing German columns. Contact sortie pilots gave commanders information of the battle which, very often, they alone could obtain and deliver. The fighting in the Arras sector more closely resembled the siege operations of the last three years; the Corps squadrons and the balloons performed their normal roles and the air force historian notes that 'many wireless calls for fire on massed German infantry were answered by the artillery, and some of the attacks were consequently disorganised before they reached the British lines.[4]'

Indeed the corps squadron pilots continued throughout the battle to indicate targets to the artillery, by message-dropping when wireless was ineffective, and a few successes were reported.[5] Increasingly, however, the efforts of both corps and army squadrons were diverted to low-flying attacks on the German infantry, both in the forward and rear areas, both with machine-guns and bombs. The air historian states that this diversion was later a subject of service controversy, admits freely that low-flying air attacks, no matter how sustained or successful, could not compare with the effect of well-directed artillery but reminds us that the artillery co-operation organisation had broken down.[6] In the circumstances the diversion of effort to low-flying attack was no doubt both wise and inevitable; there is some evidence of its success in delaying the enemy's advance and deployment. Above the battle the British fighter pilots successfully protected the reconnaissance and contact patrols and the low-level attack aircraft from interference by the German air force.

'Georg', the next stage of the German offensive and aimed at the Channel ports, had slightly lost its original point as a result of the failure of 'Michael' either to break through or to roll-up the northern part of the Allied force. Also the need to reinforce 'Michael' had weakened the German armies on their northern flank. Ludendorff could not stop, however, and he had the aggressor's advantage of being able to move reinforcements to the new front in advance of the defenders' readiness to accept that the threat had been removed from the original front. With German logic, however, he re-named the operation 'Georgette'.

From the end of March air reports began to indicate northward movement of troops to areas east of the British First Army sector between La Bassée and Armentières. The G.H.Q. Intelligence staff, however, expected the next blow to fall in the Vimy Ridge area, not far north of Arras, and there was no haste to reinforce First Army, which like the enemy facing them had been depleted in aid of the battle to their south. Meanwhile First Army's Royal Air Force squadrons and balloon sections were heavily engaged in tactical and photographic reconnaissance, the registration of targets with the artillery and the engagement of hostile batteries as they were located.

The blow fell early in the morning of 9th April, on the front of a Portuguese division due for relief. As on 21st March there was an intense artillery bombardment, including gas shell, of artillery positions, head-quarters and communications, followed by infiltration by assault parties and, at 8.45 a.m., the main infantry attack. As on 21st March, there was thick fog. The unfortunate Portuguese division disintegrated; the Germans thrust through the gap and by evening had swung north and reached and crossed the River Lys – after which this battle is usually named. On the 10th the Germans attacked north of Armentières, in Second Army's sector, and on the 11th they pressed on in both sectors and captured Messines and Merville, the latter only seven miles south-east of Hazebrouck, an important railway junction and the key German objective of this offensive. On that evening Haig issued his famous 'Backs to the wall' Order of the Day.

This message was well timed, for the next day, the 12th April, was the critical day of the battle. South of Merville and some five miles to the north of it, fresh threats appeared to Hazebrouck which were stemmed by improvised formations. In both the north and the south flanks of the enemy influx the defence held firm. French reinforcements were on their way.

From the 9th until the 11th the weather had been bad for air operations, though contact sorties and some low-level attacks on advancing infantry had been achieved by the R.A.F. On the afternoon of the 11th the weather cleared and the Corps aircraft carried out continuous contact sorties in addition to photography and close reconnaissance. On the critical 12th April the visibility was excellent and the weather fine and the British air forces made good use of it. They receive warm appreciation from the Official History.[7] Contact patrol pilots reported the progress of the battle, hour by hour, with great precision, many wireless calls for artillery engagement were answered – probably about sixty during the day – and to the south of the enemy break-through our artillery balloon observers were most successful.[8] Continuous low-level bombing and machine-gun attacks were made, particularly in the threatened sectors north and south of Merville. The German air force made determined efforts to co-operate with their infantry and to recon-noitre the British communications; they also used their balloons well forward. This led to considerable air fighting, successful for the R.A.F., and the destruction of six of the enemy's balloons. More hours were flown by the British air forces, more bombs dropped and more photo-graphs taken than in any day since the war had begun.

There was then some slackening in enemy pressure and no further headway was made against Hazebrouck. Abortive enemy attacks in the north and south on 17th and 18th respectively, the latter in rain and snow, were the occasions for further good work by the corps squadron pilots and observers, both in the form of artillery co-operation, low-level reconnaissance and contact patrols. There was a week's lull, a final Ger-man offensive south-west of Ypres which gave them Mount Kemmel and forced small Allied withdrawals east of Ypres, and the battle was over.

Though the strain had been great the defence had never seemed, after the first day, to have fallen into the confusions and dangers of the recent battles on the Somme. Nor did artillery-air communication break down, though the use of air observation of artillery fire was restricted to some extent by the mobility of some of the fighting. There was considerably less low-level bombing and machine-gunning. Above all the air force demonstrated its mastery of the arts of low-level reconnaissance and the contact patrol, calling for great skill, experience and courage from the young pilots and observers. In these two battles of withdrawal, many British aerodromes had been overrun and hurriedly evacuated. Aircraft wastage amounted to 84 per cent of the strength at the start of the March fighting. It speaks volumes for the ground crews and organisation that the efforts of the pilots in the forward area appear never to have flagged.

On 21st April, on the Somme sector, at about 10.50 a.m., a not very large-scale aerial battle started when fighters of No.209 Squadron, R.A.F., engaged German fighters who were attacking two *R.E.8s* on a photographic sortie. One of the R.A.F. pilots, newly arrived in the squadron, was in difficulties as he was pursued by a red *Fokker* triplane; his flight commander, Captain A. R. Brown, a Canadian, dived to his assistance and shot down the triplane within the British lines. Its pilot, who was killed, was Manfred von Richtofen, the great trainer and tactician of the German air force. This was a not unimportant occasion in the history of British air reconnaissance.

The British casualties in 'Michael' and 'Georgette' had been, in round figures, 260,000 but those of the Germans had been 348,000. With the spectre of the assembling American formations before him, and with nascent doubts as to his army's morale, Ludendorff could not pause for long. French reserves having been drawn north to the aid of the British, he searched for surprise in the south. He achieved it against the French Sixth Army on the Chemin-des-Dames ridge north of the river Aisne, between Reims and Noyon, aided by good natural cover for the assembly of 3,700 guns on a front of thirty-eight miles.

The British IX Corps, composed of five battle-worn divisions from the north, had, in exchange for French reinforcement of the northern front, been sent down to this quiet sector, supported by No.52 Squadron, R.A.F., equipped with *R.E.8s*. The latter's reports of dust clouds seen to the north in the early morning and late evening made no great impression on French Intelligence authorities; the Army commander made things worse by rejecting contemporary theories on 'elastic defence' and crowding the majority of his troops into the forward defence area. Upon them, in the early hours of 27th May, descended an artillery bombardment which has been described as the most devastating of the war.

This was the most spectacular of the German thrusts in the West. On the first day the Germans swept the French and British from their defences, crossed the Aisne and penetrated altogether twelve miles. By the 30th they had captured Soissons and reached the Marne at Château Thierry, a total thrust of about twenty-five miles. French reserves were found, however, and fresh defences prepared in the path of the enemy advance, which finally spent itself. Significantly, two American divisions took part in the fighting around Château Thierry. The IX Corps artillery was decimated by the opening bombardment and no artillery co-operation could be achieved by the *R.E.8* crews of No.52 Squadron, who were also harassed by German low-flying fighters. Thereafter the squadron was intermingled with the French air force in a chaotic withdrawal during which no operational flying took place.

On 9th June Ludendorff made a further thrust towards Compiègne, to the west of his last offensive; he achieved no surprise and only limited gains of territory. On 15th July he launched his last offensive, consisting of thrusts across the Marne west of Reims and simultaneously south-west from south of Reims. The attack across the Marne had some initial success but was checked by the 17th; the attack south of Reims failed spectacularly. The Germans, between Soissons and Reims, were in a large and pronounced salient, very vulnerable to the counterstroke which had already been prepared.

The British air force – whether the R.F.C. or R.A.F. – had for the most part distinguished itself in the retreat as it had in the retreat of 1914 and basically for the same reason. In the confusion and fluidity of a hurried withdrawal the need for information is at its greatest but the means of obtaining it are at their least; the eyes of the aircraft pilots are then the most regular and reliable source of information, whether those of the tactical reconnaissance pilots or of the contact-sortie pilots over the battlefield. This is a great challenge to the pilots; most ably they rose to it, both in 1914 and in 1918.

1918
Victory

—◇—

'L'édifice commence à craquer. Tout le monde à la bataille!'
MARÉCHAL FERDINAND FOCH, September 1918.

(MAP, front end-paper)

It fell to the lot of General Mangin, of the French Tenth Army, to launch the first of the Allied counter-strokes which, unbelievably to those on the sidelines, were to finish the war in four months. On 18th July Mangin struck eastwards towards Soissons from the north-west corner of the salient resulting from the last two German offensives. Three hundred light tanks made the opening assault without significant artillery preparation. Two British divisions reinforced the French at the east end of the salient, attacking north-west. In between these thrusts the French Ninth and Sixth Armies, reinforced by three American divisions, also attacked. Mangin's attack posed dangers for the Germans in the salient; its progress was not spectacular by 1918 standards but it was enough. The Germans pulled quickly out and by 4th August had withdrawn to the line of the River Vesle, some ten miles south of the Aisne.

On 8th August the British Fourth Army (reconstituted from the former Fifth Army after the March retreat and commanded by Rawlinson) attacked east of Amiens, supported by the French First Army on its right, both under Haig's command. Liddell Hart describes the attack as 'perhaps the most complete surprise of the war',[1] and certainly its most remarkable feature was the successful deception of the enemy right up to the moment of the opening assault. Among the measures to be concealed were the doubling of Rawlinson's army (including its artillery), the transfer of the Canadian Corps to that army, the concentration of almost two thousand aircraft behind the two armies to be supported and – perhaps most difficult of all – the move of four hundred and fifty tanks to their start-lines. Besides conforming to the strict and elaborate concentration plans, and limiting their activity in the key sector, the Royal Air Force built up a pattern of aircraft noise in the forward area which enabled them when the time came, to drown the noise of the tanks arriving. Inevitably, however, the rear areas and the railways teemed with activity; the most important R.A.F. and French air force contribution to the great surprise was undoubtedly their possession of air superiority and the resulting failure of German air reconnaissance to acquire evidence of Allied preparations.

As at Cambrai, the British (comprising in this case the Australian and Canadian Corps and the British III Corps) allowed themselves no

preliminary artillery preparation, launching their tanks at first light
behind a creeping artillery barrage while an intense counter-battery
programme devastated the enemy's artillery. The French, who did not
use tanks on this occasion, timed their assault slightly later to give
themselves the advantage of a whirlwind preliminary artillery bombardment. By nightfall on 8th August a penetration of five miles had been
made on a front of eight, and final objectives for the day had been
reached except on the extreme flanks; some 16,000 prisoners and 350
guns had been captured at low cost in Allied casualties. Thereafter
resistance stiffened, and an injection of some fifteen new German
divisions was made in the sector attacked, originally held by only eight
divisions. The Allies advanced a further six miles in the next two days
but did not reach the line of the upper Somme as Foch hoped; the attack
was then halted.

In addition to clearing the threat to Amiens and retaining the Allied
initiative, this battle had great moral importance for both sides. For the
Allies it was a battle they had to win; had they failed, defeat or an
indecisive outcome to the war would have seemed real possibilities. As
for the Germans, their surprise and defeat in this battle persuaded them
that they could not win the war. Ludendorff described 8th August, 1918,
as the 'black day of the German Army'. He realised that a strategic
offensive was no longer possible and that he would need to wage
defensive warfare to cover the negotiation of an acceptable peace. These
views, held now at the top of the German leadership, soon filtered
downwards to the fighting men.

In the area of the Battle of Amiens the Allies had a better than five to
one superiority in numbers of aircraft, only slightly redressed by the
high performance of the *German Fokker D7*.[2] Of the Allied aircraft some
15 per cent were Corps aircraft; of the German aircraft over 50 per cent
were of an equivalent category – an indication of differing philosophies.
V Brigade, Fourth Army's affiliated R.A.F. formation, had six Corps
squadrons, five being allotted, respectively, to the Australian, Canadian,
III and cavalry corps and to tank support, while the sixth had a
supply-dropping role – principally of ammunition. The Army Wing,
which had eleven squadrons, was to make early attacks on aerodromes
and late attacks on rail targets and was allotted sectors of the front for
low-flying attacks on infantry, artillery, transport and balloons during
the battle. Its fighters were to cover these activities and those of the
Corps aircraft. IX (G.H.Q.) Brigade was to take part, with sixteen
squadrons including two fighter-reconnaissance squadrons.

It is difficult to evaluate the actual work of the corps squadrons in the
battle. Rawlinson issued a document afterwards, in which he praised
(perhaps a trifle formally) 'the reports of the contact patrols, and the
constant and hazardous work of the artillery machines' and (rather more
enthusiastically) 'the vigour with which the balloons were rapidly pushed

forward in close support of the firing line and the valuable assistance they rendered to the staff and to the artillery'.[3] Contact sorties with the infantry seem to have been successful on the 8th but less successful on the 9th and 10th due to a shortage of signalling flares and a generally fluid situation; pilots had increasingly to observe and interpret without guidance and, the more experienced in battle, the better they did. Tank contact patrol pilots and observers, naturally enough, faced formidable difficulties of communication, whether wireless or visual, and found difficulty in distinguishing between immobilised tanks and tanks which had voluntarily stopped. Nor did they find it easy to spot anti-tank guns. Captain F.M.F. West, however, who with his observer Lieutenant Haslam flew an *Armstrong-Whitworth F.K.8* in tank contact patrols, became the first reconnaissance pilot to win the Victoria Cross.[4] He was twice wounded (as was Haslam), twice suffered aircraft damage from enemy fire and three times made emergency landings.

It would be interesting to know what the 'artillery machines' did, whether they were able to help by adjustment of fire during the successful engagement of the enemy's artillery at the start of the battle and whether they were able to help the field artillery to engage targets of opportunity during the advance; unfortunately we can obtain no information on these matters, either from air force or artillery historians or from surviving records.

Rawlinson also wrote that the action of low-flying machines on 'Z' day (i.e. the 8th), though it entailed heavy casualties, had a serious effect in lowering the enemy's morale and inflicting actual losses, as shown by captured documents. These attacks seem to have been effective in their early stages but, as the Germans recovered from the initial surprise and organised themselves, to have 'achieved increasingly less at higher cost'.[5]

Air reconnaissance reports of about midday on the 8th were of retreating Germans crowding the roads leading east and north-east towards the bridges over the Somme. This led to a G.H.Q. decision, probably inspired and certainly promulgated by Major-General Salmond, to cancel all projected bombing programmes and substitute repeated bombing attacks on seven of the Somme bridges. These attacks were continued for the remainder of the day, during the following night, during the 9th and, on a somewhat reduced scale, on the 10th; three additional bridges were added to those originally attacked. From figures provided by the air historian, which are not complete, one can deduce that on the first two days of the battle the R.A.F. lost some 110 aircraft and crews in these suicidal and futile attacks on the bridges. They were suicidal because their targets could be, and were, anticipated as soon as the pattern became apparent, and were in close proximity to the German airfields, and because the precision required to hit targets of this type demanded low and straight flight of the most vulnerable kind. They were futile because the chances of hits were exceptionally slim and the likelihood of the 25 or 112 pound bombs achieving decisive damage very nearly as small. In fact, little if any interruption seems to have been caused to enemy movement over the bridges, which was mostly towards the battlefield.

Wing-Commander Slessor, in his book *Air Power and Armies* which was published in 1936, devotes fifty pages to an analysis of the Battle of Amiens, particularly, of course, the air battle.[6] He has strong criticisms to make of the attacks on the bridges, and equally of the neglect of long-range reconnaissance in the air plans. Here are some extracts from his criticisms, by permission of the Oxford University Press.

The Intelligence Staff had anticipated that eight German divisions could reinforce the front within the first four days – and actually we know that double this number arrived; it was known that the bulk of these divisions must be brought in from other Army fronts, and in fact bombers were detailed to attack communications leading from the north; and finally we had concentrated a very strong force of bombers of which the primary task was attack on communications. Yet of the three squadrons of first-class fighter reconnaissance aircraft which were engaged in the Battle of Amiens, two were used solely as fighters, on offensive patrols and as escorts to bombers; while of the third (No. 48 Squadron, under the direct orders of the Fourth Army) two flights were used for low-flying attack, leaving only *one flight* [his italics] of seven aircraft to meet the reconnaissance requirements of this vitally important situation. . . .[7]

What actually happened was that reconnaissances were done by single aircraft at intervals throughout the day manned by flying-officers, and in one case even by a non-commissioned officer, as observers. Eight reconnaissances were done on August 8th, of which one included Péronne and all the rest were over the area well this side of the Somme; of the four reconnaissances on the 9th, again only one went as far east as Péronne. On the 10th only one reconnaissance appears to have been done, which went to Tincourt (5 miles NE of Péronne).

They produced little information which could not perfectly safely be taken for granted, or which in fact had any effect whatever on the course of the battle. . . .

What *was* [his italics] important to make sure was . . . what movements there were on the main roads and railways, not immediately behind the front, but away back at least as far as Douai, Denain, and Cambrai to the north, and Laon and La Fère in the South.[8]

Before his detailed analysis of the R.A.F.'s part in the battle, Wing-Commander Slessor had described the course of events in the battle, concluding with his opinion that the R.A.F. made two contributions of great importance to the success of the initial attack – the high degree of air superiority to which the complete surprise was largely due and the action of the low-flying fighters on the 8th. He went on:

But apart from these two factors it is impossible to assert with any confidence that the result of the battle after about 14.00 hours on the 8th would have been materially different, or that the ultimate line reached and held by our forward troops on the 11th would have been materially short of where in fact it was, if not a bomb had been dropped or a round fired by aircraft against ground objectives.[9]

On 20th August Mangin attacked successfully south of the Oise. On the following day Byng's Third Army attacked the northern flank of German salient between Albert and Arras, thus starting a pattern of continued attacks in changing sectors, frustrating German attempts to use their reserves in sensitive or threatened areas and forcing them into successive withdrawals. Byng's attack made fair progress against an enemy showing for the first time less than their normal determination in battle; Haig was quick to call the attention of his army commanders to the need for boldness and the acceptance of unwonted risks. Rawlinson resumed his advance and, when he paused again on the 26th, Horne's First Army attacked east of Arras. All three armies advanced implacably on the Hindenburg line. Bapaume was evacuated by the enemy on the 29th, the Australians stormed Mont St Quentin and, on the 1st September, occupied Péronne. The First and Third Armies had a stiff battle at the north end of the main Hindenburg defences, after which the enemy withdrew rapidly to the Canal du Nord. After a short pause, mainly for rest, the three armies, First, Third and Fourth, closed up to the main Hindenburg defences between 15th and 18th September.

During this period low-flying R.A.F. attacks continued; indeed, they had by now become part of the established air support picture, but from the air force history they would seem to have been on a slightly smaller scale and to have been very sensibly co-ordinated with artillery and counter-attack patrols by means of communication and control agencies called Central Information Bureaux. Artillery co-operation was certainly a going concern, witness a most comprehensive III Corps Heavy Artillery Operation order for the Corps attack of 22nd August, which the author was shown by Brigadier W.F.K. Thompson, son of one of the recipients of the order, and witness also favourable mentions in the air force history.[10]

The engagement of anti-tank guns remained a problem and the only acceptable solution appears to have been for the crew of the aircraft discovering the gun to engage it themselves. The artillery call procedure was clearly too slow and artillery fire too imprecise to meet the needs of tanks which were only a few hundred yards distant from the gun that threatened them.

Contact patrols seem to have operated smoothly enough, relying more and more on their unaided powers of observation and identification in face of infantry reluctance to signal. On 2nd September a delicate problem in liaison and co-ordination arose between adjoining divisions of First and Third Armies; contact pilots were given the special task of keeping both divisions informed of progress and were well praised for their performance of it.[11]

But now some of the enemy's outlying bastions started to fall.
Surprisingly, perhaps, the first of these was the Bulgarian position on
the long-static Salonika front. On 15th September the French and Serbs,
after a long artillery bombardment, attacked west of the Vardar and
after two days had broken right through on a broad front. On the 18th
British and Greek divisions attacked the strong enemy defences which
had faced the British for three years; once again no progress could be
made against them. The R.A.F.'s main role was the location of the well
protected and concealed Bulgarian batteries, demanding much low and
hazardous flying.

Against the French and Serbs, however, resistance collapsed and the
pursuit continued up the Vardar towards Uskub (Skopolje), seventy
miles to the north; the Bulgarian armies disintegrated faster than
German reinforcements could arrive. On the 21st the Bulgarian First
Army started to withdraw on the British front. The R.A.F. was now
employed principally in long-range reconnaissance; well informed by
them the Allies advanced against considerable physical difficulties and
by 26th September had captured Strumica, the main communication
centre east of the Vardar. Their stubborn enemy, bombed as they
struggled north through the mountain passes, were now near collapse,
and the Armistice was signed on 29th September.

Three days after the beginning of the final battle on the Salonika
front, Allenby made the first move of his decisive offensive in Palestine,
on the eastern flank; in the small hours of the next day his main attack
went in on the other flank, on the coastal plain north of Jaffa, after a
lightning artillery bombardment, and was everywhere successful.
Through the gap rode the British cavalry; early on 20th September they
reached El Afule and by evening Beisan, both on the Turkish armies'
line of retreat and both on the only railway. Deraa, its junction with the
Hejaz railway east of Jordan, had already been isolated by the destruction
of the railway on every side of it by Lawrence's Arabs. The main part
of the Turkish army defeated on the coast was shepherded into the
Judean hills, whence, as soon as the realities of the situation were
known, they withdrew east towards the Jordan.

Reconnaissance and contact sorties, for both infantry and cavalry,
were the main functions of the R.A.F. Corps squadrons, but in this
battle of all battles the bombing role came into its own. Before the battle
started the enemy's air force was neutralised, mainly by patrols over
their airfields briefed to attack the least sign of activity; at the start of
the main attack on the 19th Turkish headquarters and communications
were bombed with great success; as the Turkish army withdrew into the
hills they were watched from the air and attacked as they reached pre-
selected defiles. On 21st September, in particular, large columns of
troops and transport were caught east and north-east of Nablus and were
continuously attacked from the air until the passes were effectively
blocked to further movement. Turkish forces east of Jordan now
withdrew, attacked both by the British cavalry and by the Arabs, and

were eventually surrounded and captured. Damascus fell on 1st October and the pursuit continued to Aleppo against negligible opposition.

On the Western Front, at the end of September, three fresh Allied offensives were launched, one by the Americans and French astride the River Meuse, south of Sedan, a second by the British First, Third and Fourth Armies north of the Somme mainly against the Hindenburg Line, and the third, towards Ghent, by an Allied Group under the King of the Belgians which included the British Second Army. The Franco-American attack made limited progress. The British attack in the centre had remarkable success; by 5th October Horne and Byng had crossed the Canal du Nord and reached the outskirts of Cambrai while Rawlinson had captured all three lines of the Hindenburg defences. On the 8th, after the briefest of pauses, the three armies, with the French on their right, struck again, cleared up the remains of the Hindenburg line and captured Cambrai and St Quentin. They had advanced by the 10th to the Selle river, some twelve miles further east. In the north the allies recaptured the Gheluvelt ridge, east of Ypres, and reached the river Lys between Commines and Armentières.

For most of the period of these battles the weather was unfavourable for air activity. On 27th September, however, the Corps aircraft of First and Third Armies appear to have had an excellent day, both with artillery, contact and counter-attack sorties[12]; on the 28th they continued to do well in these roles and the air historian gives an interesting example of the acceleration of the pursuit of withdrawing Germans as a result of sound observation and judgement by a counter-attack patrol.[13] On 8th October the weather was favourable to the Corps squadrons, whose activities included the production of smoke screens. A considerable concentration of protective fighters, however, did not prevent German fighters from interfering to some extent with flying over the battlefield.

These offensives finally persuaded the German Government that the war was lost. On 5th October their newly appointed Chancellor, Prince Max of Baden, sent his first note to President Wilson of the United States, requesting an armistice on the basis of the latter's 'fourteen points' for peace. The German armies could do no more than withdraw from one prepared position to the next, retaining their cohesion and defending obstinately, to provide their rulers with time for negotiation.

A further Allied advance in the north cleared the Channel coast and much of Belgium. Between 17th and 25th October the First, Third and Fourth Armies forced the Selle position. Fourth Army experienced some trouble from unneutralised German artillery in the early stages of their offensive, blamed it on insufficient counter-battery work and blamed that on the bad weather which continued to dog the R.A.F. These two advances led to a massive German withdrawal from the wide salient between them, and they now stood on a line roughly north and south through Tournai and Valenciennes.

We can best sum up the Army's view of our air operations in the final phase of the First World War in the words of the Official History.

In general, the work of the Royal Air Force consisted in bombing, without important results, railway junctions, cantonments, reserves and transport; more usefully in reporting the massing of enemy reserves for counter-attack, the existence or the destruction of bridges, in ranging for the artillery, and occasionally machine-gunning enemy troops in action and on the march.[14]

Far away to the east, in Mesopotamia, the British moved forward against the main Turkish position on the Tigris, a hundred miles north of Baghdad, and at the same time towards Kirkuk to the north-east. The R.A.F. was overwhelmingly employed in reconnaissance, an important part of which was route-reconnaissance. A large force of cavalry, with artillery, succeeded on 27th October in seizing the Mosul road in the Turkish rear; fierce fighting followed but early on the 30th the Turks surrendered. Cavalry and armoured cars pressed on to Mosul, but they were anticipated by the final armistice between the Allies and Turkey which was signed on 31st October.

In Italy all had been quiet since June but during October preparations were made for the final Allied offensive in that theatre. Weather and secrecy restricted R.A.F. operations before the offensive and an intense photographic programme had to be completed in one day – the 22nd. On the 27th British and Italians attacked across the Piave and Austrian resistance crumbled. Artillery and contact sorties took place but as the retreat gathered momentum low-flying bomb and machine-gun attacks became the order of the day; as the Austrians withdrew in congested columns, on the plain but particularly in the mountains, repeated air attacks turned retreat into rout. On 30th October Austria sued for peace and on 4th November an Armistice was signed.

The final British offensive on the Western Front, from 4th November, drove the enemy back through a zone full of familiar names for those who remembered August 1914 and, in the final days before the Armistice of 11th November, 1918, brought British soldiers once again into the town of Mons. Here stood the British Expeditionary Force on 22nd August, 1914, as the Royal Flying Corps pilots, in their primitive machines, built up in twelve reconnaissances a clear picture for their Commander-in-Chief of von Kluck's advance towards, and to the north of them. Four years and three months later their successors spent the final days of this long, cruel war in an orgy of bombing and machine-gunning, of minor importance and largely ineffective.

Between Two Wars

'The principle of a unified air force –
the First Article of the Air Staff Creed . . .'
DENIS RICHARDS and HILARY ST. G. SAUNDERS:
The Royal Air Force, 1939–45, Volume 1

In Chapter 13 we referred briefly to the formation of the Royal Air
Force, as from 1st April 1918, but deferred further discussion, as
affecting post-war rather than war developments. We must now look
back to the events leading to the decision to merge the Royal Naval Air
Service and the Royal Flying Corps into a new Independent Air service;[1]
we shall find that decision preceded by a strange lack of calm logical
consideration by men of practical experience.

It is often suggested that the background to the R.A.F.'s formation
was the wasteful and inefficient competition of R.N.A.S. and R.F.C.
for the output of the aircraft industry. Such competition had undoubtedly
existed; the Navy generally had a surplus of aircraft and aircraft engines
and the Army a deficiency, and on a number of occasions the former
responded to urgent appeals to transfer their holdings or to attach naval
squadrons to army wings. Efforts were made to solve this problem by
means of committees chaired by prominent people; these committees
were at first given inadequate authority over the two services but the
third attempt was successful. At the end of 1916 the Second Air Board
was created under the able and energetic Lord Cowdray, its members
included an Army Councillor and a Sea Lord and it was made responsible
for the design of aircraft and ancillary equipment, for the quantity
ordered and for allocation between the two services.

The event which led quickly and directly to the creation of the Royal
Air Force was the first German daylight *Gotha* raid upon London, on
13th June 1917. In this raid 162 people were killed and 432 wounded,
a very large casualty list compared with Zeppelin raids or night raids by
aeroplanes. None of the *Gothas* was destroyed. A further daylight raid
took place on 7th July in which 54 Londoners were killed, 190 wounded
and a *Gotha* shot down. There was angry popular reaction to the
casualties and the War Cabinet's reaction seems to have been somewhat
precipitate. On the very day of the first of the two raids they called for
a scheme from the Air Board for R.F.C. expansion and on 21st June
they decided to increase the number of R.F.C. squadrons from 108 to
200 and the R.N.A.S. proportionately. The extra R.F.C. squadrons
were to be of bombers, reflecting a desire more for retaliation than
protection. Haig, in the meantime, lost one of his fighter squadrons,

and a further one was diverted from his planned reinforcement, to strengthen the London defences.

On 11th July the Government set up a committee of two to examine the arrangements for home defence against air raids and, secondly, air organisation generally and the higher direction of aerial operations. The two members of the committee were, surprisingly, the Prime Minister, Lloyd George, and Jan Smuts, the South African general, who had recently arrived in England. Smuts produced the two committee reports but, as Basil Collier suggests, the second of these displayed signs of Lloyd George's influence.[2] The first report concerned defence against air raids and, *inter alia*, recommended the appointment of a senior officer to command and co-ordinate all the means of anti-aircraft defence in and around London. Brigadier-General E. B. Ashmore, who had commanded IV Brigade, R.F.C. in the Somme battle, was appointed to this post and made an outstanding success of his task.

Smuts's second report appeared on 17th August.[3] It had as its starting point the statement that an air service, unlike artillery for example, *could* be used as an independent means of war operations (author's italics), that 'as far as can at present be foreseen there is absolutely no limit to the scale of its future independent war use' and that 'the day may not be far off when aerial operations with their devastation of enemy lands and destruction of industrial and populous centres on a vast scale may become the principal operations of war, to which the older forms of military and naval operations may become secondary and subordinate'. This may have been Lord Cowdray's idea or even General Sir David Henderson's – the latter was on the Air Board – but it was remarkable extrapolation from the results of the meagre R.F.C. raids with 25 lb. and 112 lb. bombs and from the two *Gotha* raids. The report went on to state that aircraft production sanctioned for the next twelve months was far in excess of Navy and Army requirements and left a great surplus available for independent operations. The maintenance of three air services was, however, out of the question and, since the War Office (Henderson, presumably) made no claim to an independent service, the Navy could not need one either. (The report could, of course, have come to the opposite conclusion – that since the Navy claimed to need its own air service, the Army must need one also – but this was not the way things were moving). The report concluded that an Air Ministry should be instituted quickly and should work out arrangements for the incorporation of R.N.A.S. and R.F.C. into a new independent air service.

The War Cabinet accepted this report without delay and formed another committee (still under Smuts) to work out details. At this stage Haig was consulted.[4] He disputed the strategic-bombing concept, starting-point of the report, both on ethical and practical grounds, and suggested that the matter should be very carefully examined 'in consultation with officers who have wide practical knowledge of the possibilities' (Haig's underscoring). As to the surplus of aircraft expected by the report, he wrote: '. . . my experience of repeated failures to fulfil

promises as regards provision makes me somewhat sceptical as to the
large surplus . . . Moreover that surplus is calculated on a statement of
requirements rendered fifteen months ago.' Haig pointed out that the
relationship between a commander and his army, on the one hand, and
'attached' units, on the other, could never be the same as if those units
belonged to the army and that it was unsound to depart from the
principle that the authority for handling a service in the field should be
charged with its training.

On 21st September 1917 the War Cabinet, now made even keener by
a fresh (though night) attack on London to carry the fight to the German
cities, nevertheless considered Haig's letter and some other difficulties
that had arisen. Some two months later it became apparent that a
governmental decision had been made in favour of the Smuts proposals.
An Air Council was formed with Lord Rothermere as Secretary of State
and Trenchard as Chief of the Air Staff; they disagreed in their
interpretation of their respective functions and in much else, and
Trenchard resigned. When General Sykes replaced him, Henderson
resigned and Lord Rothermere then did likewise. At the end of the war,
Trenchard returned from his Independent Bombing Force and took over
the post of Chief of the Air Staff once again.

If, in these pages, the background events to the formation of the Royal
Air Force have been held up to some ridicule, it does not imply that its
formation was a disaster. As aircraft became faster, more complicated
and more expensive, the existence of a third service to explore the
possibilities of war in the air became of immense value; almost certainly
it prevented the loss of the Battle of Britain in 1940, with all that could
have implied. The point to be made here, however, is that the R.A.F.'s
formation in 1918 was not the outcome of sound contemporary military
judgement; most experienced men of both services were opposed to the
idea – opposed anyway to the rape of their own air arms – and were
bound, after the war, to try to reverse the decisions of 1918. Trenchard,
therefore, was not merely confronted with the task of building and
training an air force on the basis of the lessons learnt in the field but
with the more desperate task of defending the integrity of his new
service. These two tasks were not altogether compatible.

Trenchard remained Chief of the Air Staff from February 1919 to
December 1929. During this period he suffered eight separate governmental inquiries, some initiated by successive governments in search of
economies but most of them the result of, and all of them comprehending,
efforts by the Admiralty and War Office, particularly the former, to
regain control of their air arms. These two services each had, undoubtedly, a good case; the need for their respective air arms had been proved
in war and most of the functions of their aircraft were closely integrated
with particular naval and military functions. The decision to incorporate
them into a separate independent service and had not been the result of

careful consideration of the views of those most informed but rather an emotionally inspired political decision. Nevertheless Trenchard succeeded in defending the independence of the R.A.F., and its monopoly of service aviation, against all attacks. No one can doubt the scale of this achievement or the inspiration and stamina of Trenchard, but, to succeed, it was necessary for him continually to emphasise roles suited to an independent air force rather than to naval and military air arms.

One of his most successful moves was to obtain approval for the concept of 'air control' of certain middle-east territories, where internal security problems were many but roads were few. Dissident tribes, after due warnings, could be punished by aerial destruction of their crops, their cattle and their villages. Obviously some forces of occupation would be necessary, but these could be limited to a few battalions or local levies supported by armoured cars. This system had attractions for the British government because it seemed much cheaper than the more conventional alternative. Iraq was the proving ground; the experiment was successful for, perhaps, three reasons: unfamiliarity of the tribes with air attack, a fairly dormant British conscience at the random casualties resulting therefrom and the presence at the head of the R.A.F. in Iraq of Air Marshal Sir John Salmond, an able soldier and very ready to act on his own initiative. The scheme was extended to other British colonial and mandated territories in the Middle East and, in a modified form, to the North-West Frontier of India.

'Air control' could hardly have constituted the main rock in the case for an all-embracing independent air force, however, and for this Trenchard employed the theories on strategic bombing contained in Smuts's second report – with which he had at the time disagreed.

One of the most eloquent post-war advocates of strategic bombing was Giulio Douhet, an Italian officer who became an air force general. Between 1921 and 1929 he wrote a number of treatises and articles which were widely discussed in international military circles and had some vogue, particularly in the United States where Billy Mitchell became the principal apostle.

Douhet passionately believed in the concept of the independent air force, composed primarily of bombers, but with fighters to protect them and to destroy enemy air forces which took to the air, and with a very few, very fast reconnaissance aircraft. He foresaw the independent air force first destroying the enemy's air force (mainly by bombing aerodromes and installations) and then turning its attention to the enemy's civilian population and bombing it with a mixture of explosive, fire and poison gas. The enemy's only defence, he considered, would be to put up with the bombing while mounting even more powerful counter-attacks of the same sort, first against the air force and then against the population. In this earlier writings he was adamant that there should be no army or navy aviation, or aircraft under the control of those services, until the enemy air force had been destroyed – after which some limited loans might be made.

Today Douhet's arguments, related to a pre-nuclear era, seem very naive and many of his premises patently false. No doubt, however, they were a support to those in other countries, like Trenchard in Britain, who sought justification for independent air forces. Trenchard was certainly, at this period, a believer in bomber counteraction as the main defence against enemy bombing, and bombers were predominant in the 'home defence' air force. He succeeded, nevertheless, in establishing that the R.A.F. would have overall responsibility for, and operational control of, all air defence resources, including fighter aircraft, guns, searchlights and direction-finding equipment.

The probable scale of enemy air attack on Great Britain was grossly over-estimated by the air staff; in 1924 they thought that 27,000 people might be killed in the first month's bombing of London, later the estimate rose to 66,000 in the first week. In the event 60,500 civilians were killed in air raids, throughout Britain, throughout the Second World War.[5]

In November 1920 the Journal of the Royal United Service Institution published for the first time 'Royal Air Force Notes', to match those of the Royal Navy and Army. The following extract from a note on Air Ministry policy must have made its intentions painfully clear.

. . . the main portion of the Royal Air Force will consist of an Independent Force, together with the personnel required to carry out aeronautical research. In addition, there will be a small part of it specially trained to work with the Navy, and a small part specially trained for work with the Army. It is possible that the main portion, the Independent Air Force, will grow larger and larger, and become more and more the predominating factor in all types of warfare.

The Air Ministry proposed, however, to invite secondments of officers from the other services, these officers to be trained as pilots and fly in the squadrons supporting their respective services.

The financial estimates for 1920–21 allowed for a total of eleven squadrons at home and eighteen overseas. Among the former was a single Army Co-operation squadron, and among the various static establishments authorised were the schools of Army Co-operation at Old Sarum, Wiltshire, and of Photography at Farnborough, and a small Balloon School near the School of Artillery, Larkhill. By May 1923, however, a further seven squadrons, four of them army co-operation, had been formed.

In 1933 Adolf Hitler became the German Chancellor and the possibility of another war could no longer be discounted by the British nation and its politicians. From then, progressive expansion of the R.A.F. took place; in 1935 there were sixty-seven squadrons at home, of which fifteen were for naval support, and twenty-four overseas. Of the home-based squadrons only five were 'army co-operation', supporting a prospective British expeditionary force of four divisions. The Air Component (as it was called) was also to include ten further squadrons of fighters and long-range reconnaissance aircraft. This Air Component may be contrasted with the R.A.F.'s Advanced Air Striking Force of ten bomber and five fighter squadrons which, it was planned, would deploy on the continent in a strategic role. the discrepancy between them was certainly no greater than, for example, at the Battle of Amiens in August 1918 but, as we saw in the last chapter, air reconnaissance was unwisely subordinated to bombing and other forms of low-flying attack in that battle. The post-war factors working on the R.A.F., however, made it unlikely that the Army would do better in this respect than in 1918.

The army co-operation element – the squadrons, their group headquarters and the school – could not be classed a fashionable portion of the Royal Air Force but, like most organisations with a joint-service content, it seems to have been full of enthusiasm and an earnest desire to produce good support. The squadrons took part in the Army's brigade, divisional and command training and exercises, sent detachments to artillery 'practice camps', provided lectures and demonstrations for staff-college and other students. These activities, and the initial army co-operation training at Old Sarum, taught pilots quite a lot about Army organisation and methods but did not of themselves produce a war-effective means of air observation and reconnaissance for the army. Nor did regular courses for army officers at the same school promote much general understanding, within the Army, of the essentials of army-air force problems.

Air observation – it may be said again – is a special skill to be acquired and retained only by constant practice; military exercises are not very frequent in times of peace and give limited opportunity for realistic air reconnaissance. It is possible, at other times, to sharpen the observing faculties by reporting non-military concentrations such as of cattle or railway trucks and, more generally, to look for the unusual, but this sort of training needs much guidance and supervision. Army Co-operation squadron commanders were certainly aware of this, and they also fostered the arts of using large-scale maps and of low-level navigation.

The photographic role received attention and a new camera was produced. It is sad commentary, however, on Army lack of awareness and interest in their own reconnaissance that the Air Ministry[6] found it necessary to instruct squadrons, during combined exercise, to simulate and meet the intensive and urgent demands for air photography which army staffs should be, but were not, initiating.

Few opportunities were made by the two services, in conjunction, to practise the contact sortie though there was intermittent discussion, on the same lines as in 1916 and 1917, of methods of communication from ground to air and army co-operation aircraft were eventually fitted with a device to pick up messages. By 1935 reconnaissance, but not artillery, aircraft had two-way Morse wireless-telegraphy (W/T) and speech radio (radio-telephony – R/T) was 'on the way,' but in 1938 a decision was made to revert from R/T to W/T.

Artillery practice camps became biennial, instead of annual, and live ammunition was in short supply – little being available for shoots by army co-operation pilots. Devices, misleadingly termed 'miniature ranges' were used in squadrons to introduce pilots to artillery procedure but could not teach artillery observation. The British Army was training for a mobile war and the army co-operation squadrons were organised for mobility in the field; their artillery procedure, however, remained virtually as in the siege warfare of 1917.

Because the army co-operation squadrons were essentially part of the Royal Air Force, and because the pilots pursued their careers in the widest aspect of that service, squadron commanders were constantly being urged to play a full part in 'air force training' such as air-firing and bombing and to send their officers on armament and other such courses. They were even advised in one Army Co-operation Report to cut out 'unprofitable co-operation', whatever that might have meant.[7] Presumably for career reasons R.A.F. officers remained only three years or so in Army Co-operation before moving to other spheres, while army officers who stayed too long in another service undoubtedly put their promotion prospects at risk.

Progress of a sort was apparent in the aircraft which succeeded the 150 h.p. *R.E.8* in the tactical reconnaissance role – the *Bristol Fighter* (290 h.p.), the *Armstrong-Whitworth Atlas* (450 h.p.) and the *Hawker Audax* (525 h.p.). But to some soldiers the steady increase in horse-power, weight and speed, resulting in the basing of the aircraft on quite large airfields remote from forward units and formation headquarters, seemed regression rather than progress.

Group-Captain Mann, an army co-operation pilot between the wars, probably put his finger on the main troubles when he wrote to the author: 'In retrospect, I recognise that a great failing between the wars . . . was the universal lack of proper indoctrination of line officers in both services outside the small number trained and employed in the army co-operation role. Nor was any method of tasking and control introduced which would have led to a clear understanding and confidence between the Services on which reliable and effective co-operation could be based during a major conflict.'

As we have seen, there were regular attempts at the highest levels to win back for the Army its own air arm; until late in this period between the wars, however, there seems to have been little overt criticism of the shortcomings of the army co-operation organisation or of the lack of combined training. The main reason for the apparent apathy of both services was no doubt the fatal tendency in peace of military groups to look inwards and become preoccupied with their internal affairs. The Army was concerned with the problem of the tank and its function on the battlefield, and rent with conflicting opinions on that subject; the R.A.F., which in the twenties had been developing its ideas on long-range bombing, accepted in the thirties the need for a large force of fighters for the air defence of Great Britain. At the same time the monoplane, after twenty years in the wilderness, regained respectability and offered fresh design possibities and problems.

Disquiet was expressed from time to time at the danger of Army requirements being pushed into the background, and particularly at the tendency of R.A.F. pilots to leave the Army Co-operation scene as soon as, or even before, they had built up a sufficient understanding of army organisation, functions and tactics and of the art of reconnaissance from the air.[8] It was feared that the R.A.F. would, in war, be under considerable temptation to replace fighter and bomber crew losses with army co-operation pilots and to replace the latter with new and inexperienced recruits. Nor was the army officer element in the army co-operation squadrons in any way an expert one, consisting as it did mostly of junior officers without wide knowledge of their own service.

'We do not want to go to war,' said General Sir Edmund Ironside, then, in 1924, Commandant of the Army Staff College and in 1939 to become Chief of the Imperial General Staff, 'with untrained boys directing our air reconnaissance and artillery bombardments.' Previously he had reminded his audience that the country still maintained an army with a view to its operating in the field and, for that purpose, it must be complete with all essentials of war including aircraft.[9]

Finally it was widely felt in the senior services that the R.A.F.'s preoccupation with the independent bombing role was strategically unsound. 'War cannot be brought to a successful conclusion without the action of an army', said General Ironside, and remarked that he taught as much to his Staff College students. One fears that the R.A.F. Staff College students, only a few miles away, were being taught the opposite. For the R.A.F. the independent bombing role seemed an essential, and it had indeed to be the central and major role because upon it hung (until the Battle of Britain) the one hope of preserving the Third Service. When, in 1937, the Royal Navy won back the carrier-borne portion of its air arm, Royal Air Force independence may have seemed more necessary than ever to defend.

The thirties saw the beginning of three interesting developments, all of which influenced the development of air observation for the British army. The first of these was the *autogiro* of the Spaniard, Juan de la Cierva.[10] His *C4* machine, with freely-rotating blades, was the first practical rotary-winged aircraft; it first flew in January 1923, and in 1925 Cierva brought his *C6A* model to England and the Air Ministry decided to sponsor development in this country. One of the main difficulties, the necessity to spin the blades at speed before starting the take-off run, was solved by 1931 when the 'rotor' of the *C19 Mark IV* autogiro was provided with a starting clutch and drive.

The Air Ministry was interested in the autogiro as a possible 'intercommunication' aircraft to facilitate liaison between separate parts of the battlefield. The Army's desire had always been that the army co-operation aircraft should, when required, be able to come under the command of forward army formations and be based on Advanced Landing Grounds' (A.L.Gs) near the headquarters of such formations and, incidentally, near the artillery batteries whose fire their pilots might have to observe. This was not a popular concept with the R.A.F., first because they were instinctively against the decentralisation of small groups of aircraft to the control of relatively junior army commanders and, secondly, because their heavy and fast aircraft needed comparatively large airfields which might be difficult to prepare and rather vulnerable in the forward area. The autogiro was a possible compromise, provided it could operate out of unprepared fields of average size; it would allow liaison forward even if the reconnaissance aeroplanes were based back. During army exercises in September 1933 a *C19 Mark IV* autogiro was tried out in the intercommunication role and did well enough to encourage further trials. By now, however, a fresh design advance had been made, in the shape of the 'direct control' autogiro in which the pilot exercised longitudinal control by tilting the rotor-head instead of through conventional 'control surfaces' attached to the fuselage. This allowed the autogiro to fly at the very slow speeds which its rotating 'wings' permitted without losing the control which had hitherto depended on the speed of airflow over the control surfaces. Twelve *C30A* autogiros, built by A.V. Roe and Co and equipped with direct control, were puchased by the R.A.F. for extended trials of the intercommunication role, of the role of reconnaissance by commanders and staffs from within friendly territory and of the artillery observation role. These started in 1935 and must be adjudged encouraging. Two artillery officers took part, flying alternately in the rear seat of the autogiro, which was equipped with speech radio, not reporting fall of shot in the manner of artillery co-operation over the last twenty years but rather observing *and controlling* fire in precisely the manner of an artillery officer in a ground observation post. Because they were unaccustomed to the aerial view, their shoots may not have been brilliant, but they were quick. The main difficulty they encountered was in arranging for the aircraft to be in a suitable posture for their observation at the moment that the shell burst. They believed, and recommended, that the pilot should control the shoot and, for that reason, should be an artillery officer.

In March of that year, however, Cierva had announced his final, and militarily most dramatic, autogiro development, the 'direct' or 'jump' take-off. The *C30* had been able to remain under control while flying very slowly, and thus virtually to achieve a vertical landing, but this achievement was tactically nullified by its need for a take-off run comparable to that of a light fixed-wing aeroplane. In his new development, however, Cierva incorporated the means of increasing the pitch of the rotor blades at the stage of take-off when they were still clutched into the engine and rotating at high speed; this had the effect of applying sudden lift to the autogiro and achieving a 'jump' of some six feet, after which pitch was reduced to normal and the adoption of forward drive resulted in a normal climb away. There were vibration and other troubles, however, which took time to overcome and autogiro development was overtaken by the Second World War, by the end of which the helicopter, with its ability to hover, had become a practicable proposition. The main importance of the military autogiro trials was probably to convince the army, and particularly the Gunners, that it was entirely reasonable to expect the use of light aircraft based in the forward area.

The second interesting development of the mid-thirties was the appearance of a new kind of army co-operation reconnaissance aeroplane, the *Westland Lysander* high-wing monoplane, which seemed at first to hold out the very prospects for which the Army had hoped. The Air Ministry's specification A 39/34, for which Army as well as air force must presumably carry responsibility, was issued in February 1935 and may fairly be cited as an example of the perils of asking for too much.[11]

It required a two-seater aeroplane with a good view forwards and downwards, a good view behind, and a good view for formation flying. There were to be two forward-firing Browning guns and a rear Lewis gun in a rotating turret, provision for camera and wireless set, a message pick-up hook and several alternative bomb and supply-dropping loads. An engine of 890 h.p. was specified – to be provided with a self-starter – and simplicity of maintenance was an important requirement. The Air Ministry were concerned for the need for speed to evade interception and stipulated 245 m.p.h. (at 5000 feet); they asked for an endurance of about $3\frac{1}{2}$ hours and a 'service ceiling' of 28,000 feet. With all this, the aircraft was required to take off and land within 350 yards of a fifty-foot obstacle and to have no more than 150-yard landing run on the ground. An important omission from the specification was any mention of the sort of field or other surface upon which these formidable performances were to be achieved. Harald Penrose, however, who was the *Lysander's* test-pilot, liaised closely with the army co-operation pilots at Old Sarum and with the Westland designers; the unimpeded cantilever undercarriage legs, in place of the more usual cross-axle, showed that they expected long grass and rough surface to be the lot of their aircraft.

Westland's first prototype flew in June 1936; it closely approached the specification, only its maximum speed (230 m.p.h.) and its landing run (175 yards) being slightly inferior; its take-off run was a spectacular 40 yards. It achieved its combination of fairly high maximum speed and very slow minimum speed, and thus its impressive landing performance, by automatically-operating slots across the width of the leading edge of its very wide wing, the inboard slots operating split flaps on the trailing edge of the wing. The Air Ministry ordered the aircraft in quantity.

This gallant design achieved the almost impossible in the extent to which it met the specification, but both specification and aeroplane fell between two stools. The *Lysander* could no doubt have evaded sustained attacks by a single fighter, provided its pilot made use of his ability to turn tightly at low speeds while edging downwards and homewards, but this was an alien technique at that time. Sustained evasion of co-ordinated attacks by two or more fighters, of the sort due to appear in the next few years, was to prove impracticable and the *Lysander* was too slow to win in a straight chase. It was potentially extremely vulnerable in roles such as photography and artillery co-operation. It had the ability, certainly, to get into and out of small unprepared fields in the forward area of the battlefield but, with a wingspan of fifty feet and weight of two and a half tons, it was virtually unconcealable there.

The *Lysander's* stablemate, for deeper reconnaissance, was the twin-engined *Bristol Blenheim* bomber-reconnaissance aircraft, with maximum speed lower than the Lysander's and, of course, tied to operation from established airfields. Within the contemporary concepts of air reconnaissance for armies, these two aircraft were certainly not inferior to their German equivalents, nor were there any practicable alternatives; but they demanded an impossible measure of air superiority.

Artillery, as we have seen, has a particularly intimate need for air observation – one which was accepted in the first decade of the twentieth century, was forgotten with the arrival of the heavier-than-air machine and was rediscovered and firmly established between 1914 and 1918. We have also seen, however, that artillery co-operation, as practised by the Royal Flying Corps and the Royal Artillery, was slow and not always effective; in Chapter 11 some of the causes of this situation were discussed. Soon after the end of the war, the ideas of a number of Gunner officers for improving the system found expression in their Journal; most urged the necessity for trained artillerymen to fly and observe and for two-way radio-telephony. Because of the preoccupations of the two services which have already been noted, however, it is not surprising to note a progressive falling off in the agitation for reform in artillery co-operation methods, very little change in the old procedures and no immediate sign of two-way radio in that role. Army co-operation pilots and aircraft practised their skills at artillery practice camps (as they had in 1912) but neither gunners nor airmen seem to have regarded their mutual role as being much more than a borderline activity of minor importance. An R.A.F. balloon provided sick-making ascents for Gunner officers at Larkhill and at certain practice camps, but not many believed that balloons would be plentiful in the expected mobility of the next war. The gunners were once again losing their air observation posts.

The initiative to apply new inventions to old arts very rarely stems from the old artists' yearning to make use of the inventions – indeed they usually deplore them. It is the enthusiasts for the inventions, particularly if they happen also to have practised the relevant arts, who urge their joint application. And so a key factor in the return of the Air O.P. to the British Gunners was the formation of the Royal Artillery Flying Club in November 1934. Among the Gunner officers who, within the R.A. Flying Club, flew small, light aircraft and endlessly speculated upon their use for artillery observation and fire control were Brigadier H.R.S. Massy, President of the club, Captain Charles Bazeley, its Secretary and Major Jack Parham, a notable artilleryman and pilot and the inspiration of this book.

Jack Parham first learnt to fly in 1934, in a *C19 Mark IV* Cierva autogiro – an unusual experience. He was quick to see and record the advantages of this sort of aircraft for the army, particularly that conferred by its ability to land in – and, once its jump take-off facility had been perfected, to take-off from – small fields in the area of tactical employment.[12] Later he 'converted' to more conventional light aircraft and, later still, was the senior artilleryman in the first British formation to have light aircraft, with gunner pilots, under operational command.

Massy was at this time the senior Gunner at the headquarters of Southern Command at Salisbury, Wiltshire, and it is undoubtedly to his credit that, in 1938, the first official approach was made to the War Office to provide the British artillery with light aircraft, under gunner control, for observation and fire-control. By an almost unbelievable stroke of good fortune Massy was to become in turn the Director of Military Training in the War Office and the Deputy Chief of the Imperial General Staff, in which appointments he was admirably placed to further the project which he had started on its way.

Bazeley was, in 1935, seconded to the R.A.F. as an army co-operation pilot, saw from within the inadequacy of the system and, with Massy, formulated the detailed concept of the Air Observation Post which was duly fought-for and won.[13] It coupled the essential need for a gunner pilot – to achieve a simple and thus a quick engagement – with the need for a really light aircraft, able to get into the air quickly from small fields near the gun positions and carrying simply the pilot and two-way speech radio. Such an aircraft would not be hard to fly; to teach a trained Gunner officer would be far simpler than the alternative of teaching R.A.F. pilots the complete science of gunnery. Because the small one-seater aeroplanes would be unarmed they would need to be flown low, and normally over friendly territory, the pilot observing obliquely over or around the obstacles frustrating the ground O.Ps to a depth of three or four miles. The R.A.F.'s responsibility for artillery observation would take-over there.

The War Office put their case to the Air Ministry in June 1938; the latter preferred not to make radical changes at a time when war threatened and suggested instead an effort to improve the existing procedure for observing fire. Persistence by the War Office resulted early in 1939 in joint trials by No.22 Army Co-operation Group, R.A.F., and the School of Artillery. An artillery Instructor of Gunnery, who had been a pilot in the Great War, supervised the trials, in which three gunner pilots who were seconded to the R.A.F. took part – Bazeley one of them. They flew *Audax* and *Lysander* aircraft, which not unnaturally proved too fast and unmanoeuvrable. The Army, however, felt that the trial was promising and pressed for further trials with light aircraft. Preliminary tests began of three or four types, including an autogiro.

On 1st September, 1939, however, Hitler invaded Poland.

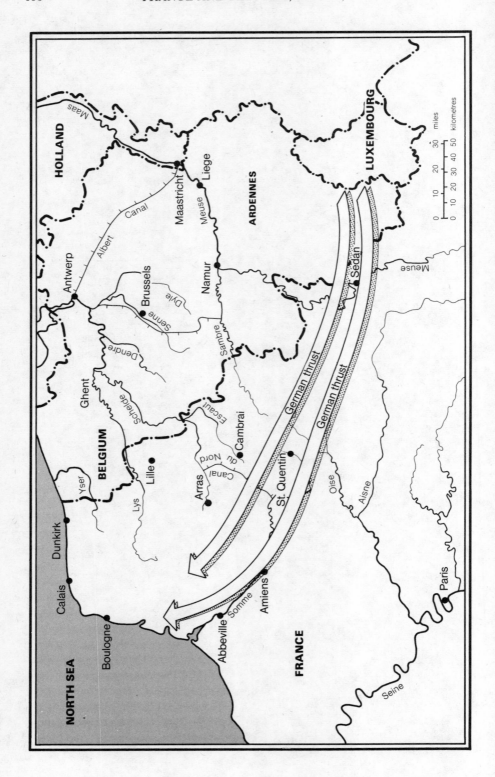

1940
Blitzkrieg
& the Air O.P.

———◇———

'The fog of war had descended over the vast battlefield'
ARTHUR BRYANT, *The Turn of the Tide*

In the first month of the Second World War the small British Expeditionary Force of four divisions was transported to France, where it took
up its position on the Franco-Belgian frontier, Belgium remaining
neutral. An 'Air Component' accompanied it, building up in due course
to a strength of five Army Co-operation squadrons (*Lysanders*), a Communication squadron,[1] four Bomber or Bomber-Reconnaissance squadrons (*Blenheims* and *Battles*)[2] and four Fighter squadrons (*Hurricanes*).[3]
General Lord Gort was the Commander-in-Chief of the B.E.F. and
initially commanded the Air Component. A re-organisation of
December, 1939, however, placed it under the command of the overall
commander of the R.A.F. in France, Air Marshal A.S. Barratt, although
remaining under Gort's 'operational control'. Also in France was the
R.A.F.'s Advanced Air Striking Force, designed in furtherance of their
philosophy of bombing German industry, which built up to ten bomber
and two fighter squadrons and a photographic squadron.

The immediate cause of war had been the German attack on Poland.
Nothing could be done to help Poland to escape her fate and when she
had been destroyed early in October, it was anticipated that a German
attack in the West would quickly develop. Instead there set in, on land
and in the air, the 'phoney war'. Neither side infringed (or was caught
infringing) the neutrality of Holland, Belgium and Luxembourg nor
attempted to break through the Maginot or Siegfried lines which faced
each other along the Franco-German frontier. Nor was either side
prepared to initiate strategic bombing. *Blenheims* were used for fairly
ineffective strategic reconnaissances and suffered severe casualties. Tactical reconnaissance being impracticable without infringing Belgian neutrality, the *Lysander* crews concentrated on training, including practice in
evasive action with co-operation of *Gladiator* biplane fighters – something
which was to pay future dividends. The B.E.F. built up to ten divisions
and carried out training and tactical exercises.

Meanwhile, in England, progress was able to be made with the testing
of the Air Observation Post concept. Tests made with a number of light
aircraft isolated the *Taylorcraft Model 'D'* – which was the latest refinement
of an American design of light cabin-type two-seater aeroplane made
under licence by an enterprising firm at Leicester. Only one Model 'D'

existed, wartime manufacture of civil light aircraft having been pro-
scribed; it was promptly lent to the trials team at Old Sarum, near
Salisbury. Meanwhile Taylorcraft Aeroplanes (England), as the firm was
called, was asked and authorised to provide a military Model 'D'. This
reached Old Sarum before Christmas, by which time the loaned model
had been used for various tests, including a test of evasion from mock
attacks by a *Spitfire* fighter.[4]

The *Taylorcraft* having proved closest to the requirement, the Air
Ministry agreed to form a unit for further trials, under command of
Charles Bazeley; the unit was to be known as D Flight and three more
Taylorcraft 'D' were ordered for it. It formed on 1st February, 1940, with
the role of testing the possibilities and limitations of the air observation
post under war conditions and of determining the most suitable type of
aircraft and organisation. From Old Sarum the flight, with three army
pilots and one air force pilot, three *Taylorcraft* and an American *Stinson
Voyager*, crossed to France for combined training with two artillery units
and some practice in evasive action with *Hurricanes* of the Air Component.
With the gunners, but without the *Hurricanes*, they moved south to the
French artillery ranges at Mailly, where they found the French helpful
though favouring the autogiro for the Air O.P. vehicle.

Germany was sensitive to possible interruption of her supplies of
Swedish iron ore which, when the northern Baltic was ice bound, needed
to be transported by rail to the Norwegian port of Narvik and thence
down her Atlantic coast. On 9th April, 1940, she invaded Norway to
safeguard this route against the British navy or even against a possible
landing by the British army. Norway resisted and small British and
French forces came to her aid (in a sense) by landing in the north and
centre of the Atlantic coast. Except in the extreme north the Allied
attempt failed, mainly because the German air force, the Luftwaffe,
established itself rapidly and crushed all Allied efforts to operate from
airfields in their bridgeheads. The German invasion forces were much
too strong for the Norwegian army and the Allies withdrew from central
Norway by the end of April and from the north a month later. A British
success in this campaign had hardly been possible, but the British people,
as ever, bayed for scapegoats. Neville Chamberlain, the Prime Minister,
resigned on 10th May and the result was a coalition government under
Winston Churchill – the most favourable of all possible outcomes for the
free world.

On that same day Germany's onslaught in the west began. The
neutralities of Holland, Belgium and Luxembourg were as nothing.
With a combination of airborne and armoured operations and a ruthless
bombing of the city of Rotterdam, Holland was eliminated from the war
in five days. The eastern frontier defences of Belgium were similarly
breached. The British and French on the western frontier of Belgium
had, as planned, moved forward to the line of the River Dyle with the

Belgians on their left. On 14th May German armoured forces advanced through the Ardennes, south of the British sector, broke through the French Ninth Army and debouched into open country west of Sedan. Wheeling north, they drove for the Channel coast, isolating the northern group of Belgian, British and French armies from the rest of the Allied forces.

A withdrawal was made between the 16th and 18th from the Dyle to the line of the Scheldt (or Escaut); on the 21st an effort was made by the British to break south from Arras but, after some early success, failed against increased enemy pressure on the flanks. The Germans had reached the Channel coast and the northern Allied group was entirely cut off; on 27th May the Belgian army capitulated and it became clear to Lord Gort that there was no alternative course to withdrawal to, and embarkation from, the area around Dunkirk. By the night of 4th June 338,000 Allied troops, mostly British and French, had been taken off from the harbour and beaches of Dunkirk, though without any of their transport, heavy arms or equipment. This was, of course, a remarkable achievement, assisted by the delay imposed on the Germans by a fierce four-day battle by the French First Army at Lille, by the heroic defence of Calais by a British force of light infantry and tanks and by the impressive defeat of the Luftwaffe by home-based R.A.F. fighters in the skies around Dunkirk.

From 10th–15th May the Air Component succeeded, to a fair degree, in reconnaissance for the B.E.F. and in providing some protection against air attack; a few artillery, contact and photographic sorties had taken place.[5] By the 12th, however, Lord Gort was becoming concerned at his fighter losses and consequent reduction in reconnaissance effort.[6] Once the encirclement of the northern group had begun, and the withdrawal from the Dyle had further shrunk its 'living space', the B.E.F.'s aircraft became increasingly vulnerable both in the air and on the ground. *Blenheims* could rarely be employed and *Lysanders* restricted their reconnaissances to the areas immediately beyond their forward troops and to the progress of the German encircling movement. Casualties were remarkably light and a fair number of enemy fighters and dive-bombers were successfully attacked. As the German armour approached the Channel ports, however, the Air Component's airfields and supply lines were menaced and fresh ones were to be found only west of the Somme or in England, both remote from the battlefield. Between the 18th and the 22nd the bulk of the Component was withdrawn from the continent to bases in south-east England; here they formed a 'Back Component' which could be tasked effectively neither by the B.E.F. nor by Air Marshal Barratt. War Office and Air Ministry together selected targets for the bombers, and an increased number of fighters helped to protect the B.E.F. from dive-bomber and other air attacks, but, as the official historian writes, there was no possibility of any sensitive reaction by the R.A.F. to increased danger at threatened points, nor could the fighters protect or replace the reconnaissance aircraft.[7]

Arthur Bryant, in his biography of General Sir Alan Brooke, whose II Corps had been bravely supported by No.4 Army Co-operation Squadron (Wing-Commander G. P. Charles), described as follows the B.E.F.'s situation at this juncture:

With the French Air Force driven from the skies and the R.A.F. Air Component reduced to half its strength and with its airfields in the path of the panzer torrent, the Luftwaffe by now had the air almost to itself. The fog of war had descended over the vast battlefield, ...[8]

On the 22nd [according to the official historian], when only one flight of the Air Component's No.4 Squadron was left in France to carry out close reconnaissance for the Army, Advanced Headquarters of the Air Component still with the B.E.F. signalled home that it was virtually impossible to continue tactical and artillery reconnaissance unless a fighter flight could be attached for duty with the remaining flight of *Lysanders* and unless fighter patrols in strength were flown over the battle area at agreed times and places. The enemy, it was said, was constantly operating flights of fighters over our entire front, and severe *Lysander* losses were being sustained to no purpose. Failing direct support, they must discontinue tactical and artillery reconnaissance except for attempts in extreme urgency. The Air Mission at Belgian Headquarters also signalled that they were getting no information from British air reconnaissance and added 'As Belgian Air Force now virtually non-existent most seriously urge undesirability leaving them blind on their front'. It is not clear that anything did, or could result from those appeals. Long-distance reconnaissance could not effectively take the place of the close observation of aircraft squadrons within easy reach of Corps headquarters.[9]

In the last days of the Dunkirk perimeter – in addition to being sent on some singularly futile bombing missions with 20lb. bombs – England-based *Lysander* pilots plotted the German forward positions on special maps, which they then dropped to the troops on the beaches. By these they were often fired upon, because of their unfortunate superficial resemblance to the German *Henschel* aeroplane.

The operations of the Advanced Air Striking Force are really no part of this history. Its *Battles* and *Blenheims* were thrown into a series of low-level attacks on the bridges on the Maas and the Albert Canal, and later in the Sedan area, which were tragically reminiscent, both in negligible effort and in dreadful casualties, of those on the Somme bridges at the battle of Amiens.[10] As a result of the German break through the A.A.S.F. squadrons had generally to make extensive withdrawals. Their fighters were thereafter able to give some protection against the German dive-bombers on the southern part of the front, while their medium bombers attacked enemy reinforcements and supply echelons. Some raids by heavy bombers were directed at industrial targets in the Ruhr area of Germany; they seem to have been ineffective[11] and they were certainly irrelevant.

After the Dunkirk evacuation there remained some fighting in France, but the outcome was not long in doubt. A force of fighter and reconnaissance aircraft (the latter *Blenheims* and *Lysanders*) known as the 'South Component' was formed with the idea of operating from bases in England in support of the British and French army formations which had formed a fresh front on the Somme. Since this component's aircraft had anyway to refuel in France, however, it was located there under Barratt's command. Between 23rd May and 7th June some thirty reconnaissance sorties, only rarely with fighter cover, achieved fair results with the loss of only two aircraft. Missions were mostly tactical reconnaissance, including the reporting but not engagement of enemy gun positions, and some air photography took place.

The movements and operations of the Allied army thereafter became increasingly confused, while the enemy's air effort increased. The *Lysanders* were soon withdrawn. The remainder of the Component's reconnaissance force, while losing and re-establishing communication with various army formations, flew about another thirty sorties and lost two *Blenheims*. The French requested an armistice on 16th June; the Component flew its aircraft home and safely evacuated its staff on the following day. The R.A.F. now awaited the Luftwaffe's assault and the Battle of Britain; the Army slowly re-equipped, digested the hard lessons of the recent fighting and, in addition to manning the coast and anti-aircraft defences, started to train itself for future campaigns.

The R.A.F. entrusted Air Marshal Sir Robert Brooke-Popham with the task of taking evidence of, and writing a report on, their experiences in France.[12] There were criticisms of the standard of training of reinforcement reconnaissance pilots, but the main reconnaissance problem centred on the *Lysanders'* inability to be flown freely in the face of modern fighter opposition. Some reconnaissance, it seems, had fallen to the lot of pilots of single-seater fighters, untrained in the art, who had simply been sent out with one single question to answer. This was no bad compromise; Brooke-Popham wondered, however, whether some single-seater pilots should not be specially trained in reconnaissance. A debate between Air Ministry and War Office on the *Lysander's* successor continued indecisively through the summer and into the winter, when the Middle East Air Force settled the matter by starting to use *Hurricanes* for reconnaissance and requesting an appropriate change in aircraft shipments from England.

Brief mention should be made of a specialised form of air reconnaissance which developed in 1939 and 1940 but of which the Army was not the principal beneficiary. This could be described as 'strategic' air photography, to distinguish it from the air photography which supplemented the observation of the tactical reconnaissance pilots. The former art had been inspired particularly, perhaps, by espionage photography over Nazi Germany by an Australian, Sidney Cotton, in a Lockheed executive aircraft, prior to the outbreak of war. Cotton was co-opted by the R.A.F. when the war started and ran a secret unit at Heston, London, operating wherever the Royal Air Force, Royal Navy, and sometimes the Army might require his rather special services.

The standard R.A.F. photographic aircraft was the *Blenheim*. It was the essence of Cotton's ideas, however, that photography should be from a great height, which the aircraft should reach quickly and where it should possess a high speed for evasion. The *Blenheim* could not match these requirements and many were lost in photographic missions in the early months of the war; Cotton wanted *Spitfires* and his thrustful and unconventional personality got him what he wanted. The *Spitfire* became the standard aircraft of the photographic reconnaissance squadrons of the R.A.F., which began to be formed after the fall of France.

Great strides were made in the science and equipment of photographic interpretation and the R.A.F. photographic intelligence organisation became 'joint-service' and 'Allied' in scope and one of the undoubted successes of the war.[13] The Army naturally needed strategic intelligence of this kind, particularly when their own or the enemy's offensives were in preparation or where supporting air attacks on enemy communications required detailed preliminary information. The other two services were even more dependent upon it, for such functions as the surveillance of enemy shipping in harbours, the assessment of possible strategic-bombing targets and of the effectiveness of the attacks upon them, and of enemy coastal activity, defensive or offensive.

D Flight, R.A.F., negotiating with the French at Mailly regarding the final (operational) stage of the Air Observation Post trials, awoke on 10th May to the sound of bombs and to the sight of hostile aircraft all over the sky. Their supporting artillery disappeared abruptly for its operational area. Bazeley, who had well assimilated the new Air O.P. doctrines which he had preached, made haste to move the flight and its aircraft away from its aerodrome (which was bombed later in the day) and to conceal it in natural scenery alongside grass landing strips. After an abortive effort to signal the Air Component for instructions, and after a briefing from the Intelligence Officer of a hard-hit unit of the Striking Force, Bazeley sent the ground party of the flight, under the R.A.F. Equipment Officer, with orders to get west of Paris and thereafter act on their own initiative. This party got itself back to England, and – more remarkably – took its equipment home too. Pilots and aircraft flew to Dieppe on the 19th, where they learnt with some surprise of the current situation. Bazeley thereupon sent Captain Davenport over to the War Office, who at once signalled recall instructions; the party landed at Old Sarum on the following day.

The Army were determined to press on with the Air O.P. idea – more determined than ever since the last month's events had proved to them that air observation of artillery fire was not readily to be had from the R.A.F.'s current arrangements for army co-operation. The R.A.F. was, naturally enough, rather too preoccupied with the threat and then the actuality of the Battle of Britain to interest themselves very much in what appeared a small-scale and long-term problem. For a little the Army made progress. D Flight trained two further Royal Artillery officers as Air O.P. pilots and a further five after they had been taught to fly by the R.A.F. The War Office somewhat prematurely decided that the aircraft they needed was the *Stinson Vigilant* and ordered a hundred from the United States.

The formation of the Royal Air Force's Army Co-operation Command in December 1940 brought a new setback, for its commander could not imagine that aircraft like the *Taylorcraft* could possibly operate in the presence of enemy fighters, discounted the whole Air O.P. idea and recommended the winding-up of D Flight and all its activities. It needed the Commander-in-Chief, Home Forces, later Lord Alanbrooke, to weigh-in on 28th April, 1941, with the strongest assurance that the Army considered the Air O.Ps essential,[14] before R.A.F. resistance ceased, the training of artillery pilots was put on a regular footing and, in August of that year, No.651 Air Observation Post Squadron, Royal Air Force, the first operational Air O.P. unit, started to form. Although R.A.F. units, the Air O.P. squadrons and flights were to come under Royal Artillery operational control. Their commanders and their other pilots were to be artillery officers, the drivers and signallers would be artillerymen too; technical aircraft personnel would be of the R.A.F. as would the squadron adjutants and equipment officers. These hybrid squadrons and flights, under apparently divided control between two services, in practice provided the best air observation posts which the British artillery has yet possessed.

An aircraft still had to be selected for the Air O.P. units. The first batch of *Stinson Vigilants* was greatly delayed and, when these aircraft arrived from America early in 1942, they were mostly found squashed beneath a cargo of cheese; this decided matters in favour of the *Taylorcraft*, the first operational version of which, known as the *Auster 1*, reached No.651 Squadron about midsummer. By then those *Vigilants* which had been rescued from the cheese and assembled had been pronounced somewhat large and complex for the role. So it all ended happily!

1940 to 1943
Learning in the Desert

◇

'Ex Africa semper aliquid novi'
PLINY THE ELDER, *Natural History, viii*

(MAP, back end-paper)

For the British Army, perhaps the most instructive campaigns of the Second World War took place along the North African coast between June 1940, when Italy entered the war at Germany's side, and May 1943, when the last German and Italian troops in Africa surrendered in Tunisia. During the course of this fighting, too, the arts of air observation and reconnaissance were developed to absorb the impact of fast aircraft and new weapons and, with fair success, to reach a compromise between the needs and wishes of two separate services and the realities of battle. These years of fighting, mostly in desert, can be considered in three phases. In the first twelve months General Sir Archibald Wavell destroyed large Italian armies in Egypt, Cyrenaiaca, Eritrea and Abyssinia (Ethiopia); in the next twelve months his successor, General Sir Claude Auchinleck, and the German General Erwin Rommel fought a series of desert battles which ended with the British Army on the defensive, seventy miles west of the Nile. In the final phase were the Battle of El Alamein, the Allied landings in Algeria and Morocco and the converging attacks which concluded the campaign.

At the end of November 1940 Italian armies were poised to invade Egypt, the Sudan and Kenya; they were, in fact, already over the borders of the first two of these. All told, the Italians had some 400,000 troops in Africa, the British opposed them with a fifth of that number. Wavell's reaction to this situation was to attack. Marshal Graziani's army in Egypt had occupied a network of fortified camps around and south of Sidi Barrani, fifty miles inside the frontier; on 7th December they were suddenly assaulted by a force of just over two divisions, with armour, under General R. N. O'Connor. A series of well-conceived, well-concealed and resolute thrusts between and around the camps overwhelmed many of the garrisons and put the rest into headlong retreat. The frontier town of Bardia and the important port of Tobruk were isolated and captured; as the remainder of the Italian army withdrew from Cyrenaica, its retreat was cut off sixty miles south of Benghazi by motorised infantry and armour, which had driven rapidly across the desert south of the coastal mountain range. At Beda Fomm, on 6th February, 1941, a day-long and sometimes fierce battle ended with the surrender of the entire Italian force.

Meanwhile General W. Platt, between January and May, 1941, pushed the Italians back from the Sudan into Eritrea, had a tough fight to overcome an outstandingly strong position at Keren, occupied the capital Asmara and the port of Massawa and invaded Abyssinia from the north. General Alan Cunningham, starting slightly later than Platt, invaded Italian Somaliland from Kenya, captured Mogadishu its principal port, and then advanced into Abyssinia from the south. Addis Ababa, the capital, surrendered on 6th April, Cunningham having by then advanced 1,700 miles in fifty-seven days. He then drove on northwards to combine with Platt's force to trap and take the surrender of the bulk of the remaining Italian forces at Amba Alagi, 120 miles from the capital, on 18th May.

The Italians had also occupied Albania and invaded Greece. The Greeks showed themselves well able to deal with this emergency, though accepting some R.A.F. assistance, but by February 1941 it seemed certain that Germany was about to intervene on her ally's side. Wavell then had to send, from his limited resources, a force of three divisions and one armoured brigade in what turned out to be a vain attempt to defend Greece. It was clear that there could now be no exploitation of the Cyrenaican victory and the British had soon to deal with the redoubtable Rommel and his German-Italian Afrika Korps. At the end of March they attacked and overran the British armour on the Tripolitanian border. Wavell quickly pulled out from Cyrenaiaca, leaving a force, however, to hold Tobruk.

Wavell was soon to be replaced by Auchinleck and to depart to the Far East, leaving in northern Africa the memory of a series of operations of brilliance unequalled in the Second World War and perhaps not often equalled in history.

As in the case of Mesopotamia in the First World War, the North African desert, because of its provision of 'open flanks' to the respective armies, because of its lack of restriction to movement and because of the difficulty of observing hostile or friendly movement except from the air, was a fruitful field for air reconnaissance. For the British army, however, there were at first formidable difficulties. Although Commander-in-Chief, Middle East, for example, Wavell did not command the R.A.F. in the Middle East, who were under the Air Officer Commanding-in-Chief, Air Chief Marshal Sir Arthur Longmore. Their subordinate commands had different boundaries and, before hostilities became imminent, there were no permanent affiliations between army and air force formations; the R.A.F.'s first role, in any case, was the air defence of the Egyptian base. Early in 1940, however, Air Commodore Collishaw and his No.202 Group controlled the air forces in the Western Desert and allotted O'Connor, during the Sidi Barrani battle and subsequent pursuit, an Air Component of No.208 Army Co-operation Squadron (Squadron-Leader R. A. Sprague but soon afterwards J. R. Wilson) and No.3 Squadron, Royal Australian Air Force (Squadron-Leader I. D. McLachlan), mostly for reconnaissance or for its protection.

The Middle East Air Force started the war with a considerable assortment of obsolete types of aircraft. By the time the fighting started, however, some *Hurricane Is* were available; at the same time it had been discovered that the *Lysander*, unescorted, was too vulnerable to be very effective. O'Connor's Air Component, therefore, was equipped with mixed squadrons of *Lysanders* and either *Hurricanes* or *Gloster Gladiators*. Sometimes the *Lysanders* operated with fighter escort and at other times the fighter aircraft were used for the reconnaissance itself.

It was essential to decide, before the battle of Sidi Barrani, the best routes by which the armour could penetrate the minefields surrounding the Italian camps which were to be attacked. This involved air photography which proved very successful. At Bardia No.208 Squadron produced air-photograph 'mosaics' of the defences, which elicited a congratulatory message from Wavell, and they repeated this service at Tobruk. *Lysanders* were used, with fighter escort, for artillery observation, and contact sorties took place. Beyond Tobruk, however, sandstorms hampered reconnaissance.

For reasons of secrecy there was no long-range air reconnaissance ahead of the British motorised and armoured force launched across the desert to Beda Fomm, but low-flying aircraft of 208 Squadron immediately preceded the force to report on the 'going'. Air reports of the enemy's withdrawal south of Benghazi resulted in a diversion southwards of the British Force which, in the event, proved important. During the battle which followed air reports of the situation of the Italian transport enabled the best direction to be given to the armoured attacks.

208 Squadron gave good warning, not altogether heeded, of the build-up of Axis forces in March 1941. That squadron was then directed to Greece, where for three weeks its small but diminishing flight of *Hurricanes* brought back information of the German influx which was, perhaps, only too apparent from other sources. In the confused conditions which accompanied Rommel's offensive in Libya, meanwhile, communications between army and air force units largely failed and tasking of the latter reverted in practice to their Group headquarters.

In Eritrea Royal Air Force and South African Air Force support of the army seems to have been good. For the final attack at Keren in March 1941 No.237 (Rhodesian) Army Co-operation Squadron (Squadron-Leader V. E. Maxwell) was under army control – a versatile unit recently re-equipped with *Lysanders*. They were used in Eritrea for tactical, photographic and artillery reconnaissance and for contact sorties. They also did dive-bombing and, soon after this campaign, were reorganised as a fighter squadron. Cunningham, in his advance into Abyssinia from the south, was also given very close support by Nos.40 and 41 Squadrons, South African Air Force. Photography was used extensively to produce large-scale maps of the main Italian defensive positions and route-reconnaissance was a significant role.

General Wavell, in his final Middle East despatch, while praising the R.A.F.'s self-sacrificing support of the army, their skill, efficiency and whole-hearted co-operation, nevertheless summarised as follows the development of air reconnaissance in this theatre:

> The forms of Army co-operation known and practised before the war, such as artillery observation and close tactical reconnaissance, have for all practical purposes ceased, since the machines designed for these tasks can no longer be flown in the presence of the enemy, and the supply of pilots trained for Army co-operation is almost exhausted. Means of photographic reconnaissance have also never been sufficient for army requirements.[1]

General Sir Claude Auchinleck took over command from Wavell in July 1941 (some ten days after the Germans invaded Russia); on 18th November he launched his desert force, henceforth the Eighth Army, in an offensive against Rommel. The battle which followed was confused. The British XXX Corps advanced northwards into the mountains south of Tobruk, to draw off Axis forces from that fortress, while the XIII Corps advanced westwards into the same area. Rommel met these threats characteristically by driving across the Egyptian frontier with two armoured divisions. Cunningham, the Eighth Army Commander, advocated a British withdrawal and Auchinleck promptly replaced him by Ritchie; the British stood fast and Rommel had to withdraw from a vulnerable and administratively impossible situation. Indeed he withdrew from the whole of Cyrenaiaca, though only to be reinforced and, in January 1942, to strike back and force the Eighth Army eastwards to a line of defensive 'boxes' running south from Gazala for some fifty miles.

In May Rommel attacked again and, after a fortnight's fierce fighting in the centre of the British position and in the south where the Free French brigade fought well, broke through. On 15th June Rommel wrote 'The battle has been won, and the enemy is breaking up'. This was unpleasantly near the truth.[2] Tobruk fell on 21st June and two days later Rommel was in Egypt. Auchinleck assumed direct command of Eighth Army which by 30th June, 1942, had occupied the relatively strong El Alamein position with its right flank on the sea and its left flank protected by an extensive saltpan, the Qattara Depression. There, in July, Rommel was twice repulsed and the situation stabilised.

Air Marshal Sir Arthur Tedder was by the autumn of 1941 Commander-in-Chief of the Mediterranean Air Command and Air Vice-Marshal Arthur Coningham commanded the Western Desert Air Force, or Desert Air Force as it later became; these air marshals were to earn high reputation for their support of the Army. Coningham's force included No.208 Tactical Reconnaissance Squadron, now led by Squadron-Leader L. G. Burnand who had commanded its *Hurricane* flight in the short but painful Greek campaign. Early in 1942 it was joined by No.40 Squadron, South African Air Force (Lieutenant-Colonel E. Biden) in the same role; each squadron had a mixture of *Hurricane Is* and *Tomahawks*. There were other, long-range, reconnaissance resources, normally employed over the Mediterranean, which could be used for strategic reconnaissance in the Army's interest. There were also seventeen fighter or fighter-bomber squadrons and nine light-bomber squadrons. Although the reports of the fighter pilots and bomber crews provided interesting and sometimes important information, it was only the reconnaissance squadron pilots who were specially trained for the job.

Efforts had been made, following the Wavell campaigns, to improve the speed and efficiency of army air co-operation. Joint-service 'Air Support Controls' had been set up at each corps and armoured division headquarters, with the necessary communications to pass to all concerned urgent reports made by pilots in the air, and fuller 'broadcasts' after the 'debriefing' of pilots at their airfields, to pass to the pilots information obtained from the forward troops and to co-ordinate and pass to the R.A.F. requests for close air support received from the forward army units.

Of the tasks of the air forces in Egypt and Malta during the coming winter, the Official Historian places first: 'To try to meet all the many demands of the army and the air forces for reconnaissance'.[3]

This particular task, he wrote, taxed the available resources to the utmost.

Because an air force squadron, equipped with fast aircraft, could not be located and moved within the tactical complex of the army formation it supported, and because the squadron-commander's leadership depended on his personal participation in operational flying, a heavy responsibility lay with the Air Liaison Officers (A.L.O.s). These army captains and majors were attached to squadrons and were permanent links between the army and corps staffs and the squadrons. They were responsible for keeping the commanders and pilots continuously informed of the army operational position and intentions and its requirements of the squadrons; they were responsible also for the passage of information and needs in the reverse direction. The disparity between their modest rank and high responsibilities called for strong personalities in militarily unambitious officers; it is apparent from the evidence of squadron and wing commanders in the Middle East and subsequent theatres of war that this quality was forthcoming and that both services were thereby fortunate.

The chaos of the opening battles of the campaign provided a severe test for the good resolutions which had been made about inter-service co-operation. For three days 208 Squadron's pilots produced much

information; in the squadron commander's opinion, however, the value
of their reconnaissances was much reduced by lack of communication
between the operations staff of XXX Corps and the Squadron, by
failures in radio and by unjustified reconnaissance demands on the
squadron from air force sources.[4] On the fourth day Rommel made his
drive towards and over the Egyptian frontier. The situation became
obscure to those in the air as to those on the ground, but the inability
of the army to protect the forward landing grounds soon became very
clear to Coningham, who wisely decided to withdraw his squadrons
eastwards. Nor was that a simple operation – 175 aircraft are alleged to
have spent the night of 24th-25th November on or around a single
advanced landing ground.[5] The Luftwaffe appeared in some force, and
the Italian air force too, but our air forces quickly got organised and by
the 26th had regained air superiority.

During the subsequent British advance through Cyrenaica 208 Squadron did well in poor flying conditions; the Official Historian, in fact,
gives them credit for most of the information gleaned about the enemy's
movement.[6] Difficulties with XXX Corps staff were ironed out while,
from mid-December, the squadron were under command of XIII Corps,
with whose staff they were clearly in great harmony.

Rommel's counter-thrust of January 1942 coincided with a period of
exceptional rainfall which had flooded the forward landing grounds and
gravely curtailed reconnaissance. The enemy were more fortunate; their
air forces were active and for a time seized the initiative. German
armour in large numbers were spotted on the Cyrenaican frontier in the
nick of time and at Antelat only just missed capturing XIII Corps
headquarters and an operational R.A.F. airstrip complete with aircraft.
For the next fortnight the need for information was so great that fighter,
as well as tactical reconnaissance, squadrons were used for reconnaissance, which was extended far to the west and south.[7]

At this unfortunate juncture the Desert Air Force, in company with
the Middle East air forces as a whole, was becoming weaker. Japan had
entered the war and some Allied resources on their way to reinforce the
Middle East were diverted to the Far East.

The *Hurricane I* had for some months been a dangerously old-fashioned
aircraft to venture out alone on reconnaissance. A single-seater aircraft
is inherently vulnerable to faster aircraft approaching from behind.
Mirrors were designed to allow the reconnaissance pilot to have some
sort of upward and backward view without abandoning, except momen-
tarily, his downward and forward view of the ground, but mirrors were
not enough and 'weaving' from side to side became necessary, clearly
incompatible with full attention to the reconnaissance. The next stage
was to provide the reconnaissance aircraft with a separate, protective
'weaver', but this was considered by some to increase the chance of
enemy interception, besides halving the reconnaissance effort. No.40
Squadron experimented unsuccessfully with unescorted reconnaissances
at a height of twenty feet. Reconnaissance pilots were required to

transmit important information from the air – this necessitated closing
the cockpit canopy and reading from scribbled notes, both unpopular
practices with pilots who expected to be 'jumped'. When they were
jumped, they might call upon a certain background of training in fighter
tactics, but too often on too little such training and experience.

Army co-operation squadrons, moreover, were under army operational control and had no automatic call on fighter protection; the
fighters and fighter-bombers were under other control and had other
tasks, which might or might not be susceptible to the respective squadron
commanders' attempts to coordinate. Casualties during air reconnaissances were increasing and their replacement by inexperienced pilot-
reinforcements tended to accelerate the increase.[8]

No replacement for the *Hurricane I* was forthcoming, but, during the
three months' lull which now took place some further efforts were made
to improve air support arrangements. Among these were the provision
of land markers – bold letters by day and illuminated Vs by night – and
the use of forward controllers, with radar, to give warning of enemy
aircraft in the vicinity. Whenever possible, reconnaissance and fighter
missions were co-ordinated, to give some protection to the former. Such
co-ordination was, however, a matter or private enterprise by reconnaissance squadron commanders and was far from simple.

Before and during the battles of May and June for the Gazala position
the pilots of 40 and 208 Squadrons seem to have supported the army
well and bravely above the complex battlefield, though the South African
Air Force historian thinks that 40 Squadron could have been used more
frequently.[9] On 17th June a failure in army-air force communications
left the latter in ignorance of the former's withdrawal from El Adem for
twelve dangerous hours. During the fairly precipitate withdrawal from
the Gazala to the El Alamein position the Desert Air Force did what it
could to harry the pursuing Germans; it was not helped by the virtual
breakdown of air-support procedure, and Coningham needed once again
to exercise more than normal direct control from his advanced headquarters.

Behind the El Alamein position the Desert Air Force was no longer
plagued by supply problems while those of the enemy, a thousand miles
east of their Tripoli base, were immense. The British, however, remained
for some time on the defensive, and 208 Squadron struggled to satisfy
the army's fever for information in a situation where about a third of
their sorties were forced back by enemy fighters. Only slowly did this
situation improve.

By the end of September, 1942, however, though the situation in
Egypt may still have looked tense, things were not as bad as they looked.
The United States, as a result of Japan's attack upon them, had joined
the Allies nine months previously; her strength had been increasing and
she now made a massive contribution to the re-equipment of the British

forces in the Middle East, particularly in tanks. She had agreed that the war in Africa and Europe should have priority and was shortly to commit her forces there. Substantial reinforcements had reached the British Middle East Command.

General Sir Harold Alexander had relieved Auchinleck and General Sir Bernard Montgomery now commanded the Eighth Army. Between 31st August and 6th September a determined effort by Rommel to drive in the Eighth Army's left flank, north of the Qattara Depression, and envelop the rest of the El Alamein position from the south, had easily been defeated in a battle named Alam el Halfa.

On the night of 23rd October, 1942, the famous battle of El Alamein began; on 3rd November Montgomery broke through at the north end of the Axis position and the long pursuit of Rommel began, to Tripoli and the Tunisian frontier.[10]

On 8th November Anglo-American landings were made in Morocco and Algeria and a composite First Army, under General K. A. Anderson, pushed east against rapidly increasing resistance from German formations landing in Tunisia by sea and air. The First Army failed to seize Tunisia by a *coup de main* but established itself in the high ground some fifty miles inland from Tunis and Bizerta, and consolidated.

Eighth Army meanwhile repelled a counterthrust at Medenine, west of Tripoli, after which Rommel, a sick man, was withdrawn. They then – with exceptionally heavy air support – forced the strong Mareth Line defences on the eastern Tunisian frontier on 21st March, 1943, and on 6th April made contact with First Army. At this juncture both armies came under the command of Alexander, who became deputy to General Dwight D. Eisenhower, the overall commander of the Allied force in north-west Africa.

The final Allied blow fell on the 6th and 7th May in the First Army sector, reinforced from Eighth Army which was faced by a strong enemy position at Enfidaville. The Americans captured Bizerta and the British Tunis. The latter's Sixth Armoured Division turned east and penetrated the Cap Bon peninsula, among the Axis reserves. Those forces which faced Eighth Army were taken in rear and on 13th May the last enemy soldiers in North Africa surrendered. This followed fairly closely the Russian relief of Stalingrad and their capture of Field-Marshal von Paulus and the remains of the German Sixth Army. The war had reached its turning point.

In the autumn of 1942, apart from any reinforcement he might expect from the Middle East Air Force, Coningham had behind the El Alamein position some 135 light bombers, 425 fighters or fighter-bombers and 70 reconnaissance aircraft. The number of reconnaissance aircraft seems proportionately very low, in comparison with that of the fighters. It had to be remembered first that *reconnaissance* was an individual art but *fighting* a 'team game', secondly that whenever the enemy air force was active the solitary and preoccupied reconnaissance pilot required fighter protection and, thirdly, that both fighters (in quantity) and bombers were essential to seize and maintain that air superiority without which armies lack full freedom of action. The Official History by General Playfair continually reminds its readers of the overwhelming importance of good information and of the dominant role of the Allied air forces in providing it.

Before and after the battle of Alam el Halfa information was particularly vital, to gauge the direction and timing of Rommel's thrust and, afterwards, to build up a full survey of the Axis defences – particularly artillery positions and minefields. No.285 Wing (Group-Captain W. D. Butler) now specialised in reconnaissance, strategic of ports and communications, photographic for battle maps, besides having administrative and technical responsibilities towards the tactical reconnaissance squadrons supporting the Corps of Eighth Army. No.40 Squadron was out of operations from late July to late September and during this period a great load rested on the shoulders of 208 Squadron (now Wing-Commander J. K. Rogers), of which the Official Historian writes: 'It has been said that in war each side gets the information it deserves, certainly the Eighth Army and Desert Air Force had good reason to be grateful to No.208 Squadron for the information it strove so hard to obtain'.[11]

The rival air forces, of course, did all possible to protect their respective armies from the prying eyes and cameras of hostile reconnaissance, particularly at sensitive periods. Before Alam el Halfa, for example, escorts of up to two or three fighter squadrons had to be provided to enable single reconnaissance pilots to discover and photograph the German concentrations.[12] The vulnerability of the *Hurricanes* and *Tomahawks* of the reconnaissance squadrons, to put it mildly, gave cause for concern, but the Air Ministry considered *Spitfires* too valuable for low altitude work – 'disappointing to those who had learned the value of good battlefield reconnaissance', comments Playfair.[13] At least *Hurricane IIs* now began to replace *Hurricane Is* in the tactical reconnaissance squadrons.

Liaison between Eighth Army and the Desert Air Force had by now become extremely close, with headquarters adjacent and commanders and staffs sharing messes. The Battle of El Alamein was preceded by a fortnight's air offensive against the Axis supply line from Italy through the North African ports and along the coast roads, while the Desert Air Force attacked and dominated the German and Italian air forces. Many steps were taken to mislead the enemy as to the intended point of attack and the outcome seems to point to their fair success.[14] The immediate prelude to the infantry assaults on the night of 23rd October was an intense half-hour of counter-battery programme by a thousand guns, followed by seven minutes' artillery fire on the enemy's forward positions. This was a programme somewhat after the 1918 pattern and, in the interests of surprise, no preliminary registration by shooting was

permitted other than a few 'air-burst' rounds, some two hours before
the assault, to test meteorological conditions. All confidence was placed
in the comprehensive photographic cover provided by the air force,
which now, once again, included 40 Squadron, S.A.A.F. (Lieutenant-
Colonel C. M. F. Murray-Gardner). In the event confidence was well
justified, enemy artillery fire being no more than spasmodic for some
hours.

From 24th October until Rommel started to pull out, fresh photographic cover was provided daily, from which hostile battery changes
were deduced for the artillery's counter-battery programme.[15] The
accuracy, and thus the effectiveness of unobserved artillery fire was
necessarily limited, however, and it would have been very useful to have
had army co-operation pilots observing for the guns beyond the limits of
vision of the ground observation posts. Two pilots of No.208 Squadron
did in fact carry out a shoot apiece, on 27th and 28th October
respectively, both described by their squadron as successful.[16] In the
mobile warfare of the last two years, however, continued pressure on the
time and activity of reconnaissance pilots and their escorts had precluded
intensive training in the art of artillery observation or the tailoring of
that art to the fast single-seater aircraft.

Tactical reconnaissance took place throughout the battle, and reports
of concentrations of enemy tanks or other vehicles were followed
promptly by fighter-bomber attacks. Luftwaffe intervention became less,
due both to R.A.F. action and to fuel shortage. From 3rd November
signs of enemy withdrawal were apparent, reconnaissance was stepped-
up and bombers and fighter-bombers attacked spectacular transport
targets on the coast road and on the tracks leading west from the enemy's
El Alamein position. In the afternoon of the 4th enemy activity on the
coast road decreased and attention was directed to desert tracks further
south. Rommel, however, extricated his forces in masterly manner and
his withdrawal was never anything but orderly. Eighth Army, after a
gruelling battle, were perhaps a trifle slow in occupying the forward
landing strips which Coningham needed to pursue the enemy with
bombs and with reconnaissance. Other factors combined to prolong
Coningham's frustrations – bad weather, supply congestion, slowness of
the army-air force support organisation to adapt itself to a new tempo of
warfare.

As Rommel's line of communication shortened his air forces came
more into the picture; he used his reconnaissance pilots successfully to
observe and avoid attempts to envelop him on his desert flank, and his
fighters to harass British reconnaissance. Coningham used his reconnaissance, as successfully, to keep watch on the enemy's preparations for
withdrawal from successive airfields, and often thwarted efforts to plough
up the latter. He was sometimes forced, however, to provide strong
escorts for such reconnaissance.

On 1st February, 1943, Coningham handed over command of the
Desert Air Force to Air Vice-Marshal Harry Broadhurst and became

Air Officer Commander-in-Chief, North-West African Tactical Air Force – much in need of his practical experience.

General Anderson of the British First Army, at the other end of North Africa, had the support of a force known as Eastern Air Command. This built up gradually to a strength of about 70 light and heavy bombers, 290 fighters, night-fighters and fighter-bombers and 60 reconnaissance aircraft. There were two army co-operation squadrons, Nos.225 and 241, equipped with *Hurricane II Es* but grouped into separate wings; one squadron was operational by 13th November, 1942, the other not until the 29th. No.682 (Photo-Reconnaissance) Squadron was partly operational by 17th November but had its airfield comprehensively beaten-up three days later. It was principally employed on strategic photography of the Tunisian ports.

There were factors inimical to good army-air co-operation. For some months there were separate British and American air commands both directly responsible to the Allied Commander-in-Chief of the North African theatre, General Eisenhower. Anderson was on the move eastwards on the 15th but by then only half of Eastern Air Command was ready; they were short of maintenance crews and there were few forward airfields. Air Marshal Sir William Welsh, the Air Commander, was responsible for the air defence of convoys, ports and airfields in the base area; he did not accompany Anderson and, though Air Commodore G. M. Lawson with a command post did so and an 'Air Support Control' accompanied the leading division, the communications were unequal to their task.

The Official Historian, very critical of the arrangements for R.A.F. support of First Army, writes: 'The two army co-operation squadrons included in the plan were first for tactical reconnaissance and secondly for fighter-bombing. In the Desert experience had shown that a tactical reconnaissance squadron had to be a highly skilled unit concentrating on that one role.'[17]

Often based on waterlogged airfields, outmatched in aircraft, their missions directed mostly into narrowly defined and predictable areas, without effective fighter protection, the two army co-operation squadrons were unable at first to produce much information for the army, while their casualties were high. Coningham's reorganisation of air tactics on Western Desert lines, and re-equipment with *Spitfires* and *Mustangs*, helped the squadrons to settle down. Very sensibly it was decided that 225 Squadron should specialise in reconnaissance and 241 Squadron in fighter-bombing. Reconnaissance now became more fruitful and 225 Squadron (Wing-Commander E. G. L. Millington) was able, after some teething trouble, to do much photography, particularly for the artillery.

The senior Gunner in First Army was Brigadier Jack Parham, whom we last met as a member of the Royal Artillery Flying Club, urging the cause of the air observation post. He had commanded a Royal Artillery regiment in the 1940 battle in Belgium and France. Back in England, he had evolved the machinery, in terms of wireless and gunnery procedure, to allow the fire of the whole of a divisional artillery – some seventy-two dispersed guns – to be brought to bear within four minutes upon an opportunity target spotted by any observation post. What is more, he had swiftly persuaded the School of Artillery and the top gunner hierarchy to accept his system – forever known as the 'Uncle Target' system – and bring it into general use. The sort of target, upon which such concentrated fire might be desirable, was, of course, as likely to be seen by the pilot of an air O.P. aircraft as by an officer in a ground O.P. When it was decided to include in the First Army order of battle for the landings of north-west Africa No.651 Air O.P. Squadron, Royal Air Force (commanded at first by Major Charles Bazeley and later by Major R. W. V. Neathercoat) Jack Parham found himself in the unusual situation of initially testing in battle two of his own concepts.

An advanced element of 651 Squadron landed at Algiers on 12th November, consisting of eleven pilots (artillery officers), thirty-nine artillery soldiers and twenty-five airmen, eight *Auster I* aircraft and a few lorries and light vans. This aircraft was no more than a standby; it had an unsatisfactorily restricted view backwards and in turns and, having no flaps, an unsatisfactorily flat angle of approach to landing. By 16th November the aircraft were assembled and on the following day the first three of them were flown forward into the unhappy air situation which has been described. By 21st November seven aircraft had joined 78th Division.

The advance into Tunisia took place in two columns, between which the seven *Austers* were divided. They were quickly involved in the abortive operations to seize Tunis and Bizerta and, until bad weather suspended those operations on 7th December, had performed thirty-seven sorties. Only ten of these, surprisingly, were to control artillery fire, five were tactical reconnaissance sorties, eighteen were for intercommunication and for the reconnaissance of landing grounds. The remaining four were contact sorties; in two of them the pilot was able to land beside the unit which he had found and identified and to bring back a written report. During this period one aircraft was destroyed on the ground and one pilot was lost.

In January 1943, after a short rest period and after the remainder of the squadron had arrived, the Air O.P.s were in action again; Jack Parham's 'Uncle Target' procedure was tried out successfully; and in due course air O.P. pilots conducted several shoots with the whole of the artillery of a division. At first there had been severe restrictions imposed on air O.P. sorties – in terms of a minimum distance behind the forward troops and maximum height and sortie-time – but, in Pemberton's words, 'these restrictions were lightly regarded by pilots'.[18] Arrangements were made, however, for 'air sentries' on the ground to give radio warning to air O.P. pilots when hostile aircraft approached and for anti-aircraft guns to cover pre-arranged escape areas. This, coupled with sensible evasive action over country selected to suit the aircraft camouflage, saved at least one life. Gradually the air situation improved for the Allies, air O.P. pilots enjoyed greater scope and army staffs learnt how best to use their services. The R.A.F. began to tolerate and then to respect the pilots of these little aircraft and the latter to value the courage, initiative and leadership of the airmen and soldiers of their ground parties. In March No.654 Air O.P. Squadron, with the new and operationally more suitable *Auster III* arrived in North Africa and joined Eighth Army for its final operations there. In Tunisia also appeared the Americans' Air O.P. organisation.

At the end of January, with Tripoli in its hands, the Eighth Army paused to build up for the expected battle for the Mareth Line. For two months the most intensive air reconnaissance covered the area of this Line and its approaches from the west and east, including lavish photographic cover, mostly by No.60 Squadron, S.A.A.F. Tactical reconnaissance detected Rommel, with a couple of days to spare, as he moved south from action against the Americans in Tunisia to strike unsuccessfully at the Medenine position on 6th March. Eighth Army, breaching the Mareth Line three weeks later with air support on an unprecedented scale, joined the Americans and the British First Army to compress the Axis forces into a diminishing bridgehead. Of the Allies' reconnaissance at this stage one can only say that it was active, continuous and effective, as indeed, almost to the end, was the enemy's reconnaissance.

Reconnaissance and observation are, as has always been emphasised in these pages, essential and intimate needs of armies; from that fact of war it follows that army commanders need to have control of their reconnaissance, whether from the air or from the ground. With the formation in Britain of an independent air force, this principle had not been forgotten and had resulted in the R.A.F. Air Components to armies, these components either under operational command of the army commanders or, at any rate, immediately responsive to their wishes. Provision was made therein not only for reconnaissance but for the protection of reconnaissance aircraft.

During the opening campaigns of the Second World War, in Belgium and France and then in Africa, sometimes in conditions of air inferiority, the limitations of medium-speed reconnaissance aircraft were discovered and the reconnaissance pilot's vehicle became a single-seater aircraft of fighter aircraft performance. Because this lonely pilot's attention was necessarily directed on objects and happenings on the ground he needed, in conditions short of air supremacy, the protection of fighters in quantity comparable to the probable size of an attacking force. Fighters were also needed however, in quantity, to win and maintain air superiority over the army's zone of operations and, as fighter-bombers, to supplement the army's artillery. The complexities of this situation effectively disposed of any practical possibility of the formation of a separate army-controlled tactical reconnaissance force. It remained necessary for the army to be assured of an adequate provision of such reconnaissance and of its proper protection, and of the quick supply of an increasing quantity of air photographs. Inter-service clashes of priority and differences of viewpoint could easily have bedevilled these problems beyond solution.

It must not be supposed that such troubles were non-existent and a few may here be mentioned.

Squadron-Leader L. G. Burnand, one of the outstanding and most articulate figures of air reconnaissance in the Second World War, left two interesting documents with 208 Squadron's Operational Record Book.[19] The first was a short note on the employment of his squadron with XXX Corps from 17th–27th November, 1941, and the second a formal report to his Wing Commander on the same operation, up to 14th December.

In the former document he wrote:

From the Squadron's point of view it is absolutely essential to have access to the highest authority for the purpose of ascertaining requirements, since these requirements are (or should be) the outpourings of the Commander's mind. The Commander wants certain information necessary for the execution of a particular move or plan. Those detailed to get it (in this case the army co-operation pilot) must know what is in the Commander's mind; only then is it possible to serve his wants.

So far in this campaign it has been a hard and winding path to the inner circle of the general staff and more often than not orders for the day's sorties have filtered through several hands and in several cases have come to this squadron's A.L.O. in a state that not only clouds the main issues but also completely disregards the capabilities of pilots and aircraft.

In the latter document he wrote:

Liaison between a Corps and its Army Co-operation Squadron is something more than a cordiality. The first principle is what might be termed operational intimacy.

In both documents he stated that the system had not initially worked. The Brigadier, General Staff, he felt, was disinclined for personal contact with the squadron's air liaison officer, his staff was reluctant to impart sufficient information to the A.L.O. about their own or the enemy's forces and the squadron was given little scope to adjust its reconnaissances to its capabilities.[20]

He claimed that in the second phase of the battle, after entreaties by himself, direct access to the Brigadier was achieved and '. . . . of sixty reconnaissances carried out during this period the majority were handled mutually with, it is humbly suggested, more fruitful results.'

Later 208 Squadron supported XIII Corps. Wing Commander J. W. Stewart, to whose 1944 *Royal Air Force Quarterly* article previous reference has been made, was, it may be deduced, in 208 Squadron at that time and mentioned in his article that XIII Corps was very good at close co-operation with the R.A.F. and that their appreciative attitude was an inspiration to the squadron in difficult times.[21]

XXX Corps was a fine fighting formation, but the understanding by its staff of army-air matters does appear to have been incomplete. Had its reconnaissance squadron been an integral part of its formation and service, who can doubt that difficulties of this kind would long since have been resolved by appropriate organisation, tactical doctrines and training? Because it was necessarily of a separate service, and because the operation of fast aircraft introduced entirely fresh factors into the problem, more than conventional attention needed to be devoted to it.

In April 1942 the Luftwaffe was gaining air superiority and severely restricting British air reconnaissance. Steps were taken to combat this, one of which was the installation of an air controller, with codename 'Jumbo', equipped with radar and radio to discover and warn pilots of the proximity of enemy fighters. On 6th April Jumbo reported much enemy activity in a certain area and 'ordered' pilots not to fly there. Later a pilot of No.40 Squadron, South African Air Force, which was then in support of XIII Corps, was ordered by an officer of the Corps's headquarters to disregard Jumbo's order and carry on with a reconnaissance which had been arranged. The pilot did so and was shot down; his squadron was resentful and the matter was taken up with the service heads. As a result Jumbo was made the final arbiter.[22]

This unfortunate occurrence affords an excellent example of the contradictions inherent in the performance by an air force unit of a basic army function.

We do not know of the specific reconnaissance need of XIII Corps on this occasion. Had it been within the province of an armoured reconnaissance regiment, the Corps commander or his staff would – almost subconsciously – have assessed the relative 'need' and the 'risk' and would have given appropriate orders. The reconnaissance had, in fact, to be an aerial one; since 40 Squadron was under command of the Corps, however, one might infer that its position was entirely analagous to that of the armoured reconnaissance squadron. So thought, evidently, the XIII Corps staff officer who overruled Jumbo.

But there were two important differences between the respective positions of the 'armoured' and 'tactical' reconnaissance units, firstly the army background and upbringing of the Corps officers, which did not collectively fit them to assess air factors as against military needs and, secondly, the essential personal involvement of the tactical reconnaissance squadron-commander, as a leader, in operational flying, which unavoidably prevented a relationship with the Corps commander similar to that of the armoured reconnaissance regimental commander.

Nor was Jumbo's position militarily logical. He was certainly best qualified to assess the air risk taken by pilots who flew, escorted or unescorted, in particular areas. But he can hardly have been qualified to determine what risk was operationally justified, for he was not 'in the mind' of the Corps commander. Nor, probably, was he aware of the possible military penalty to be paid for lack of the information which the

Corps commander so urgently desired, nor was he entitled to accept or reject such penalty. The logic of events in due course made this clear to all and reduced Jumbo's status to that of a very necessary information agency.

The problem of providing fighter protection for reconnaissance missions, which has already been mentioned, is linked with that of the ultimate control of air reconnaissance. In the conditions of 1941 to 1943 in North Africa it was apparently inescapable that, because army reconnaissance and fighter missions were under the operational control of separate services, fighter cover was only possible by private negotiation between squadron commanders. This was not a tolerable situation. Strengthening air force opinion was, however, in favour of their overall surveillance of air space and control of all friendly movement therein, implying, of course, a lessening of Army control of their air reconnaissance.

The great contribution made by the air marshals in the Middle East and North Africa, their staffs and, above all, their squadron commanders was to develop, in defeat and in victory and in co-operation with the army, a joint-service method relevant to battle and satisfactory both to army and air force to minimise, and almost always to find a way around, the difficulties, and to provide the vital requirement of reconnaissance.

With the failure of the *Lysander* to survive in modern battle had collapsed the whole philosophy of, and training for, 'army co-operation'. A new reconnaissance philosophy and training machine had to be provided, based on fighter-type aircraft, in the midst of war. Fighter and reconnaissance pilots came thereafter from the same source; dash and aerobatic skill on the one hand, restraint and high sense of responsibility on the other, helped to separate them into appropriate streams and imaginative (though necessarily hurried) training both at home and in Egypt, culminating in that by their operational squadron commanders, produced in aggregate a very high standard of pilot. The standard needed to be high to enable discriminating reconnaissance for the army, coupled often with difficult navigation and with attention to hostile fighters. As Air Marshal Broadhurst has written, 'They missed out on the glamour'.[23] This could be said of many fine fighting men and it is not of first importance; what is important is that their high qualities and achievements should not now be forgotten.

As for the air O.Ps, they had demonstrated their ability to operate in the forward part of the battlefield in conditions of air inferiority and to perform their artillery functions with light loss. The voices of the doubters were at last stilled and an air O.P. squadron, under artillery operational command, became an integral part of each army corps.

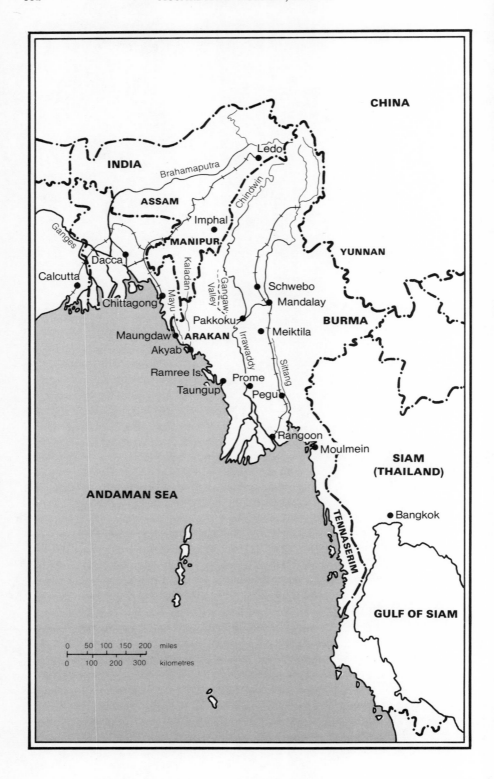

1941 to 1945
Asia and Australasia

◇

'And here were forests ancient as the hills'
S. T. COLERIDGE, 'Kubla Khan'

Although the war in the Far East did not end for four months after the war in Europe, it had begun, of course, over eighteen months before the Allied landings in Italy. It is convenient to consider the Far East fighting next.

The war in the Far East began with the Japanese air attack of 7th December, 1941, on the United States Hawaiian base of Pearl Harbour, and ranged over most of the Indian and Pacific oceans, Hong Kong, Malaya, Singapore, the Dutch East Indies, the Philippines, New Guinea and Burma, until the Japanese surrender on 15th August, 1945. We shall in this chapter confine ourselves to the land operations in which British and Dominions' forces were principally engaged.

From the surprise of Pearl Harbour and from British preoccupation with the war in Africa and the Atlantic, the Japanese held the initiative. They quickly overran Hong Kong, Malaya, Singapore and North Borneo and, by June 1942, had added Burma, Java and Sumatra to their bag. An attempt at a British counter-offensive on the Arakan coast of north-west Burma at the end of 1942 had failed by March 1943.

The Japanese also thrust deep into the south-west Pacific, seizing early in 1942 the port of Rabaul in New Britain and landing in several places in the Solomon Islands and on the north coast of New Guinea. From Buna, on that coast, they thrust south, across formidable jungle-covered mountains, towards Port Moresby – only about four hundred miles from the coast of Australia. Australians and Americans reacted quickly, however, and prevented any further exploitation of these initial gains. The United States General Douglas MacArthur assumed command of the Allied Forces, South-West Pacific, in March 1942, and in New Guinea, by the end of that year, the Australians had driven back the Japanese to the Buna area.

In early 1944 the Japanese launched strong offensives into India, first in the Arakan and then on the central (Imphal) front, with the aim of cutting the Allied rail and river lines between Dacca and Ledo. These supply lines served both the British and Indian formations in the Imphal area and also a Chinese army under the American General Stilwell which had begun to move slowly south from the extreme north of Burma. For the Japanese their major offensive, after promising well, proved a disaster and soon developed into obstinate but continued withdrawal. Stilwell's Chinese and General Wingate's second long-range penetration ('Chindit') operations in central Burma, between them, put the Japanese in northern Burma into similar withdrawal. The central Burmese plain, north-west of Mandalay and of the great bend in the Irrawaddy river, appeared to offer an opportunity for a final engagement of the Japanese in more open country, exploiting British superiority in armour, but the Japanese withdrew to the Irrawaddy. General Sir William Slim's Fourteenth Army, however, now achieved a masterpiece of deception; IV Corps, disguised as a small outlying detachment, moved down the Gangaw valley, crossed the Irrawaddy near Pakkoku and seized the Japanese complex of communications and airfields around Meiktila on 4th March, 1945. The inevitably fierce battle of retention followed, but the XXXIII Corps had now crossed the Irrawaddy west of Mandalay and by the end of March the Japanese armies in Burma were clearly in no state to offer sustained resistance.

It took IV Corps just a month to push down the 'railway valley' to Pegu, forty miles short of Rangoon, while XXXIII Corps, in the Irrawaddy river valley reached Prome, some 140 miles north of it. At this stage a British seaborne descent was made upon Rangoon; the Japanese did not wait for it but withdrew east to the line of the Sittang river. In the Arakan, meanwhile, having weathered the Japanese offensive at the beginning of 1944, XV Corps advanced down the coast and occupied the important port of Akyab on 3rd January, 1945. A series of navy-supported operations down the Arakan coast concluded with the British on the Taungup-Prome road.

In the south-west Pacific, between February and October 1943, Americans, Australians and New Zealanders recaptured the South and Central Solomon Islands and Lae and Salamaua, important bases on the north coast of New Guinea, west of Buna. In the next nine months Australians, with Americans in increasing number, occupied virtually all the rest of New Guinea and much of New Britain.

The United States fleet, marines and army, meanwhile, supported in the closing stages by the Royal Navy, had closed in upon the Japanese mainland by way of Iwojima and Okinawa and, on 6th and 9th of August, 1945, the atomic bombs on Hiroshima and Nagasaki made the way clear for the Japanese Emperor to announce his country's unconditional surrender.

The Japanese assault upon British territories in the Far East somewhat naturally revealed the latter's air, like their land, forces to be extremely weak and outmatched both in quantity and quality. In Malaya this disparity was never overcome to the extent of providing the retreating soldiers with information or with close air support in measurable quantities.

In the Japanese invasion of Burma, which followed, the Royal Air

Force, with the Indian Air Force and a very gallant and effective American Volunteer Group, were still outmatched but were now able to give their ground forces some support, if only by engaging the Japanese bombers. Reinforced with more modern aircraft in much greater numbers, and helped by Japanese withdrawals of aircraft to the South West Pacific, they were able in 1943 and 1944 to establish air superiority all over Burma, first for limited periods and then permanently. Before the Trenchard theories of strategic bombing could be translated into practice, the natural development of land operations in this vast, largely impenetrable theatre, and the basic thinking of the United States Army Air Force, resulted in a more direct and much sounder use of air power, to permit the full use of air transportation.[1] Transport aircraft were used initially for the emergency supply of units and formations isolated by Japanese envelopment, then on a much larger scale for the supply of the Chinese armies in the Yunnan province and as the sole means of supply of the two Chindit operations and, finally, as virtually the entire means of supplying General Slim's Fourteenth Army in its recapture of southern Burma. These aircraft were used also for troop movements on a large scale – for example for the second Chindits' descent on central Burma and for the reinforcement of the Imphal front against the main thrust of the Japanese invasion.

As in North Africa Allied air resources were also, to some extent, diverted from reconnaissance to the close support of ground forces. The problem of achieving, in jungle, the accurate location of targets and the accurate delivery of bombs, cannon-shell or bullets was intense; it demanded, and eventually received, control by the ground troops through the medium of radio communication with flight leaders – control closer and thus more efficient in the case of the uninhibited army pilots of the Tenth United States Army Air Force on the northern front.[2] This form of support, replacing that of artillery, was fully justified in this theatre, because of technical difficulties of gunnery in jungle, the absence of artillery from Chindit columns and, during most periods of intense air supply, the rationing of artillery ammunition.

Both sides, however, used the air for reconnaissance. Over the sea this was essential and along the coasts always useful, but the air forces naturally found difficulty in observing detail in jungle terrain. In the earliest days of the Japanese invasion of Burma a faulty air report of enemy vehicles on a certain road culminated in prolonged bombing of British columns by both Allied and Japanese aircraft.[3] A flight of No.28 Squadron, R.A.F., under Squadron-Leader A. S. Mann, supported 14th Division's abortive Arakan offensive in early 1943. Their airfield was a hundred yards from divisional headquarters, commander and staff frequently visited the flight, the flight's pilots attended the divisional commander's daily meetings. Liaison could not have been closer. But, though contact sorties were successful, it was rarely that tactical or photographic reconnaissance over the jungle revealed the enemy. A year later (28 Squadron no longer present) everything was on a larger scale and liaison less close; the Japanese started their 1944 Arakan offensive with a flank envelopment through thick jungle by a force of about five battalions; although a Japanese offensive was thought to be imminent, tactical reconnaissance saw nothing of this move.[4] On the central front, however, at much the same period, road construction and the appearance of rafts along the Chindwin river gave, by way of the reconnaissance pilots, important warning of the second phase of the offensive while, later on, occasional glimpses were had of Japanese road columns approaching Imphal.[5]

Hurricanes had soon replaced *Lysanders*, missions were usually flown by two aircraft, one the protective 'weaver'. Pilot survival had been enhanced but not the ability to search through the jungle canopy. Reconnaissance became more and more strategic, rather than tactical, directed on such objects as roads, railways, rivers and airfields. The Japanese adopted the policy of basing their air forces out of range of all but the longest-range Allied bombers and of flying them forward, by staging airfields, for specific operations; air reconnaissance and photography sometimes detected such movements in time to punish them severely. The United States First Air Commando, a task force in direct support of the second Chindit operation and equipped with aircraft for a variety of roles, had two big successes of this kind, against Anisakan airfield (east of Mandalay) on 4th March, 1944, and against Shwebo on 8th March.[6] The Chindit operations had necessitated initial reconnaissances, by Wingate himself and others, of the operational area 150 miles inside enemy territory, and it was an air photograph which sensationally revealed, a few minutes before the Chindits' gliders were due to be towed off from an Assam airfield, that one of the two planned landing zones had been comprehensively obstructed.[7]

Air reconnaissance over the central, more open, Burmese plain was naturally more effective. Contact sorties became more frequent, to report progress of forward units, and it was from air reconnaissance that Fourteenth Army received the earliest indication that the Japanese were not to be brought to battle between Chindwin and Irrawaddy.[8] During the Irrawaddy crossings west of Mandalay *Hurricane* pilots made the unusual discovery of a group of Japanese tanks. During the last battle in Burma, in July 1945, resulting from the attempted break-out by Japanese troops trapped west of the Meiktila – Pegu railway and road, R.A.F. reconnaissance gave useful information regarding the escape routes used.

Japanese air reconnaissance, it must be understood, was markedly less effective than ours, due to the degree of air superiority gained by the Allies. The decisive move of IV Corps down the Gangaw valley, for example, was never recognised by the Japanese as more than that of a relatively small detachment. It was the attainment of such air superiority which, more important still, allowed the British and American transport aircraft to rove far and wide over Burma, normally without escort and without excessive loss.

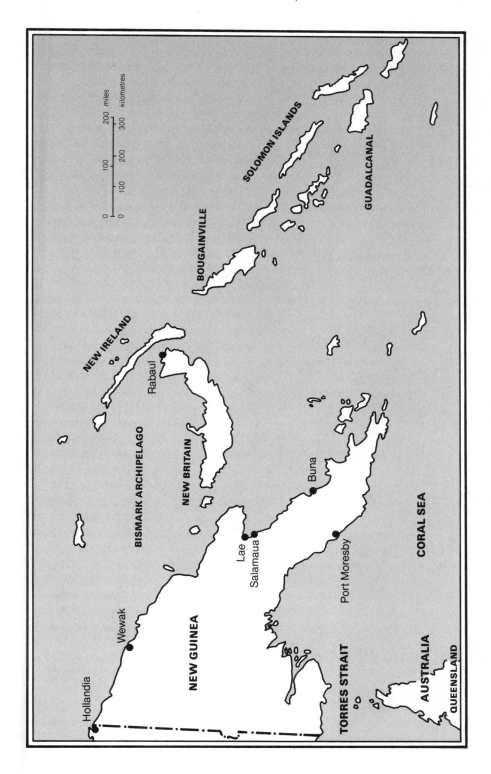

In New Guinea air supply was as vital as in Burma but the observation and close reconnaissance provided for their army by the Royal Australian Air Force was also most successful. The Australian Army's official history is full of tributes to this and particularly to the pilots of No.4 (Army Co-operation) Squadron, R.A.A.F., (Wing-Commander W. F. Allshorn) 'equipped with slow, almost weaponless *Wirraways*[9] and manned by skilful pilots and observers'.[10] Artillery observation was regular and effective, visual reconnaissance of Japanese positions and movement invaluable and contact reconnaissance and reporting of friendly forces equally so. A striking indication of the relationship between the ground forces in New Guinea and the men who observed for them in the air is provided in the following extract from the Australian Army's history of the operations of 1943–1944:

> On New Year's Eve occurred a loss which upset the fighting men of the 7th Division. One of the *Boomerangs* from No. 4 Squadron, piloted by Flying Officer Staley, was lost on reconnaissance near the 5,800 Feature.[11] These manoeuvrable tree-skimming aircraft, piloted by their valiant crews who seemed to know the tangled country so well, had appeared indestructible.[12]

It is interesting to speculate why air force reconnaissance for the army in New Guinea was, apparently, more intimate and tactically productive than that in Burma, topography and conditions in each country being fairly similar. The Japanese air force in New Guinea and New Britain was operating at the end of a long line of sea-communication much more vulnerable than their land line to Burma; they could never operate numbers of aircraft comparable to those of the Australians and Americans and the latter very quickly seized and held air superiority. The R.A.A.F. army co-operation squadron in New Guinea (like the R.A.F. and Indian A.F. army co-operation squadrons in India and Burma) started their war equipped with slow, out-of-date aircraft. Because air superiority was quickly gained, however, the Australians did not need to change these for aircraft fast and modern but less convenient for reconnaissance over jungle – the kept their *Wirraways* and *Boomerangs* and flew them boldly in accordance with the role. To quote, once again, from the Australian Army's history, 'the soldiers soon became used to seeing them circling slowly, seeming almost to hover, over the Japanese lines . . .'[13]

In Burma, air observation returned to the British army in a new and exciting form with the appearance of No.656 Air Observation Post Squadron, R.A.F., in January 1944, commanded by Major Denis Coyle, Royal Artilllery. His squadron was equipped with *Auster IIIs*, in which the pilot's view had been greatly increased and in which landing flaps much improved the *Auster I's* performance in and out of small fields and strips. The unit was organised in the same manner as the other Air O.P. squadrons, that is to say with artillery pilots, drivers and signallers and air force aircraft technicians; it came under artillery operational command.

The arrival of 656 Squadron more or less coincided with the beginning of the big Japanese offensive, first in the Arakan and afterwards on the central front, the main feature of which was the Imphal plain. In the Arakan, early in February, the Japanese outflanking movement, to which we have referred, isolated the 7th Indian Division from its neighbours, the 5th Division, and from all rearward supply links. They stood fast, supplied by air, for eighteen days, after which they and relieving formations took the offensive and restored the situation. These were unpromising conditions in which to introduce air O.P.s to the Burma theatre of war; very wisely the corps commander withdrew them from the forward area to rearward strips, from which sorties were made to one small strip in a forward brigade position to deliver messages and medical supplies.

It was not until March 1944 that conditions permitted operations in the normal Air O.P. role and, soon afterwards, leaving A Flight in the Arakan, the rest of the Squadron moved to the Imphal Plain and Kohima fronts.[14] They were employed in other roles besides artillery observation and control of fire, including short-range reconnaissance (often with artillery fire 'on call') and contact sorties, particularly valuable in this theatre. With the defeat and withdrawal of the Japanese, 656 Squadron began to filter back to India at the end of June for the aircraft to recover from the inroads of the climate upon their fabric and for a period of intensive training.

In September and October, 1944, 656 Squadron moved up to the Burma frontiers again, C. Flight under XV Corps in the Arakan, the rest of the Squadron under Fourteenth Army on the central front, A and B Flights supporting the advance of IV and XXXIII Corps but being placed under command of various divisions of both corps as operations demanded. They had reached maturity and the army reached maturity in their understanding of how they could be used. The artillery role was now paramount and accounted for about half the sorties; these included the spotting of enemy batteries, the registration of these and other targets for future engagement and the immediate engagement of targets on other occasions. Enemy batteries were often silenced by the simple expedient of putting up an *Auster* to look for them, sometimes by night. About a quarter of the sorties were for short-range tactical or photographic reconnaissance, the former often illustrated by sketch maps. Of the remaining sorties, contact patrols proved as important as ever. Orange umbrellas were often used by infantry patrols and others to reveal themselves to the pilots, conspicuous signals which could, nevertheless, be displayed quickly and for a minimum period. Message bags were used to drop instructions to such parties, radio problems being difficult to overcome. Occasionally it was possible to land, for direct liaison, on patches of open country, on beaches on the Arakan coast or on strips prepared, as standard procedure, by army formations.

During this period the Army's appreciation of the work of these skilful and enterprising pilots reached full flower.[15] It must be remembered, however, that the air superiority won by the air forces permitted the *Auster* pilots to fly with far more freedom than, for example, in Tunisia. 'We were very rarely influenced by Jap air', Coyle has recorded, 'therefore all we had to avoid was the trajectory of our own shells and enemy ground fire.'[16] It was normal to fly at heights between two and three thousand feet, to observe from positions almost vertically over the targets and to use binoculars.

January and February 1945 were busy months, in the last six weeks of which six pilots of A Flight flew for six hundred hours in over six hundred sorties, supporting XXXIII Corps' crossings of the Irrawaddy river either side of Mandalay.[17] Many of these were contact sorties to locate units which had slipped across the river, surreptitiously by night and in 'wireless-silence'. B Flight supported IV Corps' crossings near Pakokku, its advance east to capture Meiktila, its subsequent battle as the Japanese reacted and its final advance to Pegu.

C Flight had remained in the Arakan, supporting XV Corps' advance on Akyab, Ramree Island and Taungup, the latter part of which consisted of a series of amphibious operations in which the air O.P.s directed the fire of warships' guns in addition to land artillery.[18] The flight's part in the occupation of Akyab on 3rd January, 1945, possibly the best air O.P. story of the war and certainly a good example of the type of reconnaissance of which only air O.P.s were capable, will do well to conclude this chapter.

Akyab, whose airfield was very necessary to the British as a staging point for aircraft supplying Fourteenth Army in southern Burma, lies on a small island at the south end of the Mayu peninsula where most of the Arakan fighting had hitherto taken place. Twenty-fifth Indian Division, of XV Corps, had reached the tip of the peninsula by Boxing Day of 1944 and two West African divisions had simultaneously cleared extensive territory north-east of the peninsula. The Japanese, however, had strongly fortified Akyab island and were expected to fight hard for it; consequently British arrangements to assault it were on a most generous scale. A strong naval bombardment force was to concentrate for the reduction of the strongest seaward defences, while six squadrons of heavy and medium bombers and sixteen other R.A.F. or U.S.A.A.F. squadrons would take part. The contribution of the land artillery was, as compared to these, fairly modest but included medium and heavy guns. Zero hour was 10 a.m. on 3rd January, 1945.

Captain Jimmy Jarrett, commander of C Flight, returned on the evening of the 1st January from a conference with the Navy, to learn that one of his pilots had flown a reconnaissance sortie over Akyab that day in which, from lack of enemy reaction, from lack of shipping in the harbour and from the excited demeanour of the inhabitants, he had formed the opinion that the Japanese had left the island. Brigadier John Daniell, commander of the divisional artillery, sent Jarrett out next day to see whether the local inhabitants were actually occupying the main target areas for the bombardment on the 3rd. They were. They were also running about waving flags and, a mile to the east of the town, Jarrett found an open space which had been levelled to some extent and where the crowds had been marshalled off a landing area by eight men with large white flags. After a close look at the proffered landing strip, he landed. The crowd surged round his aircraft; he did not stop the engine but shook hands with a number of people through the window and was told that the last Japanese had left. He, on his part, said that the British were coming soon, as friends, and then took off and returned to Daniell.

Jarrett then interviewed a succession of commanders of ever increasing rank up to General Christison, the Corps Commander, and learnt that the calling-off of the complex bombardment of the following day was not the straight forward matter he had assumed it to be. Everyone regretted the probable loss of life and, perhaps more cynically, the waste of ammunition, but who could be sure that the Japanese had really gone or, if they had, that they would not return? And how should one contact the heavy bombers, beyond the Bay of Bengal, or the Navy, at sea and preserving wireless-silence? At about midday on the 2nd Daniell asked Jarrett if he could fly over to the island again and try to return with a 'representative'. Daniell meanwhile spent his time 'quelling an almost mutiny among C.O.s and air O.P. officers who refused to take part in any fire plan aimed at Jimmy's friends on the Island'.[19]

On this trip Jarrett took his batman, Gunner Carter, and left him on the island as 'temporary military governor'. He had, of course, to switch off the engine and get out and, thus released from any remaining inhibitions, the inhabitants crowded round and over the aircraft, which began to look unlikely to do the return trip. A measure of order was restored, however, and a representative selected from the six who tried simultaneously to enter the aircraft. With him Jarrett returned to the mainland. By evening, to everyone's relief, particularly Jarrett's, the word came through that although the landing would go ahead on the morrow the fire programme would be 'on call' only.

On the following morning Jarrett flew back with the representative to the island, while another of the flight pilots flew out to sea to meet the fleet, establish radio communication and, much to the fleet's suspicion, inform them that the shooting was off. The Commandos, who had not been brought up to date, did a fighting landing, were surprised at the absence of either enemy or fire support and even more surprised to find a battalion of British infantry resting half a mile inland. And, in Jimmy Jarrett's words: 'General Christison himself was flown over shortly in an L5 and so took over the military governorship from Gunner Carter.'[20]

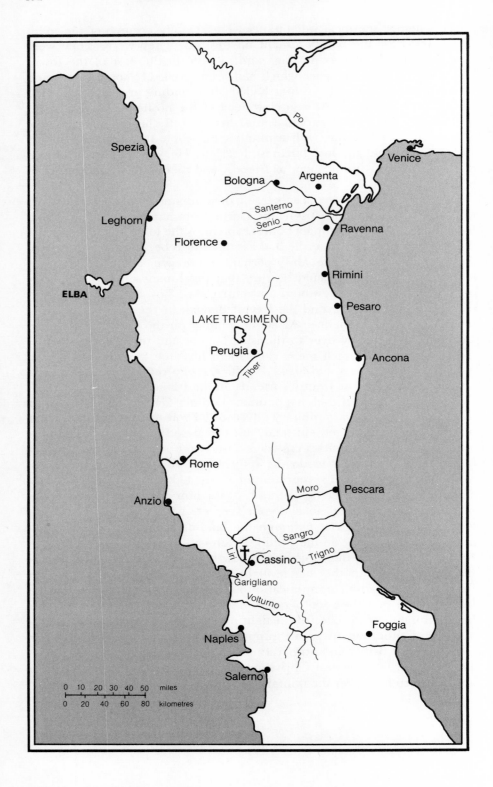

1943 to 1945
Italy

◇

'A bird of the air shall carry the voice'
Ecclesiastes X, 20

From Akyab of January 1945, we must return to the Tunisia in which the Axis forces were rounded up in May 1943.

Planning for the descent on Sicily and Italy had been going on for the last six months, and the Anglo-American invasion of Sicily was launched on 9th July. This was quickly successful, although it is mostly remembered for the disaster to a large proportion of the gliderborne assault force prematurely released from their tug-aircraft in unexpected meteorological conditions. The British Eighth Army advanced up the east coast, where the main defensive system was based on Mount Etna; the United States Seventh Army struck across the island to the north coast and followed the latter east to converge with the British at Messina on 16th August.

The Germans withdrew in good order to the mainland of Italy but for the Italians the war against the Western Allies was nearing its end. Their dictator, Mussolini, had been arrested on 26th July and Marshal Badoglio had started secret negotiations with the British and Americans. An armistice was signed on 3rd September, on which day the Eighth Army started to cross the Straits of Messina, and an Italian government was in due course set up on Allied occupied territory. On 9th September the main landing was made at Salerno, south of Naples, by the United States Fifth Army under General Mark Clark (containing a British corps). The Eighth Army established contact on 16th September and thereafter advanced up the east side of Italy, confronted for the rest of the war by a succession of defended river lines. The Fifth Army occupied Naples on 1st October and Kesselring, the German commander in Italy, withdrew to a strong position, the Gustav Line, based upon the Garigliano river. By the close of 1943 Eighth Army had crossed the Trigno, Sangro and Moro rivers and their advance had come to a stop in face of bad weather. Eisenhower and Montgomery now returned to England to play their parts in the forthcoming invasion of northern France, Alexander and General Sir Oliver Leese replacing them.

On 22nd January, 1944, a surprise landing was made by the American VI Corps, in which were the 1st, and later, in turn, the 56th and 5th British Infantry Divisions, at Anzio on the west coast of Italy, fifty miles behind Kesselring's main position and forty miles south of Rome. A decisive eruption onto the German communications might, perhaps, have been made; instead the Germans blocked off the bridgehead and remained generally on the Gustav Line. There followed the well-known abortive assaults upon, and the final futile bombing of, Monte Cassino and its monastery. At last, on 11th May, the Fifth and Eighth Armies combined in a deliberate attack on the Gustav Line and up the Liri Valley, and Kesselring withdrew. On 4th June, two days before the Allied invasion of Normandy, the Fifth Army entered Rome.

Alexander's forces in Italy were milked to provide for the invasion of Elba in June and of the south of France in August; later they were to be further depleted for operations in Greece. For the remaining Allied troops the Italian campaign became a hard slog. Kesselring had prepared another strong position, the Gothic Line, spanning the country from, roughly, Spezia to Pesaro, and withdrew from it in September only after a month's bloody fighting.

Through the winter the two Allied armies closed up to the last of the German positions in Italy, based on the River Senio in the east and the north-eastern edge of the Appenines – south and south-west of Bologna. Here in April 1945 the final battle of the Italian campaign began. The Eighth Army attacked across the Senio, crossed the Santerno and, with the Fifth Army, entered Bologna. By 28th April the line of the River Po was forced and then resistance collapsed. The German formations in the Italian theatre surrendered unconditionally on 2nd May, 1945.

These Allied operations incorporated three major landings upon hostile shores and innumerable river crossings; for obvious reasons the air forces bore more than a normal share of responsibility for the preliminary reconnaissances. These were chiefly photographic and had three main objects in view; first to produce vertical photographic cover as a basis for large-scale maps, secondly to deduce enemy activity from the scrutiny and comparison of successive sets of photographs taken at frequent intervals and, thirdly, to provide military planners and unit leaders with, usually, oblique-view photographs of beaches, river banks and other future objectives. For long-range photographic reconnaissance the Royal Air Force used *Spitfire XI* and *XIX* and *Mosquito* aircraft;[1] their tactical reconnaissance squadrons, which dealt with the immediate requirements of the armies whether before, during or after the landings or crossings, were equipped mostly with *Spitfire Vs*. The American equivalent was the *P 51 Mustang*, probably the best reconnaissance aircraft of the Second World War.[2]

Supplementing observation from the ground in the immediate battle zone of the army were the air O.P.s in their *Austers*. Now they have taken their place in this narrative we need to be careful with our terminology. The air O.P.s, and the squadrons to which they belonged, were of the R.A.F. but, since they were under army operational command, their missions were not included in the statistics of the Allied air forces. It we remember this situation it will probably not be too confusing to use the terms 'air force' and 'air O.P.' to distinguish between the fast and the slow.

The British or British-affiliated air force squadrons most concerned with tactical reconnaissance for the army were Nos.40 (South African Air Force), 208, 225 and 318 (Polish) Squadrons[3] and, for longer-range photographic reconnaissance, Nos.682 and 683 Squadrons. The first four of these, together with detachments from the other two, were contained within No.285 Reconnaissance Wing (Group-Captain E. G. L. Millington from September 1943), which now began to exercise a greater degree of operational control than previously over the tactical reconnaissance squadrons. In principle, reconnaissance requests were made, through Army Headquarters and the Headquarters of the Desert Air Force (whose title remained unchanged in the orchards and vineyards of Italy), to 285 Wing Headquarters, who then suballotted and set up the missions. Much of the planning emanated from daily evening conferences but the system necessarily allowed for urgent requests to be made and met. At the Squadrons, air force operations and intelligence officers briefed pilots on 'air' factors and air liaison officers (A.L.O.s) on the military position and the army's needs. These A.L.O.s, army majors and captains, were of immense importance to the standard of reconnaissance support. They needed to arm themselves not only with every detail of the Allied and enemy situation known to the army staffs but, far more difficult, with an understanding of the Army Commander's operational philosophy and aims and, of course, the requirement behind each one of the reconnaissance tasks requested of the air forces. Group Control Centres, sited conveniently for communication with the fighter, fighter-bomber and reconnaissance airfields, and with the pilots and flight-leaders in the air, controlled in detail the operations which the Army and Desert Air Force had planned together. At the end of a reconnaissance mission A.L.O.s, among others, debriefed the pilots and fed reports rapidly to army headquarters, to the original source of each reconnaissance request and to intermediate headquarters. Photographs were sent to the Army Photographic Interpretation Section for first-stage interpretation and onward passage with the reports. Provision was made to receive 'flash reports' from pilots in the air and to broadcast information regularly to all army formations. A very high standard of intelligence, ability and resource was clearly required of the A.L.O.s and of the army's air staff officers; from the reports of R.A.F. commanders this standard seems almost always to have been attained.

This procedure may have seemed slow, unwieldy and remote to those who, in the desert, had experienced reconnaissance by an air force squadron under command of a corps. There were, however, compensating advantages in the new procedure. Inter-service co-ordination at higher army-air force level relieved squadron commanders, essentially leaders in the air as on the ground, from the additional anxious task of serving army masters; fighter-protection (though rarely needed) was readily arranged between Wing and Desert Air Force headquarters or at the evening conference; above all it became possible for a single air force authority to view together the whole complex of air operations, to co-ordinate, to warn, to re-brief whenever necessary, and to economise vastly in the use of aircraft. This centralised system became an article of faith with the British and American air forces and it undoubtedly worked well in the Italian and North-West Europe campaigns of 1944 and 1945. Whether, in less advantageous conditions, under air inferiority for example or in the stress of hurried withdrawal, it would not have proved too slow, remote and impersonal for those at the 'sharp end' is less certain.

In Italy, a complication resulted from the incorporation of X and XIII British Corps, at different periods, within the American Fifth Army and from the necessity of providing them with air reconnaissance; some of Millington's units were, from time to time, detached operationally to the United States XII and XXII Tactical Air Commands.

Four British air O.P. squadrons took park in the Italian campaign, Nos.651 and 654 throughout (Major T. B. Laird commanding the latter from July 1944), No.655 from the end of 1943 and No.657 from April 1944. Although the intention had been for each Division's artillery to incorporate an air O.P. flight and for each Corps to incorporate the squadron headquarters, such a tidy organisation did not survive the constant redeployments of British formations and the changing tactical emphases and needs. The measure of the air O.P. success was its complete acceptance by armies and air forces as an integral part both of the artillery and of the army as a whole; in Italy the air O.P. idea was finally established. The existence of the army-controlled *Austers* within the battle area, furthermore, encouraged their use in forms of reconnaissance other than the observation of artillery fire, for low-level oblique photography, for example, for the carriage of engineers and other specialists on technical reconnaissance and – most important – to enable infantry and armoured unit commanders to view in advance the ground over which they were to lead their troops, often a slow process from viewpoints on the ground.

In Sicily, four days after the first landings, there were fighter-bombers based in the beach-head with, no doubt, a certain reconnaissance potential, but the professionals in the shape of 40 Squadron were not there for a further two days. Not for four days more did the first air O.P.s appear. Much of the tactical and photographic reconnaissance from Sicilian airfields was over the mainland of Italy; pilots from North Africa found the change in scenery presented novel observation problems. For the air O.P.s artillery and contact sorties predominated and 651 Squadron pilots directed, for the first time, the gunfire of ships of the Royal Navy. So, as we shall see, did 40 Squadron.

At Salerno the air O.P.s were first in the field, 654 Squadron being ashore and ready to fly on the morning following the first landings. Three days later there were fighter-bombers ashore and after another two days 225 Squadron was using an airfield in the beach-head. 654 Squadron was under command of X British Corps of the United States Fifth Army. In the weeks following the landing the pilots directed the fire of naval guns as well as of their own artillery upon targets out of sight of ground O.P.s, particularly enemy in the surrounding hills. As the Fifth Army advanced north the country was flat and good ground O.P.s very rare, giving fine opportunites for the air O.P.s.

No.225 Squadron's *Spitfires* in the beach-head, with the particular role of watching for movements of enemy reinforcements into the area or of signs of withdrawal therefrom, were for some time plagued by hostile artillery fire. The Official History states that 'Allied army-air co-operation was creaking a bit at this stage'.[4] By the end of September, however, reconnaissance units were based both in the Salerno area and in the Foggia group of airfields, seventy miles to the north-east. From the latter much air photography took place during the next three months over the Sangro river battlefield, and it is clear that Eighth Army fully appreciated its value.[5] Light bombers were used at this period to carry out night reconnaissance of the roads leading into the battle areas from the north.

On the Sangro No.651 Air O.P. Squadron was strenuously employed in its primary role and received from its corps headquarters a mild rebuke for over-boldness on the part of its pilots. They often used, as they had begun to use in North Africa, oblique air photographs cunningly gridded to enable 'map references' of spotted targets to be directly read from them. These were named, from their inventor, Merton photographs. Oblique-photography to produce these led quickly to its requirement for many other purposes.

The Anzio beach-head presented a considerable problem of air support. Tactical and Photographic reconnaissance had generally to be carried out from airfields in the Naples area, 150 miles away, although a small detachment of 225 Squadron was based on an advanced landing ground within the beach-head from 8th–18th February, 1944, when it came under enemy artillery fire. The Luftwaffe had airfields close to the beach-head but the Allied air forces maintained a high measure of air superiority and their reconnaissance pilots kept commanders at Anzio pretty well informed of the enemy's situation and movements.

For continuous short-range observation, however, the Anzio garrison, confined in a small area almost devoid of adequate ground observation, relied to a great extent on air O.P.s based within the beach-head. No.655 Squadron (Major D. P. D. Oldman, R. A.), which had joined 651 Squadron on the Sangro near the close of 1943, sent two flights (Captains W. G. Gordon and P. H. Henderson) to Anzio while American air O.P.s were also there. These air O.P.s of both nations were given a great opportunity, which they took, to demonstrate their value and their ability to operate in conditions far below optimum, thus confirming what 651 Squadron had demonstrated in North-West Africa. Tanks, infantry and artillery were their targets as the enemy strove to destroy the beach-head; the fire of naval as well as army guns was directed by their pilots. Here, as in the first world war and as in the Burma campaign of the present war, enemy artillery were often silenced by the mere appearance of an artillery aircraft.

Perhaps it would be of interest to illustrate briefly the procedure by which large concentrations of artillery fire could be directed against an enemy target, by means of an example from the Anzio battle.

Pilot (on his radio): Hello, Peter Six (this was his own call-sign), Mike Target, Mike Target, Mike Target (this indicated that a regiment of artillery of some 24 guns should fire.) Two hundred enemy forming up . . . (here he indicated by map-reference the position of the centre of the target) . . . Fire by order (in other words, when the pilot gave the word). Scale twelve (that is twelve rounds from each gun). Report when ready. Over.

C.R.A. 1st Division (on the same radio frequency): Big Sunray (senior gunner) here. Cancel last order Peter Six. Give him Victor Target (indicating that the whole of the Corps artillery, 172 guns including heavier natures of gun, should fire). Scale twelve. Fire by order, report when ready to Peter Six. Carry on, Peter Six, well done. Out.[6]

The Germans soon associated the air O.P.s with their difficulties. The Official History, for which the air O.P.s were usually rather junior objects, records:'. . . the great activity of American and British spotter aircraft, which were unaffected by the weather because they hopped off and on to their airstrip and flew very low, gave the Germans the impression that all their preparations were observed, and lowered morale'.[7] Whatever degree of air superiority the Allied air forces might hold in Italy, it could not prevent German low-level fighter sorties against the light aircraft from the airfields closely surrounding the bridgehead. Two British air O.P. pilots were shot down and killed; three more, with artillery and anti-tank guns closely packed in a small area, were hit by their own shells and, of these, two died. Procedures were developed to give pilots some warning of enemy fighters and to minimise the risk from their own artillery; a relatively large concentration of light anti-aircraft guns gave them considerable protection against the Luftwaffe.

For the Allied break-out from the beach-head a comprehensive artillery plan was prepared, with great secrecy, registration of targets being conducted over a long period and almost entirely by the air O.P.s. As the Germans withdrew many inviting targets presented themselves, while the first link-up with the main Allied force was achieved by a British air O.P. pilot who landed alongside American armoured cars.

The air O.P. flights did very well at Anzio, and this must assuredly include their ground parties, particularly the Royal Air Force technicians who had to work under conditions they could never have anticipated but whose efforts resulted in no single sortie needing to be refused for unserviceability nor being abandoned for engine failure.

After four years of virtual neglect, there was in Italy a great revival of the air force role of artillery reconnaissance. We can trace the first renewal of interest to the influence of Jack Parham (probably) and of the very air-minded senior artillery officer of V Corps, Brigadier Ambrose Pratt (certainly), in Tunisia early in 1943. During the preparations for the final Allied offensive there, appropriate radio sets had been provided for the artillery, pilots of Nos.40 and 225 Squadrons had carried out special training and trial shoots and 225 Squadron had done the necessary oblique photography for the earliest Merton photographs. The shoots, however had not been vastly successful, mainly because of radio failures, and, in the battle which followed, the pilots had confined themselves to reporting the activities of hostile batteries without subsequently observing fire.

No.40 Squadron (Lieutenant-Colonel W. A. Nel) appears to have been bitten by the bug of 'arty R', however, and to have set out to be masters of the art. Arrived in Sicily, their pilots observed for guns of the Royal Navy, first off the Sicilian coast and later off the 'toe' of Italy. At the Sangro battle, based now in Italy, they began to observe for the Eighth Army's medium and heavy artillery – the targets being hostile batteries. Through the winter of 1943–4 this role formed a greater and greater proportion of 40 Squadron's missions until, in April, eighty artillery missions were logged (60 per cent being pronounced successful) as compared with forty-eight tactical and eleven photographic reconnaissances.[8]

No.225 Squadron (Lieutenant-Colonel R. H. Rogers, D.F.C., S.A.A.F., from December 1943), after its spell at Salerno, was deployed in two detachments in the Naples and Foggia areas. They too had acquired an enthusiasm for the artillery role and, in the interval between Tunisia and Sicily, had done some training with artillery in North Africa. They, like 40 Squadron, seem to have opened their artillery account in Italy with the Royal Navy, directing fire against targets which included a super-heavy gun in a railway tunnel. Subsequent co-operation with the Royal Artillery increased steadily until in April 1944 the Squadron flew sixty-nine artillery missions as compared with forty-six tactical and seventeen photographic reconnaissances.[9]

No.208 Squadron (Lieutenant-Colonel J. P. D. Blaauw, D.F.C., S.A.A.F.) arrived on the scene in March 1944 and was quickly swept into the artillery whirl. In April they flew seventy artillery, fifty tactical-reconnaissance and six photographic missions.[10]

Finally, in May, No.318 Polish Squadron (Commander Wing-Commander L. Wielochowski) arrived from North Africa. In the course of the next twelve months' operations, entirely in the eastern half of Italy, this squadron probably flew more artillery missions than any other squadron, observing for British as well as for Polish artillery.[11]

The pre-war artillery air-observation system had been streamlined a little, to take account of pilots flying fast single-seater aircraft equipped with two-way speech-radio and of artillery able to shoot more accurately and consistently than in 1918. The clock-code had disappeared; instead the pilot gave corrections in yards either for 'line' or for 'range', aiming to 'bracket' the target with burst beyond and short of it. Once the centre point of an area had been registered the Uncle Target procedure, and extensions of it, enabled concentrations of medium and heavy artillery quickly to be applied to any enemy activity in the area. Sometimes, however, the pilot's task was simply to report whether hostile batteries on a given list were manned, unmanned or dummies; as a result his own artillery might decide to engage and he would notify results in general terms. Provision was sometimes made for the weaver escort pilot to be allotted a separate medium or heavy battery with which to engage enemy flak interfering with the main shoot. Pilots engaged in artillery missions, incidentally, were often a fruitful source of other important tactical information.

However streamlined this system, it was still slow, and usually unsuitable for mobile operations. It was, however, very relevant to deliberate attacks against prepared defences such as those on the many successive river lines and such as the Allied attack of May 1944 through the Gustav Line and up the Liri valley, which finally turned the Cassino position and forced the German withdrawal to the north of Rome. Nos.40, 208 and 225 Squadrons all took park, predominantly in the artillery co-operation role. Before the battle there was much photography and a large number of shoots against bridges; during the battle continuous artillery patrols were maintained over the battlefield to report on the activity or otherwise of the hostile batteries on the counter-battery lists, to observe for their engagement if necessary and to engage impromptu targets such as new hostile batteries, transport on the move and the like. The Royal Navy and the United States Navy participated, their guns being directed mostly by air force pilots.[12]

Nos.654 Air O.P. Squadron and 657 Squadron (Major J. R. Ingram, R.A.), and those pilots of 655 Squadron who were not deployed at Anzio, were also engaged in this battle, doing much of the preliminary oblique photography, maintaining continuous cover, reporting on the activity or otherwise of hostile batteries and engaging with their artillery the enemy reinforcements.

From Rome northwards the Allied air forces may be said to have achieved the air supremacy which they held in this theatre until the end of the war – of immense significance to the soldiers as they negotiated congested routes through the Appenines, and to their air O.P.s. The latter now flew at heights of seven thousand feet or more, out of range of enemy machine-guns on the high ground, using binoculars to aid observation. They were also able to fly above and sometimes beyond the leading elements of the advance, to spot at an early stage, to report and to engage with the long-range artillery the enemy strongpoints on and to the flank of the route. This was the sort of integration of air with ground reconnaissance which had been anticipated by War Office teaching as far back as 1912,[13] though nullified by the trench warfare of 1914–1918; in theory the role was a dangerous one, bold flying and air superiority made it less dangerous and there were few casualties. A liaison began to be built up with R.A.F. tactical reconnaissance pilots who sometimes indicated fruitful targets for air O.P.s to engage with their artillery. In this phase contact missions were frequent; often it was radio which achieved the contact, but Very light and Aldis lamp signals were also used.[14]

The greatest problem was to find suitable strips to enable air O.P.s to keep up with the advance. The *Auster IV*, which started to replace the *Auster III*, was an excellent aircraft, with better visibilty for the pilot and greater endurance than that of its predecessor, but could not match the latter's spectacular take-off performance.[15] The air O.P.s would have been unable to keep pace with the advance had it not been for the swift and regular support of the Royal Engineers in the preparation and improvement of airstrips.

The air force reconnaissance squadrons benefited equally from air supremacy; tactical reconnaissance and contact missions replaced artillery missions as the battle became more mobile. By now it had become common practice for tactical reconnaissance aircraft to carry cameras and for their pilots to bring back oblique photographs to confirm or supplement visual reconnaissance.

At about this stage of the Italian campaign the Royal Air Force launched an intensive 'interdiction' programme, in which continuous attacks were made against the enemy's lines of supply, deployment and reinforcement, with the object of isolating the battlefield. This attempt undoubtedly met with a fair measure of success and, without it, the German resistance would have been even more obstinate and prolonged than in the event; most air force chroniclers, however, have greatly exaggerated this while almost totally ignoring the reconnaissance role. Their army counterparts also tended to be mesmerised by the bursting bombs and the clatter of cannonfire and to overlook the inconspicuous and silent accumulation of information in which the tactical and photographic reconnaissance squadrons played so large a part.

With the interdiction role there emerged the form of mission called 'armed reconnaissance', in which fighter-bomber pilots were given a comparatively free hand to find and harass movement on the roads and railways, and to report concentrations worthy of bombing by formations of larger aircraft. This may remind one of the unproductive R.F.C. missions of 31st July, 1917,[16] but in Italy in 1944 and 1945 such missions were doubtless justified by the requirements of interdiction. In a sense they were reconnaissance, but reconnaissance for the air force bombers rather than for the army, carried out by pilots untrained in the art and rarely productive of important information. The tactical reconnaissance pilots were professionals, trained in the arts of reconnaissance; they did not seek armed clashes with enemy aircraft nor did they attack ground targets – indeed they expressly avoided combat in the cause of obtaining information and bringing it back to the Army. This was not always understood, either by Army or R.A.F. commanders.

A word must be said of Nos.682 and 683 Photographic Reconnaissance Squadrons (Squadron Leaders J. T. Morgan and H. S. Smith, respectively, at first, R. C. Buchanan and R. T. Turton later). These squadrons flew deep strategic missions, unescorted, unarmed, over Germany, Austria, Hungary and Jugoslavia, but they also maintained small detachments with Fifth and Eighth Army, for more tactical photography, and they sent a further detachment to participate in the landings in the south of France. The Fifth Army detachment of 682 Squadron took part in the Gustav Line – Liri Valley battle, providing fresh daily photographic cover of the whole enemy position. The Eighth Army detachment of 683 Squadron later photographed the German Gothic Line positions in great detail.

In their missions beyond the Italian frontiers, pilots of these squadrons met rather more enemy fighters than did the tactical reconnaissance squadrons and, in addition, they were attacked on a number of occasions by Allied fighter pilots insufficiently acquainted with the photographic reconnaissance *Spitfires*.

In the fighting in the northern half of Italy the German army tended to use their tanks, which were not very numerous, as static strongpoints, and various methods of engaging them proved unsuccessful. New methods were now tried, with air O.P.s working in pairs using the fire of large-calibre guns to frighten the tank from place to place. The sort of accuracy needed for this game was hard to achieve with long-range artillery. Attempts were also made to use air O.P.s to indicate tank targets to ground-attack aircraft; these failed by reason of the different radio frequency bands on which the two types of aircraft worked and the delays inherent in retransmission by R.A.F. 'Visual Control Posts'. When, by private enterprise, an Air O.P. squadron commander installed an American radio into his *Auster*, the R.A.F. rather absurdly considered it unwise to allow army pilots 'direct control' of R.A.F. formations.[17]

The penetration of the Gothic Line was assisted by Kesselring's misappreciation of the strength of Eighth Army's thrust on the east coast, the fruit of inadequate air reconnaissance under Allied air supremacy. In this battle for the Gothic Line, and thereafter, the counter-battery role once more became of special importance, both for air forces and air O.P. squadrons. The German artillery stopped firing when Allied aircraft were about; much ingenuity was expended by the latter in deceiving the enemy into presuming their departure, opening fire and thereby being located. Tactical and photographic reconnaissance seem to have provided Eighth Army headquarters with much early information,[18] and contact missions were also effective. Enemy mortars became rather a menace and air O.P.s were widely, though not particularly successfully, used against them;[19] like their artillery, however, the German mortars tended to silence when the air O.P.s were about.

Of the final phase, following the Senio crossing, an artilleryman has written of 'the perfection of artillery reconnaissance shoots with the R.A.F.'[20] As the tempo of the pursuit accelerated, however, the tactical reconnaissance pilots flew far ahead, calling for fighter-bomber strikes against the more congested concentrations of enemy vehicles and, in this manner, often providing the Allied headquarters with the best information of the progress of their own forward troops.

The air force reconnaissance squadrons which served in North Africa and Italy were all of high quality. Such quality is created by commanders, by pilots and – not to be forgotten – by ground crew. Though it is perhaps invidious to mention particular squadrons, when all were so good, one must nevertheless pay special tribute to No.40 Squadrons, South African Air Force, and to No.208 Squadron, Royal Air Force. From many sources of evidence it is clear that these units were exceptional and approached their roles with single-minded determination to excel. In North Africa they developed very close relationships with the fortunate army formations which received their support; their pilots lived dangerously and so, at times, did the devoted men who kept their aircraft serviceable. In Italy the change in system made army-air force relationships somewhat less intimate but the support – if fully apparent only to a diminished coterie of the Army staff – no less effective.

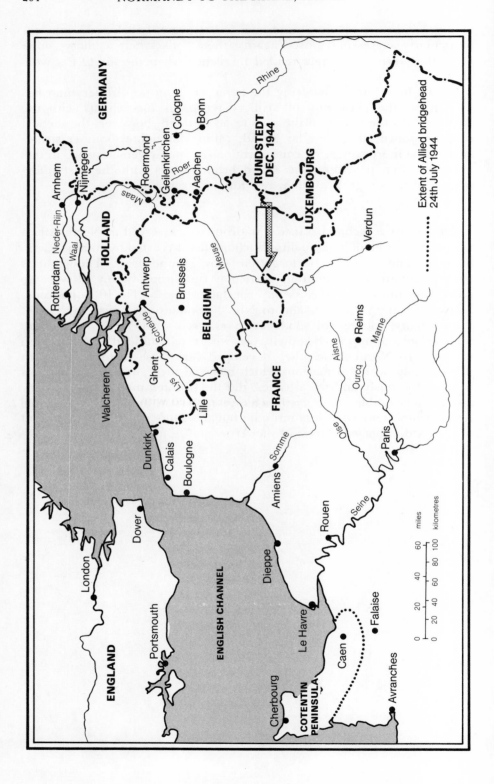

1944 to 1945
Normandy to the Elbe

——◇——

'. . . . it is doubtful if any single factor
contributed more to our success in the field than air reconnaissance.'
Air Vice-Marshal E. C. HUDLESTON, *c.* 1946

'The Air O.P. . . . . a necessary part of gunnery.'
Field-Marshal the VISCOUNT MONTGOMERY, Despatch, 1st June, 1946

On 6th June, 1944, a successful lodgement was made by British and American forces on the Cotentin Peninsula of Normandy, and was slowly expanded. By 25th July the British, on the east flank of this bridgehead, had attracted to itself the bulk of the enemy's defence and the Americans, on the west flank, began their planned break-out. Five days later they had reached Avranches at the base of the peninsula and were fanning out into Brittany. The Germans thereupon attempted an armoured attack against the left flank of the American thrust; this failed and by 18th August a considerable proportion of their force was trapped in the area of Falaise, twenty miles south of Caen, between the encircling Third United States Army to the south and the First Canadian and Second British Armies to the north. Thus confined, they were violently attacked from the air and the roads soon choked with wrecked tanks and transport. Three days later the remaining Germans were in full retreat and the Allied armies in headlong pursuit. Paris was liberated on 25th August, Brussels and Antwerp on 3rd and 4th September. The American Third Army had, by then, crossed the Meuse at Verdun. Difficulties of petrol supply now brought the advance to a halt; soon afterwards Allied forces which had landed in the south of France linked up with the right wing of Eisenhower's armies.

To maintain the advance it was decided to force the three river lines of the Maas, Waal and Lower Rhine by three airborne operations, to outflank the German Siegfried Line at its north end and perhaps trap German formations in west Holland. The farthest of these endeavours failed at Arnhem, the other two succeeded. The Canadians cleared the Scheldt estuary by 6th November and thus opened the port of Antwerp to shipping.

But the Allied momentum had been lost and it was the German Field-Marshal Rundstedt who launched the next offensive, in the Ardennes on 16th December, a dangerous onslaught which penetrated fifty miles before it was finally stopped. The Allies' advance was resumed in January 1945, with hard battles as they closed up to the river Rhine.

On the night of the 23rd, and on 24th March the crossing of the Rhine was made on a broad front with parachute and glider landings in the enemy artillery areas and, from then on, resistance was slight. The

Russians were within Berlin, the American Third Army had crossed the Czecho-Slovak frontier, the British were across the River Elbe and the Canadians had liberated northern Holland when the final German surrender took place on 4th May, 1945.

The overall air plan for the assault on the Normandy coast had the following aims:

To prevent effective interference by the Luftwaffe.

To provide continuous reconnaissance of the enemy's dispositions and moves.

To disrupt enemy communications and channels of support ('Interdiction').

To support the landing and subsequent advance.

To strike at enemy naval forces.

To provide airlift for airborne forces.[1]

The reconnaissance portion of this plan may be said to have started to operate in 1942. From then onwards, in addition to many deep reconnaissances, the air force carried out with their high-flying *Spitfires* continuous, and many times repeated, photographic reconnaissances of a strip of European coast, thirty miles wide, from Holland to the Spanish frontier; this served both to inform the military planners of developments in the defences which had, in due course, to be overcome and also to indicate targets for the Allied fighter-bombers. A discouraging number of these photographic missions failed by reason of cloud and it became necessary to supplement them with photographic missions at low-level, using tactical-reconnaissance *Mustangs*. Skilled interpreters detected the continuous changes in the enemy's situation and defences, including the appearance of artillery and other strong-points and, incidentally, the *V1* missile sites being prepared for the 1944 summer offensive against London.

An early and traumatic opportunity to test the Allies' training and operational philosophies of invasion occurred with the 2nd Canadian Division's reconnaissance-in-force at Dieppe on 19th August, 1942 – a tactical failure and very costly in casualties. Nos.35 and 36 Reconnaissance Wings had, since early in the year, been carrying-out continuous visual and low-oblique photographic reconnaissance of the coast, in general co-operation, respectively, with South-Eastern and Southern Army Commands, with an arbitrary dividing line passing thirty miles east of Dieppe. 35 Wing received forty-eight hours' warning of their participation in the operation, then planned for early July; no photographic cover existed, for the simple reason that 36 Wing had never been asked for it. A late request to 35 Wing for very low-level oblique photographs of the beaches in front of the Dieppe casino resulted in a hazardous but successful mission by Flight-Lieutenant C. D. Harris St. John.

The Dieppe operation was then cancelled, but re-mounted under conditions of extreme secrecy. Shortly before the new assault date, photographs revealed evidence of enemy emplacements built into the cliffs east of Dieppe. It was too late to act upon this unconfirmed information, which was, however, murderously confirmed during the landings. Air Marshal Sir Trafford Leigh-Mallory, the Air Force commander, hoped to attract and destroy a sizeable Luftwaffe contingent over and around Dieppe; he succeeded, though at the cost of rather greater casualties to his own forces, 35 Wing losing seven per cent of its sorties.

As D-day approached, the Army's reconnaissance requests became more and more closely related to their forthcoming areas of operation and to enemy movements in the hinterland. Many low oblique photographs were produced, to show terrain configuration, beach obstacles and defences, landing-craft approach routes and inland routes from the beaches. They were widely used by reconnaissance pilots to supplement visual reconnaissance. Intense secrecy needed to be kept regarding the selected assault area and a comprehensive deception plan suggested the Pas de Calais as the intended invasion point. The volume and nature of reconnaissance had to support that suggestion. An Allied and joint-service Combined Reconnaissance Centre co-ordinated all visual and photographic reconnaissance and a Central Reconnaissance Committee ensured that every individual mission, and the sum of such missions, conformed to the deception plan.

Equally vital to the deception plan was the concealment from enemy reconnaissance of the enormous Allied concentrations of troops, equipment and invasion craft in the south of England. One of the outstanding successes of the Allied air forces was the achievement of this concealment.

Army and Air Force were, of course, educating themselves and each other, during these years, in the capabilities and limitations of air reconnaissance and in the methods and procedures best calculated to obtain the best results. Security inhibited the planning staffs from revealing – even to their own Air Force – the problems behind the reconnaissances requested. Air Commodore Peter Donkin, who commanded 35 Wing at that time, comments on their tendency to specify too exactly the type of photograph, the height from which to be taken and so on, rather than to inform the air force of the problem and of the information needed, while leaving the airmen to set up the mission.[2] He quotes as an example an occasion where, several sets of vertical photographs from 10,000 feet having failed to satisfy, their object was revealed as the discovery of whether certain fields had been protected against glider landings by the planting of poles or other obstables; low-oblique photographic runs, when the sun was low and shadows long, thereupon provided a quick answer. In 1944, when 35 Wing, under 84 Group, started to support the First Canadian Army, Donkin found an army staff well content to pose its questions to the reconnaissance wing and to leave the latter to find the answers by the most suitable methods.

In addition to the enemy's fighters, Allied air reconnaissance missions had to contend with the more serious menace of flak, particularly intense near the coast.[3] This they avoided as far as possible by study of flak and radar maps, compiled from every source of intelligence but particularly from up-to-date air photographs and pilots' reports, by very accurate, very low-level navigation to the selected crossing-point, by constant variations of course and height and by never returning for a 'second look' at anything. When intercepted, the *Mustangs* were invariably outnumbered, but were distinctly more manoeuvrable than the German fighters and seldom outpaced at low level.

For the invasion Eisenhower was, of course, the Supreme Commander; his deputy was Tedder. The air forces under their command consisted of Coastal Command, the Allied Strategic Air Force and the Allied Expeditionary Air Force, the latter commanded by Air Chief Marshal Sir Trafford Leigh-Mallory. The latter's command was of four parts, the Air Defence of Great Britain, Airborne and Transport operations, the 2nd Tactical Air Force under Coningham and, initially, the Ninth United States Army Air Force. Coningham's force, which was to support Montgomery's Twenty-first Army Group, included Nos.83 and 84 Groups to give direct support, respectively, to the Second British and First Canadian Armies.

Both Groups contained numbers of fighter and fighter-bomber squadrons. In 83 Group (Air Marshal Harry Broadhurst) was also No.39 Reconnaissance Wing, Royal Canadian Air Force (Group Captain E. H. Moncrieff at first, G. H. Sellers from February 1945), comprising Nos.414 and 430 Tactical Reconnaissance Squadrons and 400 Photographic Reconnaissance Squadron (initially Squadron Leaders C. H. Stover and F. H. Chesters and Wing Commander R. A. Ellis respectively) and, until October, 168 Tactical Reconnaissance Squadron, R.A.F. (Squadron Leader P. W. Mason).

In 84 Group (Air Marshal L. O. Brown at first, E. C. Hudleston from December) was No.35 Reconnaissance Wing, R.A.F. (Group Captain P. L. Donkin until August 1944, A. F. Anderson thereafter), comprising Nos.2 and 268 Tactical Reconnaissance Squadrons and 4 Photographic Reconnaissance Squadron (initially Squadron Leaders M. J. Gray, A. S. Mann and C. D. Harris St. John respectively).

The photo-reconnaissance squadrons had *Spitfire XIs* and the tactical-reconnaissance squadrons *Mustangs I, IA or II*, modified to carry a camera.[4] A special 'air spotting pool' was formed of naval and air force pilots and aircraft, detached temporarily from their parent units and the pilots specially trained to observe and report the fire of naval guns in the early stage of the invasion. Air O.P. squadrons, in both 83 and 84 Groups, were tactically integrated into the artillery of the various corps, and of the Army Groups Royal Artillery (A.G.R.A.s) into which heavier artillery was concentrated. They had mostly *Auster IVs*,[5] which were gradually replaced by the very similar *Auster Vs*.

In No.2 Group of the tactical Air Force were light and medium bombers and further *Spitfire*, and also *Mosquito* and *Wellington*, photographic reconnaissance aircraft. *Mosquitos* and *Wellingtons* of two squadrons were equipped with night photographic equipment in which flare-development and film exposure were mechanically linked. This proved useful to detect German night movement but pilots had to fly comparatively low and were vulnerable to flak.

One of the main tasks of the Allied air forces, as we have seen, was the isolation of the Germans in the Normandy bridgehead from reinforcement and supplies. For this a widespread interdiction plan was made, and considerable internecine strife took place to secure the participation of Bomber Command, who had not been persuaded by four years of failure, aircraft losses and casualties that their separate war against German industry was not on the point of success.

The first reconnaissance aircraft in action on D-day were those of the air spotting pool, observing for naval guns. 160 aircraft were so involved on this day and the role continued on a lesser scale for many weeks.[6] Visual and photographic reconnaissance took place over and beyond the bridgehead, interpretation of the latter taking place at Odiham, in Hampshire, England, and the results wirelessed to Second Army in the bridgehead. This worked surprisingly well.

Air O.P. units mostly got their reconnaissance parties ashore on 7th June; they had provisionally selected landing fields from air photographs but some were still under hostile artillery fire. On 8th June the first aircraft of Nos.652 and 662 Squadrons, supporting I and XXX Corps respectively, flew over the Channel, landed in the bridgehead and were at once in action.[7] They were followed successively, during the next three weeks, by 653, 659 and 658, and later by 660 and 661 Squadrons.

The enemy's reaction to the air O.P.s was sharp, particularly on the east side of the bridgehead, and it was necessary at first to fly low and tactically, in the manner Bazeley had conceived, and to carry rear-observers to give warning of imminent attack. When cloud-cover was suitable, however, sorties sometimes took place at three or four thousand feet, penetrating a little over enemy-held territory. Various early-warning systems were used to help the pilots and observers, some based on forward artillery observation posts, others on the light anti-aircraft artillery system. In spite of every precaution, however, air O.P.s were shot down both by enemy fighters and by ground fire.

No.652 Squadron (Major R. R. Cobley) had made itself expert, within the air O.P. fraternity, in air photography and set up a makeshift processing-station in the bridgehead. By 12th June the whole of the I Corps front had been photographed. From then onwards the local demand for low-level oblique and vertical photographs increased steadily and was met more and more by the air O.P.s, whose organisation was in due course adjusted to provide a photographic flight in each squadron.

The air O.P.s were used extensively in the counter-battery role, either actively engaging the enemy's field artillery or keeping it quiet by their mere presence. They gleaned much general reconnaissance information in the process. As an example of air O.P. activity may be mentioned the fifty-seven sorties flown by 652 Squadron on 23rd June, in support of an attack by 51st Highland Division. Twenty hostile batteries were located and engaged, seven by one pilot in one sortie. By afternoon all enemy artillery fire had died away. Some thirty enemy fighters attempted interception, four being shot down by our light anti-aircraft guns. One *Auster* was shot down and its observer wounded, another made a forced landing after hitting a tree while evading a fighter attack.

As more and more Allied artillery squeezed into the bridgehead, without much enlargement of the latter, it became difficult to choose air O.P. 'fly lines' clear of the trajectories of their own guns. On the other hand the pilots had the disposal of an immense weight of gunfire. An occasion is recorded when Major A. Lyell, commander of 658 Squadron and supporting 8th A.G.R.A., used the artillery of three corps with supporting medium and heavy artillery – between five and six hundred guns in all – to engage forty enemy tanks in cover.[8]

The success of the Allied invasion clearly demanded air superiority over the bridgehead from the very beginning. The confidence of the air forces that this could be achieved, in spite of the initial barrier of English Channel between air bases and armies, was entirely justified by events. Air superiority in such conditions, however, could not be absolute. As over the Anzio beach-head in Italy, so over Normandy the Luftwaffe was able, regularly if not too frequently, to intercept both high-flying photo-reconnaissance and lower-flying tactical-reconnaissance missions and to encourage escorts (if only a single 'No.2' aircraft) to be provided for the latter. The German flak always commanded respect and reconnaissance casualties were at times as high as seven per cent of sorties, threatening early in July (though not actually achieving) a suspension of tactical reconnaissance except for special tasks.[9] The Official History mentions, too, in connection with Second Army's offensive of 18th July, that the Germans 'had sufficient air reconnaissance to detect any unusual activity'[10] and, as we have seen, their fighters made periodic appearances over the bridgehead to attack the air O.P.s.

It must be recorded therefore that, for the third time, the air O.P.s proved that they were able to operate under conditions well short of air supremacy. They adjusted their flying to the conditions and received good support from their anti-aircraft guns; their operations were not often frustrated and were undeniably effective. The German 10th S.S. Panzer Division published at the end of July a document 'Lessons of the Normandy campaign' which, after recording the damage to the German supply system from Allied low-flying fighter-bomber and rocket attacks, continues: 'The biggest nuisance, though, are the slow-flying spotter-planes which in utter calmness fly over our positions and direct fire, while our infantry weapons cannot reach them'.[11]

Tactical and photographic reconnaissance were, of course, continuous, some fourteen thousand and five thousand sorties, respectively, being flown between 6th June and 30th September.[12] Close liaison between air reconnaissance and army formations was not at first possible, with the former based in England and tasked through a joint-service headquarters at Uxbridge. Tactical reconnaissance areas were delineated, some fifty miles in front of the forward troops and some seventy-five miles wide, where, failing specific requests, search was made for enemy movement of all kinds. Because of the Allied interdiction programme information was often negative, and it is doubtful whether many soldiers understood the individual risks these pilots took. The following unexceptional extract from 35 Wing's 'News Sheet No.37' of 11th June, 1944, describes a typical mission of the preceding day, the squadron being still based in England:

At about 19.30 a special demand came from T.A.F. for a reconnaissance of the road leading from the south to Le Mans and of the two roads leading from that city to Laval and Alençon. Large columns of heavy M.T. and armoured cars were reported to be approaching Le Mans and it was of the utmost importance that the direction of their advance after leaving Le Mans should be determined. A penetration of such depth was only just within the range of a *Mustang* and the hours of daylight that remained were few. Flying Officer Hope, with Flight Lieutenant Gent as No.2, took-off at 20.26 hours. The Section was instructed that if there was any doubt of their being able to get back to base, they were to land on the strip at Cabourg and refuel, if necessary staying the night.

Shortly after taking off No.2 was forced to return owing to engine trouble. Flying Officer Hope, realising the importance of the mission, went on alone. He crossed the coast at Trouville and set course for Le Mans, but had to sheer off a little to avoid some *Thunderbolts*. Inland he ran into variable weather, alternating patches of clear sky and low cloud.

He reached Le Mans without incident, reconnoitred the road leading up from the south and then following the Le Mans – Laval road where he saw some tanks. Not far away he saw some *Typhoons* doing a dive-bombing attack and shortly afterwards two *M.E.109s* with yellow noses and black and white striped wings coming in on his beam. He went into cloud for three minutes but on emerging saw more of the same Huns so he set out for home. On the way back he saw Argentan and Lisieux burning. When over the Channel, as dusk was falling, he called up for a homing . . . .[13]

As procedures and communications developed, R.A.F. 'visual control posts' or 'contact cars' on the ground provided a means of communication between the army's forward formations and the tactical reconnaissance pilots, in addition to their better-known use for directing air-to-ground attack. Reconnaissance missions could thus be briefed or rebriefed by radio as they came over, and debriefed on the way home.

Such missions were termed 'contact reconnaissance'; they had, of course, a somewhat different object from the standard contact sorties of the Great War. The VIII Corps account of operations in the bridgehead mentions particularly the early information, from air reconnaissance on 29th June and again on 31st July, of enemy movement towards their front as the Corps's attacks developed.[14]

High-level photographic reconnaissance of river-lines, airfields, coastal areas and railway marshalling yards tended to anticipate future operations. Success was very dependant on the weather. On a good day, 6th July, 35 Wing flew sixty-three photographic missions and produced 28,000 negatives.[15] On a less suitable day, 4th August, 39 Wing needed to fly photographic missions under low cloud, at the dangerous height of 9,000 instead of the customary 30,000 feet – to produce comprehensive cover over the Second Army front, which proved very valuable.[16]

The bridgehead did not expand as quickly as had been planned. Although an advanced landing ground was in operation from 10th June and was in fairly regular use, and although Nos.168 and 430 Reconnaissance Squadrons were based within the bridgehead from 29th June, numbers built up slowly. During this period of build-up, demands for, and control of, reconnaissance were only gradually transferred from the Uxbridge headquarters to the Army and Group headquarters in France; 83 Group and 39 Wing were based in the bridgehead, and in full control, by the middle of July, 84 Group and 35 Wing about a month later.

The trapping and destruction of much German armour in the Falaise pocket represented a formidable success for the Allied fighter-bombers and equally for the tactical reconnaissance pilots. In the stress of hurried advance and pell-mell retreat, German army formations were not always able, as they had earlier contrived, to restrict movement to the hours of darkness. 39 Wing gave early information of German movements against the left wing of the American advance on 6th August, as early as 12th August signs were detected of withdrawals to the east and throughout the next seven days tactical reconnaissance missions of both 35 and 39 Wings gave timely locations of an average of three thousand hostile vehicles a day. Later, as premature reports of the closing of the gap began to come in from army sources, the cameras of the tactical reconnaissance pilots were called upon for confirmation. This proved difficult and, before the matter was resolved, important German armour had slipped out of the trap.

For the Canadians' final advance to Falaise a photographic mosaic of their entire Army front was requested. Two 4 Squadron *Spitfires* were used for this and six thousand prints produced at Odiham. Thence they were flown to Gosport and from there, due to bad weather, travelled by motor torpedo-boat, arriving at Canadian Army headquarters within twenty-four hours of the demand. Deeper reconnaissance, meanwhile, gave evidence of German withdrawals over the Seine and of the condition of bridges, enabling maps to be made of potential Allied crossing points.

Those air O.P.s in a position to bring fire to bear on targets in the pocket or on the escape routes had an active time. 653 Squadron (Major G. P. Pollitt) was supporting XII Corps as it pressed in upon the withdrawing Germans and had a particularly full day on 18th August, one pilot flying for six hours forty minutes and controlling twelve shoots on tanks and other vehicles, five of them with a complete divisional artillery.[17]

There followed an intensely mobile phase in which Air O.P. reconnaissance parties sometimes tangled with retreating Germans. This was especially true of 662 Squadron (Major G. A. Hill), supporting XXX Corps, one of whose flights was on 3rd September first onto Brussels Civil Airport, only to find it ringed by German flak. Another flight had a battle west of Antwerp and captured twenty-four prisoners. The Guards Armoured Division took its Air O.P. flight, behind its tanks, from Brussels to Nijmegen, the aircraft derigged and carried on lorries. At this time the need of army formation commanders for communication aircraft became apparent and, since no adequate provision had been made, they began to 'misuse' their air O.P.s, thus depriving their artillery of observation.[18]

Between 3rd and 8th September, as is clear both from army war diaries and R.A.F. operational record books, 83 Group, including its tactical reconnaissance, was lagging seriously behind Second Army's pursuit.[19] The main cause of this lag was, probably, delay in the forward delivery of aviation fuel, this due perhaps to insufficient priority being allotted in planning. The long-range *Mustangs* should have given the tactical reconnaissance squadrons some advantage but, by an even worse priority decision, they had already started to lose these attractive aircraft to Bomber Command and to receive less suitable *Spitfires IX* and *XIV* and *Typhoons*.

The British failure at Arnhem was due to several causes, one of which was the presence in the area, re-equipping, of 9th and 10th S.S. Panzer Divisions. Their presence was known to the airborne formations[20] but their battle-effectiveness was undervalued. During this operation the air O.P.s with XXX Corps, moving up the Eindhoven-Nijmegen road, flew dangerously along a corridor never very wide and for a time cut by the enemy. Three *Austers* of 658 Squadron were forced or shot down by enemy fire, within thirty minutes, beside a short stretch of this road. A fourth *Auster*, with Jack Parham as passenger, got through to Nijmegen.

The First Canadian Army needed to reduce the Channel ports of Le Havre, Boulogne and Calais by siege operations, Dunkirk being deferred until later. Air O.P.s were involved in all three operations, as were 35 Wing's reconnaissance squadrons. Photography of the port defences was no doubt the most important air force role but a number of artillery missions also took place. Air O.P.s located a large number of hostile batteries in these operations but perhaps the most notable air O.P. occasions were the shoots by 660 Squadron (Major F. N. Lane) against Cap Gris Nez batteries, using the long-range 14-inch and 15-inch guns at Dover.

Both air O.P.s and the R.A.F. reconnaissance squadrons were involved in siege operations of a different kind north of the Scheldt estuary, where an unusual but vital task was to produce daily flood reports.[21]

In the First World War the Germans had often been lucky, so it had seemed, with fog. So was von Rundstedt as he prepared for his offensive of December 1944, mostly immune from Allied air observation. As the battle proceeded, however, the weather cleared and both American and British air O.P.s made good shooting against tanks, headquarters, vehicles and guns, confined in the hilly country to roads or areas adjoining them. Tactical reconnaissance by 39 Wing was more intensive than during the bridgehead fighting and a squadron was detached for a short period from its Wing airfield. Air photography dispelled rumours of a coming extension northwards of the German offensive.

On New Year's Day, 1945, the Luftwaffe appeared in strength in a well-planned attack on Allied airfields. Considerable damage was inflicted; 35 Wing, however, escaped lightly, some aircraft being in the air and others (owing to the unwonted appearance of a few German aircraft on the previous evening) comprehensively dispersed and concealed. 39 Wing had some fifteen personnel casualties and nine aircraft destroyed on the ground.

Among the battles fought as the Allies closed on the river Rhine may be mentioned XII Corps's January offensive in the Roermond – Geilenkirchen area and the February battle of the II (Canadian) and XXX Corps for the Reichwald forest. No.653 Air O.P. Squadron receives a favourable mention in the Official History for their performance in the former battle: 'Artillery fire had been most effective throughout, the forward observation officers being greatly helped by air observation planes, which were able to fly in weather that denied the area to other aircraft for most of the day.'[22]

Before and during the Reichwald battle the squadrons of 35 and 39 Reconnaissance Wings seem to have produced particularly valuable results, whenever weather permitted. 35 Wing kept track of German movements to the north-west and north and, later, located by photography their rearward positions and observed their preparations for withdrawal. A similar service was provided by 39 Wing to the south and south-east. There was the usual amount of 'armed reconnaissance' and it is interesting to find, in the report of the battle by the new A.O.C. 84 Group, the comment that 'tasks for armed reconnaissance should be defined clearly, to avoid missions "swanning" around the flak areas.'[23]

In this battle Major Hill of 662 Air O.P. Squadron had no less than eleven flights under his command. Landing grounds were hard to find in waterlogged country, one flight operating for a few days from a field just over a mile from an enemy position. Fly-lines were also hard to find. In spite of these difficulties, however, this was a particularly active period for air O.P.s, with many registration and neutralisation shoots and concentrations of the fire of divisional and corps artilleries onto important targets. Arrangements were also made for air O.P.s to call up R.A.F. rocket-firing *Typhoons* through a radio set at the R.A.F.'s control room. Aided by the almost complete absence of the Luftwaffe and by effective early warning of its few appearances, pilots were now flying as high as 4,000 feet and using binoculars for observation. It was recorded, however, that observation of enemy movement was not very successful under these conditions.[24]

A few air force 'artillery co-operation' missions took place during the Reichwald battle, with unspectacular results.[25] They had previously taken place in the Normandy bridgehead and during the siege-operations on the Channel coast and in Holland. Only in Italy, however, during the Second World War, can air force observation of artillery fire be said to have paid big dividends. There many deliberate operations were mounted against deep fortified positions behind river lines. The Allies brought up their heavy artillery and, with its longer range, it required air observation from aircraft of a type which could regularly penetrate enemy air space. In these conditions, although radio-telephony had speeded up the procedures, the tempo of artillery shoots was still slow; this did not matter unduly in such static operations and the frequency of the shoots ensured that a body of trained and experienced pilots existed. This in turn ensured that a large proportion of shoots were successful. In more mobile conditions a slow tempo was less acceptable; the air force pilots, with many quite different types of mission to perform, could not easily maintain their skills of artillery observation; it was found moreover that the air O.P. pilots, in the favourable air situation which pertained in 1945, could cover most zones with their observation.

The pilots of Nos. 4 and 400 Photographic Reconnaissance Squadrons made perhaps the major air contribution to the Allied crossing of the Rhine by the production and continual renewal of comprehensive cover of the river and the territory to its east and north-east.[26] From a carefully interpreted series of photographs a great array of targets was set up for the Allied artillery, including a large number, but unfortunately not all, of those German flak batteries in position to engage the aeroplanes and gliders of the airborne troops.

During the week before the crossing the remaining squadrons of 35 and 39 Wings covered the same areas with regular tactical reconnaissance. Both wings, in addition, flew missions at extreme low level to obtain oblique photographic cover of both banks of the river; these involved modification of the standard camera-fits and intense flying hazards both from flak and ground obstructions.

At first light on the morning of 23rd March photographs were taken of that portion of the battle area which was of particular interest to the airborne troops. These were printed, interpreted and, with reports, flown to England for the briefing of the airborne troops that same evening – at which each platoon commander was thus provided with an air photograph of his objective, only twenty-four hours stale.

A thousand British guns of all calibres took part in the fire programme of 24th March and air O.Ps were at some risk from it; four were hit and the crews of three of them were killed. Air O.P., R.A.F. and R.C.A.F. pilots directed artillery fire upon enemy flak and other batteries. The air forces (84 Group reinforcing 83 Group) flew many tactical and photographic missions; smoke, widely used to conceal Allied movement before and during the crossing, unfortunately served also to conceal the enemy from Allied ground and air observation. By the evening, however, concentrations of artillery fire were being brought down by ground and air O.P.s to assist their infantry to enlarge, and burst forth from, their bridgeheads over the river.

The final pursuit then began. The 39 Wing squadrons flew boldly, sometimes well ahead of the ground pursuit. Requests for close reconnaissance in front of the leading troops were also frequent, however, and, as the tempo increased, contact cars began once again to act as the communication link between forward troops and tactical reconnaissance pilots. The air O.P.s had varied roles – their own brand of contact sortie to keep track of the leading armour, route and bridge reconnaissance, photography of enemy positions, 'air O.P. cover' to keep enemy artillery quiet during bridging operations and, towards Bremen and Wilhelmshaven, rather more artillery shoots.

Once the headquarters of 83 and 84 Groups were fully established on the Continent, in operational control of their respective wings, air reconnaissance was requested, planned and executed in accordance with a clear-cut preconceived procedure. This continued the process of centralisation which had begun in the Italian theatre in 1943 and early 1944 but which, because of local factors, had not there been brought to its logical conclusion; now, in north-west Europe, air force reconnaissance became centralised at the level of the two army headquarters and those of their supporting air force groups. Much of its planning took place at daily evening meetings between the two services, at which the Reconnaissance Wing representative played – according to the situation – a greater or lesser part. Subsequent modifications to reconnaissance plans were often necessary, as the intelligence acquired from reconnaissance and other sources was interpreted, sifted and compared, or in response to urgent calls from the junior army formations. Army air staffs, air liaison officers, reconnaissance wing headquarters and contact cars combined to meet the new requirements and to ensure that the 'Group Control Centre', the tactical headquarters of each group, was fully informed and able to tailor the overall air operations to the overall situation.

The First Canadian Army were confirmed believers in air reconnaissance. In September 1944 their headquarters published a review of the Army's use of air reconnaissance since the arrival of 84 Group's headquarters in the bridgehead.[27] The review stated in its first paragraph: 'Tactical reconnaissance has been one of the most productive and authoritative sources of information for the First Canadian Army throughout the campaign to date. On days when tactical reconnaissances and photographic reconnaissances could not be made it has been difficult to get a clear idea of the enemy picture.' This statement it illustrated with examples from the bridgehead phase, the battle of the Falaise gap, the German withdrawal across the Seine, the pursuit which followed, the reduction of the coastal fortresses and fighting on the Scheldt estuary. It emphasised the value of reconnaissance by pilots trained in the art, paid tribute to the accuracy and restraint of the tactical-reconnaissance pilots and discounted the value of 'armed-reconnaissance' as a source of intelligence.

The review went on: 'The present arrangements for Air Reconnaissance are working to the complete satisfaction of the First Canadian Army. We feel that we are getting all the information that can be reasonably expected from this source'.

And it finally recorded the Army's opposition to any change in the type and scope of air reconnaissance.

It seems possible that this review was partly inspired by the news that Coningham proposed to replace Air Marshal Brown as commander of 84 Group. The close association of Montgomery and Coningham in the desert had not survived the centralisation of R.A.F. support in the ensuing years and a revival of air force chauvinism. The relationship of an air force Group to the Army it supported was not regarded in contemporary R.A.F. opinion as analogous to that of a Corps or Division of that Army, but the idea of equal partnership was widely ventilated. Brown was considered too subservient to the Canadian Army and too reluctant to modify the latter's demands; these suggestions are outside the purview of this book since the conduct of reconnaissance was not under criticism. Donkin, who commanded 35 Wing up to August 1944, and Anderson, his successor, have both expressed the belief that the job of a reconnaissance pilot was basically 'to obtain information and get it to the people who could make use of it;[28] this basic principle may have seemed vulnerable to the Canadian Army when Brown's methods were under fire. Under Hudleston, however, the highly successful reconnaissance arrangements continued unchanged. At the end of the war Army, Group and Wing combined to produce a publication, *Air Recce*,[29] in which they outlined their reconnaissance achievements and the system which governed them.

No doubt the quality of the reconnaissance conducted by the very experienced and professional squadrons of 35 Wing was very high. Air Chief Marshal Sir Theodore McEvoy, who was Senior Air Staff Officer of 84 Group, gives credit also to the Wing Commander, Operations, of the Group, none other than Lewis Burnand, the former Commander of 208 Squadron in the Western Desert, who, writes McEvoy, 'made sure that reconnaissance was efficient and that it was used efficiently.'[2] The Canadian tactical reconnaissance squadrons of 39 Wing were initially inexperienced, as compared with the squadrons of 35 Wing, with their leavening of experience from North Africa and Italy. Before D-day the Canadian reconnaissance pilots were widely employed in low-level attacks on road and rail transport in France. From D-day, however, they concentrated on the reconnaissance role and there is no evidence that inexperience remained a valid factor during the 1944 and 1945 campaigns or that the Canadian reconnaissance pilots did not operate with the same competence and courage as their counterparts in 35 Wing. A high aircraft serviceability rate, maintained in the difficult conditions of the Normandy bridgehead, is proof of the Wing's morale and efficiency.

One cannot feel, however, that the understanding of air reconnaissance and the importance attached to it by First Canadian Army and 84 Group were matched in the corridors of Second Army and 83 Group. In 84 Group's intelligence bulletins[30] first place was normally and logically given to the activities of 35 Reconnaissance Wing; in corresponding 83 Group documents little mention can be found of 39 Reconnaissance Wing except where its pilots left the strict paths of tactical reconnaissance to shoot down an enemy fighter or to attack a railway train. Second Army's intelligence summaries devoted little space to tactical reconnaissance while quantifying, under 'smokers', 'flamers', and so on, the claims of armed reconnaissance pilots' attacks on vehicles.[31] In the volumes of the history of the Royal Canadian Air Force, *The Fifth Year* and *The Sixth Year* respectively, it is mentioned that there were repeated expressions of appreciation by the Army, and a few messages from certain divisional and corps headquarters can be found in the Public Record offices and elsewhere. A brief and rather formal message was sent by General Dempsey, commander of Second Army, at the close of hostilities.[32] There hardly seems to have been in Second Army headquarters, however, the enthusiasm for, or belief in, reconnaissance that was so conspicuous in First Canadian Army. There could be several explanations of this, from the anonymity of items of intelligence as they became mingled with other such items from other sources, to the strains of mobile operations which left little time for intelligence staffs to observe, detach and report reconnaissance achievements of special significance. It is to be feared that in Second Army and 83 Group headquarters air reconnaissance came to be regarded as a routine affair which could safely be left to the joint staffs, while high-level interest was centred on the fighter-bombers.

For a possible explanation of these different attitudes towards air reconnaissance we might perhaps look to the airmen at the top. Air Marshal Brown, who set the 84 Group reconnaissance standard, had been a soldier, had served in the old Army Co-operation organisation and – in the difficult 1941 days in the Western Desert – he had co-ordinated tactical reconnaissance both on the headquarters of the G.O.C. Cyrenaica and later, commanding the air force during the withdrawal. He took the attitude simply that 84 Group existed to support the Canadian Army and he would naturally have understood and placed first the soldier's inherent need for information. Air Marshal Broadhurst had grown up with the young R.A.F. as it fiercely guarded its indepen-dence; he had been a Fighter squadron commander, was imbued with the spirit of the offensive and determined, no doubt, that it should animate the operations of his Group wherein, in consequence, the aggressive roles had priority. Second Army was, perhaps, swept along with his views, or else they preferred to fall in with them rather than to risk internal and unprofitable disputes.

Another possible explanation stems from the undoubted fact that the greatest devotion to reconnaissance is found amongst those who have been in direst need of it in battle. In the vast spaces of the Western Desert, in 1941 and 1942, the successes and failures of air reconnaissance were in many soldiers' minds; in north-west Europe, two years later, as the British Second Army rolled forward in superior numbers and under their formidable air umbrella, the soldiers' lives were less gravely affected by variations in reconnaissance results. Perhaps they took things for granted? Canadian soldiers, however, had undergone, in the Dieppe raid of August 1942, an unpleasant experience in encountering enemy defences and resistance of unexpected strength. For this reason, perhaps, they were, in their next and final campaign of the war, best qualified to recognise, and very ready to acclaim, the results achieved for them by air reconnaissance.

What have we Learned?

'Yesterday this Day's Madness did prepare;
To-morrow's Silence, Triumph, or Despair.'
Edward Fitzgerald: *Rubaiyat of Omar Khayyam*, LXXIV

1945 is the point at which this history must close, far enough back to avoid the distorting lenses of so-called peace, of terrorism, of economics and politics, of the services' struggle for survival, of sectional interests within the services – must close, above all, in the realistic environment of major war. From 1945 we may look back briefly through our 150 years of air observation and reconnaissance for armies, to see what we have learned and to remember those who taught us.

'What is the enemy doing? Where exactly is he? Where exactly are my people?'

These three questions have animated all military observation and reconnaissance from the beginning of warfare. They have preceded all other military considerations because, no matter how large the caveman's club, how true the bowman's arrow, how sharp the cavalry sabre, how deadly the rifle and gun, how overwhelming the tank, only reliable and regular information enabled the weapons of victory to be profitably deployed. 'The side that has the greater amount of information about the other generally wins.'[1]

Within the period covered by this history the human eye was the most effective means of observation. To the eyes of spies were added the eyes of soldiers ranging deep and wide on horseback and of other men concealed on hills. As men learnt how to rise into the air the implications on military observation were quickly understood by the aeronauts and aviators, often less quickly by the earthbound soldiers.

First came the spherical balloon, France's perils of the Revolutionary Wars hustling it into military service close on the heels of its first ascents. Jean-Marie-Joseph Coutelle, chemist, aeronaut and only by force of circumstances soldier, we must name the great pioneer of air observation; he recognised not only the tactical uses of the balloon and the need for effective communications but also the need for an efficient ground-servicing organisation. John Money was the first British pioneer. An aeronaut as early as 1785, he saw clearly the military need for the observation balloon, was exasperated by the lack of response from soldiers and statesmen and never ceased to belabour them. George Edward Grover assumed his mantle after the War of American Independence and by his persistence at least kept the idea alive. It was left to the stern and forceful James Lethbridge Templer finally to achieve the British military balloon and to guide it into service.

The South African War confirmed the military need for air observation; the same war established the particular artillery need for observation posts, both on the ground and in the air. The spherical balloon's instability, however, impaired its efficiency as an observation platform except in calm weather. The Cody kites were soon able to replace balloons in high winds but neither spherical balloon nor kite was to prove a military answer, which was found in the Continental development of the kite-balloon. British attention in this direction was diverted by the apparent attractions of the 'dirigible balloon' or airship, with its promise of reconnaissance deep over enemy territory. Airship development was slow, however, and as a means of army reconnaissance was soon overtaken by the aeroplane.

The British pioneers of aeroplane reconnaissance were the artillery officers, Lancelot Gibbs, John Duncan Bertie Fulton and Bertram Dickson. In their own primitive aircraft they took part in the 1910 army manoeuvres, establishing a precedent which, in 1912, suddenly convinced an uneasy British Army of the discomfort of being observed by hostile aeroplane pilots and, by deduction, of the uses of their own air reconnaissance. The formation of the Royal Flying Corps and its development into an army-controlled organisation ensured that air factors would receive proper attention when the army went to war.

The first mobile weeks of the First-World War saw a triumph for the Royal Flying Corps. Before and after the battle of Mons, and after Le Cateau, the closest air watch was kept on the movements of von Kluck's First German Army and information of the greatest value was placed in the hands of the British Commander. Von Kluck's moves south and then south-east were faithfully reported to the British and French. Pre-war training had paid dividends, and particularly the R.F.C.'s understanding that air observation was not a natural human skill but one only to be mastered by constant practice.

On the Western Front a three-year siege set in. Specialised forms of air reconnaissance predominated – artillery observation, air photography and the 'contact' role ('Where exactly are my people?'). The pre-war work of men such as C. J. Aston and H. P. T. Lefroy, of the Royal Engineers, and the exertions and clear thinking of Donald Lewis and Baron James, of the Royal Flying Corps in France in 1914 and 1915, culminated in the provision of a tolerable wireless transmitter for the artillery aeroplane, together with the 'clock-code' system for reporting fall of shot – in time for the big artillery battles of 1916 and 1917. Kite-balloons were also provided for artillery observation, with telephone communication to the guns. A distinction was already appearing between an aircraft like a kite-balloon, which merely gave extra height to an observer, and air reconnaissance which took the observer a greater or lesser distance over enemy territory.

Although the R.F.C.'s artillery role was dominant on the Western

Front, tactical and strategical reconnaissance perpetually took place to view the enemy's preparations and help to gauge his intentions. Elsewhere, particularly over the deserts of Mesopotamia, tactical reconnaissance was the major role. Air photography was an invaluable confirmation and extension of the airborne eye which was used to a steadily increasing extent. Contact missions were, in the fog of artillery-battles on the Western Front, essential to commanders; the problem of communication between the infantry and tank soldier and the pilot was, however, never adequately solved.

These 'working aircraft', as they were sometimes called, usually needed protection, which led to fighter aircraft and to combats sought with enemy air formations to establish and maintain air superiority. This role was very satisfying to the spirited young pilots of the R.F.C. and to Trenchard, their leader and mentor, and it was far more interesting to the general public than were the various natures of air reconnaissance.

Other forms of aggressive air warfare, such as bombing and ground-strafing grew in frequency, in the importance with which they were regarded inside and outside the flying corps and in the resources devoted to them. In the closing stages of the campaigns in Palestine and Italy, during the pursuit of beaten enemy, these roles achieved decisive effect; otherwise they rarely stampeded seasoned troops.

The decision to form the independent Royal Air Force in 1918 was not based on military considerations. Fortunately the Great War ended before this decision had had time to divide the loyalties of the squadrons between the army formations and their new service. Fortunately, too, the independent Royal Air Force proved in due course the ideal means of forming and training the fighter force which won the 1940 Battle of Britain, and of fighting battles for air superiority which alone gave their armies tactical freedom of action and the ability to use air reconnaissance. Less fortunately, on the other hand, it became obvious to Trenchard and to the Royal Air Force that their successful resistance to the efforts of the other services to win back their air arms depended largely on the pursuit of the philosophy of strategic bombing – the main and quite unjustified assumption in the 1917 'case' for an independent air force. This in turn relegated to comparative obscurity the air roles in support of Royal Navy and Army, mainly reconnaissance of one kind or another. Although the British Army, at the higher levels, did its best (though in vain) to recover its air arm, it cannot be said that enough was done, at the lower levels, to achieve that continuous and close contact between demanding and providing services which alone could have made air reconnaissance and observation effective. The impact of the fast monoplane fighter came too late for adequate tactical reconnaissance to be ready, on either side, for the 1940 battles.

Although in the siege conditions of the Western Front the R.F.C.'s artillery role had been paramount, neither artillery nor flying corps believed themselves to have solved the problem of controlling artillery

fire from an aeroplane in a mobile battle, nor was it supposed that a
kite-balloon would be able to operate in such conditions. Virtually
nothing was done, between 1918 and 1939, to correct this. It was left to
Captain Charles Bazeley and other members of the Royal Artillery
Flying Club to propound the simple and audacious 'Air O.P.' solution,
combining the most primitive and slowest of aircraft with two-way
radio-telephony and with a philosophy of low flying designed to confound
enemy fighters by means other than speed and power. This fitted
nowhere into the R.A.F.'s philosophy but, fortunately, there were, then
and later, senior army officers – the future Lord Alanbrooke in particular
– with the inspiration to support the unlikely air O.P. idea and with the
military weight to prevent its suppression.

War straightened things out. In the unambiguous conditions of the
Western Desert it was quickly understood that single-seater fighter
aircraft were essential to the reconnaissance role. By the end of 1942, by
perseverance, by trial and error, but above all by the loyal and gallant
support of the army formations by the air force squadrons allotted to
them, air reconnaissance had reached a high standard and effective
methods and procedures had been devised for initiating it and for
profiting quickly from its results. Air Marshals Tedder and Coningham
must, of course, receive high credit for preserving inter-service relationships, often in difficult conditions, and thus for allowing air reconnaissance to develop as it did. The men, however, whose leadership, sense
of co-operation and ingenuity did most to advance the new science of
tactical reconnaissance during these years were the squadron commanders, particularly Wing Commander L. C. Burnand, of 208 Squadron, R.A.F. and Lieutenant-Colonel E. Biden of 40 Squadron, S.A.A.F.

In Italy this pattern continued but here, due to the successive river
lines upon which the Germans based their lines of resistance something
like siege warfare developed. With it returned the air force's artillery
observation role, streamlined since 1940 and now carried out unaided
by the pilots of single-seater fighter-type aircraft. In these particular
circumstances the role was most successful. Photographic reconnaissance
developed in two directions, very high vertical photography of large
areas for photographic interpreters to convert into detailed intelligence
of enemy defences, weapons, vehicles and numbers, and low-level,
oblique photographs to confirm and extend visual reconnaissance by
tactical-reconnaissance pilots. Air reconnaissance began to be centralised
and controlled at Wing or even Group, instead of Squadron, headquarters; this became the final pattern in the 1944–45 operations in
North-west Europe.

Meanwhile the long struggle for the artillery air O.P.s had ended
when the first Air O.P. squadron went into action in Tunisia at the end
of 1942. These squadrons were an ideal compromise – artillery pilots
and signallers with R.A.F. ground-crew, organised into R.A.F. units
for general and technical supervision but under the operational control
of artillery commanders. From the hostile air conditions of Tunisia in

1943 the air O.P.s moved to conditions of increasing air superiority in Italy, although in the Anzio beachhead they had to prove themselves in a confined area under frequent local air attacks. In Italy, the Far East and north-west Europe the air O.P.s were everywhere successful; they had become in words used by Field-Marshal Montgomery, 'a necessary part of gunnery'.

With a combination of fast and very slow aircraft, supported by radio-telephony, specially designed cameras and suitable ground-servicing organisations, the British and most other armies of the West had advanced air observation about as far as Coutelle could have foreseen in 1794. He would have looked askance, perhaps, at the large communication gap between the front-line troops and the tactical reconnaissance pilots, imposed by the necessity for the long-semi-permanent airstrips needed by the fast aeroplanes. Jourdan, Coutelle's General, though he thought little of the balloons, would have been outraged at the idea of observation or reconnaissance for his army being entrusted to a separate service not fully responsible to himself; and indeed the idea is, basically, militarily, outrageous. Both Coutelle and Jourdan would have to admit, however, that development in air observation had more than kept pace with the advance from the captive spherical balloon to the 400 m.p.h. aeroplane.

One of the most encouraging features of this development has been the part played in it by comparatively young men – Coutelle himself, the successive British aeronauts who hammered away at a reluctant War Office until Templer was finally allotted the first British military balloon, the triumvirate of Gunner officers who flew their own aeroplanes in the 1910 Army manoeuvres, Major Frederick Sykes and the R.F.C. squadron commanders who so ably trained their pilots in 1914 and those other R.F.C. pilots who so rapidly developed the artillery procedures of 1915. We must add to these the members of the Royal Artillery Flying Club of the nineteen-thirties who had the confidence to press forward with the air O.P. idea in the face of scepticism and sometimes ridicule, and the artillery pilots who proved the idea in battle. Last, but certainly not least, we must remember the balanced, cool courage of the reconnaissance pilots and the moral, as well as physical, courage of their squadron commanders who, particularly in North Africa, proved in battle the new methods and machinery appropriate to the single-seater fighter aeroplane.

Summarised briefly, what we learned about air observation and reconnaissance, up to 1945, was as follows:

An army's need for the earliest possible information is elemental and vital.

The basic requirements for air observation are the eye of a highly-trained observer, a good platform for his observation, a camera to record his vision and communications for his earliest reports.

Artillery, because of its ability to strike at the enemy as soon as he is seen, and at long range, has a particular and continuous need for air observation.

In many war situations observation and reconnaissance aircraft need protection from hostile aircraft.

The Air O.P. idea, and its success, should encourage armies and air forces to look for simple solutions to their problems, even if out of keeping with current philosophies.

The dependence of an army, for such vital and integral matters as observation and reconnaissance, on a separate and independent service results in difficulties, particularly of priorities and control.

It is not the author's intention to reach any further conclusions in this book, nor to describe in detail developments in air observation and reconnaissance since 1945. When the lessons of the hundred and fifty years before 1945 are considered, however, it must be in conjunction with developments of the following thirty years, some of which should, therefore, be briefly discussed, against the sinister background and threat of nuclear warfare.

The human eye, assisted for many years by camera and in slow-moving aircraft by binoculars, can now be reinforced by colour-film (to penetrate camouflage), night photography, radar, infra-red sensors and other devices to detect the presence and movement of transport and individuals. Pre-programmed 'drones' can carry these equipments over selected routes and areas, and in-flight transmission could place the record of their observations continuously before monitoring observers alongside military commanders on the ground. Very soon it may be possible for such an observer, supplied on television screen with a 'pilot's view' from the drone's flight path, to vary that flight path at will. The observation and air O.P. requirements might perhaps be met by similar equipments projected vertically above the forward battle area and transmitting their observations as they slowly descend by parachute, or hover – sustained by kite or by rotor blades.

The replacement of direct observations by the human eye by indirect observation of the sort we have just considered would make formidable economies in the number of human observers and would reduce human casualties. It would abolish the wasteful and never fully efficient joint-service operation of air reconnaissance for armies. It would, however, call for extensive technological backing that might divert to industry significant numbers of potential fighting men. The division of national resources between observation and strike equipments (between reconnaissance drones and tanks, for example) might be hard to plan and impossible to vary at short notice.

Whether the battle-reliability and durability of such observation equipments will prove acceptable, and to what extent enemy counter-measures can be resisted, remain to be seen. Perhaps – under the impact

Two Air O.P. pioneers.
42 [ABOVE] Charles Bazeley.
43 [ABOVE RIGHT] Jack Parham.

44 [RIGHT] Air Vice Marshal C. H. B. Blount, Commander of the Air Component of the British Expeditionary Force, France, 1939–40.

◀ overleaf

| 40 |
| 41 |

40 *Hawker Audax* picking up a message, Kohat, India, 1939.

41 C30A autogiro at Larkhill for artillery observation trials. On the right, Hawker Hart reconnaissance aircraft, not participating in the trials.

◄ overleaf

45
46
47

45 *Lysander* of the Air Component in arctic conditions, France, winter of 1939–40.

46 10 May 1940, D Flight *Austers* 'in natural scenery'.

47 The First Air O.P. course, October 1940: Left to Right: Back, Captains Willett, Ingram, Morgan, Tetley-Jones, Lane; Front, Captain Cobley, Squadron Leaders Davenport and Joyce, Captain Neathercoat. Davenport and Joyce were in D Flight; all but one of the remainder were to command squadrons.

48 [ABOVE] R.A.F. oblique air photograph of a Rhine bridge, October 1939.

49 [TOP] *Hurricane I* over the Western Desert.

50 [ABOVE] No 208 Squadron in Libya. Advanced Landing Ground LG 134, late 1941.

51 [LEFT] Lewis Burnand, commander of 208 Squadron, 1941–2, one of the outstanding figures from air reconnaissance in the Second World War.

52 [TOP] Air Marshals Coningham and Tedder, November 1941.

53 [MIDDLE] Spitfire Vs in the Western Desert.

54 [ABOVE LEFT] *Auster I* the first operational Air O.P. aeroplane.

55 [ABOVE RIGHT] *Auster III*, probably of 654 Air O.P. Squadron in Tunisia.

◀ overleaf

| 56 |
| 57 |
| 58 |

56   Hurricanes IId operating from an Advanced Landing Ground in the Arakan.

57   Sensational Photographic Reconnaissance.
5 March 1944: photograph showing 'Piccadilly' one of the two planned Chindit glider-landing-zones, blocked by tree trunks.
58   Lalaghat airfield, Assam: the photograph examined by General Wingate (second from right) and officers of the assault force a few minutes before due to take-off.

59 [ABOVE] No. 4 Squadron, R.A.A.F., in New Guinea.
Wing Commander W. F. Allshorn.

60 [BELOW] Wirraways at Nadzab, West of Lae, 1944.

61   Air O.P. photograph 1944. The Myittha Gorge, not far short of the River Chindwin in the advance from Imphal.

62   Akyab, Burma, January 1945. Captain Jimmy Jarrett, C Flight, 656 Air O.P. Squadron.

63   Gunner Carter, 'Deputy Military Governor' at a period of uncertainty.

64 Geoffrey Millington, commander of
285 Reconnaissance Wing, Italy 1943–5.

65 Anzio beachhead, 1943–4.
Auster III approaching to land.

66 [BELOW] *Spitfire PR XI*

67 [RIGHT] Lieutenant-Colonel W. A. Nel,
commander in Italy, 1943–4, of 40
Squadron, South African Air Force.

70 [ABOVE] Photographic sortie by Major R.
W. V. Neathercoat of 651 Air O.P. Squadron:
bridge reconnaissance on the Ronco river,
Route 9 between Rimini and Bologna,
October 1944.

71   [RIGHT] *Auster IV* of 654 Air O.P.
Squadron using a road strip, Russi, eight
miles west of Ravenna, 1945.

◄ overleaf

68
69

68   40 Squadron on Forli airfield, northern
Italy, December 1944.

69   654 Air O.P. Squadron workshop, Italy,
1944, Leading Aircraftsmen J. Kershaw (left)
and J. J. Barker.

72 Marshal of the Royal Air Force
Sir Charles Portal with officers of 35
Reconnaissance Wing, Autumn 1944. Left
to Right: Group Captain A. F. Anderson
(Commander 35 Wing), Sir Charles,
Squadron Leaders C. D. Harris-St. John
(4 Squadron), C. E. Maitland (who relieved
M. J. Gray, 2 Squadron, September 1944)
and A. S. Mann (268 Squadron).

73 [BELOW LEFT] Air Vice Marshal L. O.
Brown with HM King George VI, 1944.

74 [BELOW RIGHT] 24 May 1944: German
'Chimney' radar at Boulogne, photographed
by Squadron Leader A. S. Mann in a *Mustang*
of 268 Squadron , at about 500 mph after a
dive from 9000 feet.

75 39 Reconnaissance Wing, RCAF.
Group Captain G. H. Sellers, 39 Wing Commander
from February 1945, with (right) his Wing Commander
(Operations), R. C. Waddell, *c.* March 1945.
76 R. A. Ellis (left) and E. H. Moncrieff with Lord
Trenchard, September 1943.
77 Squadron Leader Cal. D. Bricker in the cockpit of
a *Spitfire XIV,* Germany 1945.

78   *Mustang Mark I* of 2 Squadron.

79   *De Havilland Mosquito Mark XVI* (*Photographic Reconnaissance*)

80   Normandy bridgehead, July 1944, 652 Air O.P. Squadron *Auster* being wheeled
out of its blast-pit.

81   'Oblique', looking east-north-east from 2000 feet, of part of the Diesfordter Wald
between Rhine and Issel. An air photograph used for the airborne operation in support
of the Rhine crossings of 24 March 1945. Taken by 414 Squadron on 7 March.

of modern, perhaps nuclear, warfare – the technological fronts would be the first to crack, leaving the human observer in the primitive aircraft supreme. The human eye and brain together constitute a hardy, computerised piece of equipment of considerable adaptability, and it may be many decades or even centuries before military commanders are ready to dispense with it.

The aeroplanes which have been the platforms of the reconnaissance pilots have since 1945 increased still more in speed but have incorporated sufficient aids to enable pilot or observer, after very considerable training, to navigate, to conduct visual and photographic reconnaissance and to communicate by radio. A special manifestation of fast, modern, military aeroplanes is the direct-lift *Harrier*; whether this can be fully developed into a forward field-operated, field-maintained vehicle of army reconnaissance is difficult to forecast. At the slow end of the scale the light helicopter has mostly replaced the light aeroplane as the air observation vehicle of armies, adding flexibility to the choice of landing areas but also, surprisingly, difficulty of concealment in the field and, less surprisingly, expense and complexity. The units of light armoured cross-country vehicles which now perform the classic cavalry reconnaissance role can usefully employ light helicopters, integrating their tactics with those of the armoured vehicles. Most Western armies now incorporate their own Army Air Corps and the latter have already acquired certain armed and aggressive roles to which helicopters seem well suited.

The artillery arm has become potentially more powerful than ever, with guns and projectors of longer range and nuclear ammunition, but for full effectiveness it needs air O.P.s more than ever before. In the British Army, however, the artillery-controlled air O.P., that 'necessary part of gunnery' in 1945, has virtually disappeared, and the British artillery is similarly situated to its predecessors of 1914 and 1938. This, and a like situation in some other armies, seems less the result of new warlike factors than of peace time pressures which have caused us to forget a lesson thrice learned.

Other new factors of considerable importance are the guided and homing missiles which create fresh problems in the protection of aircraft, especially perhaps slow-flying army aircraft in the forward part of a battlefield. The threat cannot yet be considered as fully evaluated, but the counter-measures of which the theorists think all tend towards greater size and weight and less simplicity. Thus, in a much more humble way, had things developed from 1918 to 1938, from *R.E.8* to *Lysander*. Harsh necessity led in 1940 to the use of the single-seater fighter for reconnaissance but it was inspired simplicity which produced the all-successful air O.P. organisation, the fruit of peacetime thought which ignored preconceived ideas untested in war.[2]

It is not easy, in these days of advanced technologies, to search for simplicity. The technologists will not support such a search, for their bread and butter depends on its failure. Nor are the most professional of army and air force aviators on the side of simplicity; they are throughly bored by it but inspired, on the other hand, by the challenge presented by complex and sophisticated aircraft and associated flying procedures. For those who operate the necessarily fast deep-penetrating reconnaissance aircraft simplicity must have a limited meaning; for the army observation pilots, living and working in the forward part of the battlefield, a small and simple aircraft would seem a tactical essential.

We have left until the end the most difficult problem of all – one which did not appear until 1918 – the division of control of reconnaissance between the services. This has already been described, in the present chapter, as outrageous; having regard to an army commander's first, vital and inherent need for information, no lesser adjective would be sufficient.

For the greater part of the Second World War, Army and R.A.F. commanders strove to maintain an acceptable relationship between their services and an acceptable machinery of co-operation. They succeeded to a degree which did them the greatest credit, but many of their combined actions needed to be compromises while relationships sometimes became strained which, in a single service, would have remained unimpaired. As we have seen, the Army failed sometimes, in North Africa, to safeguard the forward airfields of their reconnaissance squadrons or to give the latter adequate warning of hostile penetration. We find fairly regular R.A.F. criticism of the selection of air reconnaissance tasks by army commanders and staffs, as displaying ignorance of the capabilities and limitations of the art. The Air Force failed sometimes to provide such adequate fighter protection for the army's reconnaissance missions as to enable them to operate as the army wished. The outcome of these difficulties was not closer integration but greater centralisation of air force support, and thus the organisation and control of the army's air reconnaissance at the highest joint-service levels. The Army accepted such centralisation, with the loss of intimacy and thus of tactical speed which it implied, and the Air Force ensured that centralisation worked. The advent of continuous Allied successes in the field under almost continuous air superiority, however, made this joint-service experiment indecisive. To the soldier in the field reconnaissance and observation must remain *integral* requirements; to the airman the air is *indivisible*.

The logical solution to this problem of control is to give to each of the three services the aircraft, pilots and servicing resources which it needs to fight its battles. Logic, however, breaks down in the face of our unhappy nation's reluctance to spend money on defence and of the high cost of modern military aircraft. And, while it would be simple enough to identify and to separate from the air force a sufficiency of tactical and photographic reconnaissance squadrons, the separate permanent provision of fighter protection for air reconnaissance, scaled to the most adverse situations, would clearly demand considerable extra resources of aircraft, equipment, manpower and money. So long as reconnaissance continues to be based partly upon direct observation by the human eye, therefore, it seems likely that the Royal Air Force will remain responsible for deep fast-flying reconnaissance for the Army, and the Army Air Corps for the activities of the observation helicopters.

The Army Air Corps' role should raise no control problem. The main problems of the Army commanders in the field, as related to R.A.F. reconnaissance on their behalf, must be:

The numbers and performance of their allotted reconnaissance aircraft.

The ability of these aircraft and their pilots and observers to operate effectively in the prevailing air situation.

The commanders' powers of operational control over their means of reconnaissance.

If these requirements are recognised as part of the 'elemental and vital' need for information, then means must be found to meet them. The first of them is a matter of joint-service and industrial forward-planning and needs no further comment here. The other two requirements need some elaboration.

The ability of reconnaissance pilots to operate effectively requires either a high degree of air superiority or other effective protection of reconnaissance missions. The R.A.F. has often seemed to postulate air superiority, if not air supremacy, as a *prerequisite* of any attempt by the Army to operate at all, and to reserve the right – during the fight for air superiority – to make use of whatever aircraft-resources they wish, if necessary at the expense of reconnaissance for the army and of other army needs. The British Army, however, particularly at the beginning of a war, almost invariably operates under the burden of enemy superiority of many kinds. A measure of air inferiority must be expected and, as in North Africa in 1941 and 1942, air reconnaissance must still take place – in dangerous conditions. It is at such periods that joint-service organisation and resources must exist to provide appropriate fighter protection for urgent reconnaissance missions, and also a close and flexible liaison, effective at the lowest levels – such as did not need to be, and was not, provided by the highly centralised systems developed in 1944 and 1945.

A military commander's absolute operational control over resources placed absolutely at his disposal must be accepted as an essential of complete battle-efficiency, and nothing short of complete efficiency is likely, in the early days of war, to achieve a victory. Among those resources, the most vital and urgent in these early days will be those of reconnaissance. The commander's control over his *air* reconnaissance squadrons should be as absolute as his control over his *armoured* reconnaissance squadrons. Relations, furthermore, between a *tactical reconnaissance* squadron commander and the staff and commander of the army formation he supports should be as intimate as that of the equivalent *armoured reconnaissance* commander. If, while supporting an army formation, the tactical reconnaissance squadron was fully integrated into that formation, and if R.A.F. officers filled certain staff appointments within the formation, it might be possible to dispense with the present machinery for joint-service discussion and agreement of individual reconnaissance requests, and with some of the functions of air liaison officers, thus saving, perhaps, vital time.

There are two well-known air force counters to this doctrine of integration, first that it is wasteful to keep small bodies of airmen and aircraft within army formations not all of whom are in active need of their support all of the time and, secondly, that uncontrolled and unco-ordinated use of airspace is wasteful, inefficient and dangerous. The former argument will not hold water; it could be applied to any other of the resources of an army formation – artillery, engineers, armour or infantry – which, as every soldier knows, can be moved from formation to formation as required; because of their speed and flexibility, aircraft can switch their support from formation to formation more readily than most of the other 'arms'.

The second argument has, however, considerable force. We have noted the difficulties that reconnaissance squadron commanders often experienced in the desert in obtaining fighter escort or cover for the missions which the army required; we have noted the inordinate scale of fighter cover sometimes required for essential reconnaissances of sensitive enemy areas; these are small problems among the many which must confront all operators of fast aircraft within a disputed airspace. It is not unreasonable to argue the need for central surveillance of the whole airspace in which combat aircraft are involved, a central communication system to tell units and aircrews what is happening in this airspace and a central control to ensure the adequate protection of aircraft and to co-ordinate swift reaction to enemy threats.

What has to be done is to reconcile these needs – the need of the army commander to control absolutely all the resources he must use to defeat the enemy and the need of the airman for an airspace in which he can operate freely and with reasonable safety. The task will not be easy; it will certainly not be impossible. However it is approached, considerable Air Force understanding and sacrifice will be required.

An urgent contribution, however, is required of the Army. The organisation for army-air co-operation which developed before and during the Second World War accepted the separation of army formation commanders and their operational staffs, on the one hand, and reconnais-sance squadrons, on the other, save for a tenuous air-liaison-officer link. It is apparent, from many army and air force opinions, that the A.L.O. and Army-Air staff posts of the Second World War attracted officers of intelligence, character and responsibility far in excess of the demands of their rank. These officers, almost entirely from sources outside the Regular Army, maintained the vital link between the Army and its air reconnaissance. It cannot be expected that such high-grade, yet militarily unambitious, personalities will always be available, and appointments outside the main stream of regimental and staff appointments are not popular with Regular Army officers. More important still, the present system results in the great bulk of army officers pursuing their careers in near or complete ignorance of the methods by which an air force obtains for an army one of its principal requirements – and certainly its earliest requirement – information. At whatever cost, this ignorance must be dissipated; if army officers are not brought up to understand the minutiae of air reconnaissance as well as they understand that of other forms of reconnaissance, then there will be a lack of good commanders, good staffs and good information.

It is right that we should conclude this chapter with a tribute to the men of air reconnaissance, and we might mention first those who have repaired, maintained and serviced the aircraft, sometimes in close proximity to the enemy and often in conditions unfavourable to their role. The technicians of the Reconnaissance and Air O.P. Squadrons, as of other Royal Air Force squadrons, set and maintained high technical standards, undeflected by any of the dangers or discomforts of their position.

Most of all, however, there must be mentioned in these closing paragraphs the bravery of reconnaissance pilots, a matter imperfectly understood by both services. The loneliness of the pilot, particularly of a single-seater aircraft, his essential concentration on the reconnaissance in hand, the acceptance of increased risk in the cause of increased information and the need to avoid combat whenever possible, all these demand cold courage, only marginally modified when working in pairs. Because a description of the mission could only be provided, afterwards, by the pilot himself, such descriptions have often been in low key.

From the pilots of 1914, from the artillery, photographic and contact patrol pilots and balloon observers of 1915–18, from the R.A.F. reconnaissance pilots and Air O.P. pilots of the Second World War, the same type of sustained courage has been required and has been forthcoming.

If this short history of air reconnaissance and observation for the army has called attention to its notable anomalies, to the vital importance in war of the information obtained and to the readiness with which this is forgotten in peace, to its often decisive impact on the army's battle and to the air force wish to control it, to the bravest and most devoted men of whom the least is generally known, then this book will not have been wasted.

Notes

---◇---

CHAPTER 1

1. Jeremy Taylor, p. 14.
2. *Holy Bible,* Numbers XIII.
3. See *Holy Bible,* Joshua VII. Ai, however, may actually have been Bethel, so some experts say.
4. Denison, pp. 271, 272.
5. Maurice, *History of the War in South Africa, Vol. I,* p. 334.
6. Robinson, Part III, p. 523.
7. Von Muffling, p. 2.
8. Von Muffling, p. 13.
9. Liddell Hart, p. 126.

CHAPTER 2

1. Burne, p. 172.
2. Churchill, *Marlborough, Vol. II,* pp. 449, 450.
3. Churchill, *Marlborough, Vol. III,* pp. 113–15.
4. Napier, Vol. II, pp. 175, 177.
5. Guedalla, pp. 220, 221.

CHAPTER 3

1. Collier, *History of Air Power,* p.1. Hart (p. 27) says likewise.
2. *Royal Artillery Historical Affairs Committee Proceedings, April 1965,* p. 128.
3. Gamble, p. 9.
4. Gamble, p. 27.
5. An incomplete copy of this pamphlet is held by the Library of the Royal Aeronautical Society. It contains also some interesting material on the Battle of Fleurus.
6. Phipps, pp. 170, 171.
7. Tissandier, Chapter XIV.

8. Money, pp. 6–8, a paper by Lieutenant G. E. Grover before the Royal Engineers' Institute, 23rd April 1862 and Gamble, p. 19.
9. Tissandier, p. 138.
10. Observation platforms or ladders.
11. Money, p. 18.
12. In 1862 Coxwell was credited with a 'height record' of five miles and he was probably the first aeronaut to experience and survive annoxia.
13. Alexander, p. 358.
14. Gamble, p. 54.
15. Gamble, p. 56.
16. Gamble, p. 56, footnote.
17. Readers who are interested may read *Parkinson's Law,* John Murray, 1958, pp. 63–72.
18. Shrapnel: shell filled with small shot, burst by time fuse.
19. Penrose, p. 38.

CHAPTER 4

1. Waller.
2. Potgeiter's Drift and Vaal Krantz, both south-west of Ladysmith and east of Spion Kop.
3. Headlam, Vol. 3, pp. 350, 351.
4. Headlam, Vol. 3, p. 365.
5. Waller. This and the following accounts of the activities of No.3 Balloon Section at Fourteen Streams are condensed from the Section reports in Waller's History.
6. Walker, p. 33.
7. It depended, of course, on who held the high ground. A balloon might have been useful to the British before Colenso – see Chapter 1.
8. See Chapter 2.
9. Walker, pp. 34–36. Lynch, while in Paris, contested Galway successfully for the British Parliament, repaired to Westminster, was arrested, condemned to death and pardoned and, in 1918, became a Colonel in the British Army.
10. See his lecture to the Aeronautical Society of Great Britain, 1906 – *The Aeronautical Journal,* July 1908.
11. Walker, pp. 43 et seq.
12. Headlam, Vol. 2, pp. 166, 167.

CHAPTER 5

1. Colonel Capper told an artillery audience in November 1909, for example, that one of the essentials of aerial observation was to be stationary – *Royal Artillery Journal*, January 1910.

2. Gamble, p. 114.
3. Broke-Smith, Chapter VI.
4. It received the Royal title in 1918.
5. Raleigh, p. 206.
6. *Army Review,* January 1913.
7. *The Aeronautical Journal* of July 1913.
8. Gamble, p. 245.
9. *Royal Artillery Journal,* August 1912 – lecture to the Royal Artillery Institution of 22nd February 1912.
10. Gamble, p. 233.

CHAPTER 6

1. Later, of course, replaced by roundels.
2. Edmonds, *History of the Great War, 1914, Part I,* pp. 66, 67.
3. *PRO* AIR 1/2162.
4. Edmonds, *History of the Great War, 1914, Part I,* pp. 193, 194.
5. Edmonds, *History of the Great War, 1914, Part I,* pp. 273, 274.
6. Raleigh, p. 329.
7. Raleigh quotes (p. 335) a congratulatory message from Joffre in which he praises the professionalism and high training standards of the 'English Flying Corps'. Unfortunately Raleigh gives no reference.

CHAPTER 8

1. Sortie – one flight by one aircraft.
2. Anstey, p. 36. At Raleigh, p. 341, will be found a verbose sequence of messages, said to have been transmitted by wireless on 24th September 1914. Remembering that the wireless communication available, then and for long afterwards, was restricted to one-way Morse code signals, Raleigh's version (widely repeated in later accounts) seems inconceivable.
3. In 1917 Caquot became Director of the French Military Aviation Technical Section and greatly increased aircraft production. He received many honours including, from the British, the Distinguished Service Order. After the war he returned to civil engineering, particularly in the field of bridge design but, when the French Air Ministry was formed in 1928, he became Director-General, Technical. He died in November 1976, in his ninety-sixth year.
4. Edmonds, *History of the Great War, 1915, Part II,* p. 54.

5. A rough analysis of R.F.C. operational communiqués from 25th July to 31st December indicates that 50 per cent of the sorties were for artillery tasks, 18 per cent photographic, 27 per cent for short-range reconnaissance and 5 per cent for strategic reconnaissance. Cole, *Royal Flying Corps, 1915–16.*
6. The 'clock-code' procedure will be described in Chapter II.
7. Edmonds, *History of the Great War, 1915, Part II,* p. 142.
8. Raleigh, p. 446.

CHAPTER 9

1. Neumann, pp. 216–218.
2. Courtney, p. 52.
3. Neumann, p. 201.
4. Jones, Vol. II, pp. 164–168. Trenchard enshrined his beliefs in a now famous paper of 22nd September, 1916.
5. Courtney, p. 58.
6. *Morane Parasol,* a French two-seater, high-wing reconnaissance mono-plane.
7. British Expeditionary Force, France, Headquarters Leaflet No.SS 553 (von Below), para 196.
8. Jones, Vol. II, p. 212.
9. The division of duties between pilots and observers varied between R.F.C. Brigades, Wings, Squadrons and probably crews. The training manuals of 1916 and 1917 stated that either pilot or observer might undertake a shoot. The word 'observer' has often to be used to indicate merely a 'person who observes'.
10. Neumann, pp. 219–221.
11. Edmonds, *History of the Great War, Part II,* p. 114. Blount, as Air Commodore, was to command in 1940 the 'Air Component' to the British Expeditionary Force in France.
12. Jones, Vol. II, p. 250.
13. Cole, *Royal Flying Corps, 1915–16,* p. 235.
14. Jones, Vol. II, p. 272.
15. Statistics here are from, or derived from, Edmonds, *History of the Great War, 1916, Part II,* p 576 and Cole, *Royal Flying Corps, 1915–16,* p. 312.

CHAPTER 10

1. Edmonds, *History of the Great War, 1917, Part II,* p. 363.
2. This calculation includes four Royal Naval Air Service squadrons attached to the R.F.C. for these operations.

3. The *R.E.8* was designed by the Royal Aircraft Factory to meet an R.F.C. requirement in the autumn of 1915. It was a tractor aeroplane with a Vickers synchronised gun for the pilot and Lewis-gun with Scarff ring for the observer. Many flying and other weaknesses were discovered and it was withdrawn from service, largely redesigned and reissued.

4. Courtney, p. 102. Writers of the R.F.C. part in the Great War have made much of the severe casualties experienced, particularly by pilots fresh from England. It is a fact of war that the greenest soldier is the readiest victim. As to the casualty rate, the Royal Air Force made an investigation of this matter and their findings will be found in the Public Record Office (*PRO* AIR 9/36). The investigation covered all pilots sent to France from July to December 1917, inclusive, not including flight commanders and others who had previously served overseas. The Arras battle lies outside this period. 24 per cent of the new pilots lasted less than three months though only 8 of the 24 per cent were killed or missing. 13 per cent lasted between three and six, and 36 per cent between six and nine months, the remaining 27 per cent over nine months.

5. Edmonds, *History of the Great War, 1917, Part II,* p. 94.

6. A special leaflet (SS 170) was published after the battle, remarking on the high standard of co-operation between aircraft and artillery which had been attained therein and recording the principles and procedures which had led to this. In fact, it contained little new, the real lesson being in the first paragraph: 'The very successful co-operation between the artillery and the Royal Flying Corps during the operations was largely due to the fact that the principles laid down in the various official manuals were followed.'

7. The Germans had, independently, devised much the same procedure.

8. Jones (Vol. IV, pp. 161, 162) regards the R.F.C. as blameless, but this seems improbable.

9. Jones, Vol. IV, pp. 162, 167, 168.

10. Edmonds, *History of the Great War, 1917, Part II,* p. 170, footnote.

11. Jones, Vol. IV, pp. 166, 167.

12. Edmonds, *History of the Great War, 1917, Part II,* p. 197.

13. Jones, Vol. IV, p. 177.

14. Edmonds, *History of the Great War, 1917, Part II,* p. 284.

15. Edmonds, *History of the Great War, 1917, Part II,* p. 273.

16. 'Observers' undoubtedly embrace balloon observers, see Jones, Vol. IV, p. 184. During September 1917, 9559 artillery targets were engaged with air observation, mostly hostile batteries. In the same period the Germans engaged 943 – see Jones, Vol. IV, p. 202.

17. Jones, Vol. IV, p. 238.

18. Jones, Vol. IV, pp. 257-9.

19. Miles, *History of the Great War, 1917, Part III,* pp. 30, 70.

20. See, for example, Raleigh, p. 448 and Courtney, p. 82.

21. B.E.F. Training Leaflet No. SS 135, *Co-operation between Aircraft and Infantry,* France, 1918.
22. Jones, Vol. II, pp. 472–5.
23. Collier, pp. 59–61.

CHAPTER 11

1. Chapter 2.
2. The German infantry reacted in a similar manner – see British Expeditionary Force, France, Headquarters Leaflet SS 553 (von Below), para. 97.
3. See Chapter 8.
4. Anstey, p. 119.
5. Edmonds, *History of the Great War, 1917, Part I,* pp. 296, 297.
6. Anstey, p. 153.
7. Anstey, pp. 163, 164. It is doubtful whether it was general practice to photograph at the end of each shoot.
8. Rawlins, pp. 124, 129.
9. Jones, Vol. IV, p. 213.
10. Insall, pp. 170–175.
11. The Germans did not use the clock-code system but indicated broad degrees of error left or right and over or short.
12. Jones, Vol. III, pp. 308, 309. We shall return presently to this letter, of 1st November, 1916, in another context.
13. Note, for example, the detailed description of artillery sorties in Courtney, pp. 55, 56 and Insall, pp. 170–173 and a lecture by Colonel A.C.H. MacLean reported in the *R.A. Journal* of February 1918. Note also Imperial War Museum, Department of Sound Records, tapes nos. 000013/05, 000014/04, 000023/02, 000171/02 where four pilots testify separately to separate practices. In two cases it was evidently normal squadron practice, during 1917, for the observer to carry out the artillery duties and in another there was 'no hard and fast rule.' The General Staff, War Office, pamphlet 'Co-operation of Aircraft with Artillery (Revised December 1917)' stated that either pilot or observer undertook these shoots; both, in their individual training, were taught to do so.
14. Insall, pp. 170–173.
15. Edmonds, *History of the Great War, 1917, Part I,* pp. 296, 297.
16. After the end of the war the R.A. Journal published a number of essays by gunner officers on the problem of how to improve co-operation between aircraft and mobile artillery. A prize was awarded to the winner. All essays emphasised to some extent the slowness of the existing procedure and recommended ways to improve matters. See *R.A. Journal,* various numbers, April 1918 to August 1920.
17. Jones, Vol. IV, p. 213.
18. *R.A. Journal,* July 1920, p. 165.

19. Jones, Vol. II, p. 116.
20. Jones, Vol. III, pp. 307–310.
21. Jones, Vol. III, p. 308.
22. Neumann, p. 90.

CHAPTER 12

1. Aspinall-Oglander, Vol. I, pp. 86, 87.
2. Aspinall-Oglander, Vol. I, p. 322.
3. Aspinall-Oglander, Vol. II, pp. 393, 394.
4. Jones, Vol. II, p. 71.
5. The Zeppelin *L. 59* attempted the voyage from Germany but was recalled by wireless when over Khartoum – much, no doubt, to the relief of Lettow-Vorbeck's administrative staff. Jones, Vol. III, p. 67.
6. Jones, Vol. V, p. 353.
7. Single-seater fighters.
8. Falls, *Official History, Egypt and Palestine, Vol. I,* pp. 60, 61
9. Jones, Vol. V, p. 204.
10. The Official History does not mention this performance, but Jones (Vol. V, p. 218, footnote 1) quotes an authority.
11. Single-seater tractor fighter.
12. Falls, *Official History, Egypt and Palestine, Vol. II,* p. 141.
13. Falls, *Official History, Egypt and Palestine, Vol. II,* p. 309.
14. Neumann, p. 263.
15. Moberly, Vol. IV, p. 132.

CHAPTER 13

1. Edmonds, *History of the Great War, 1918,* Vol. I, p. 167.
2. Anstey, p. 235.
3. Edmonds, *History of the Great War, 1918,* Vol. I, pp. 168, 169.
4. Jones, Vol. IV, p. 337.
5. Jones (Vol. IV) mentions: (p. 310) a successful LL call answered by field batteries on 23rd March; (p. 331) a number of calls answered and concentrated artillery fire brought to bear on enemy moving to attack on 28th March; (p. 339) two undermanned and withdrawing batteries going into action against enemy infantry reported by message-drop, also on the 28th; (p. 343) the break-up of a German attack by artillery fire in reply to wireless calls on the 31st. Delap writes (pp. 39, 40) that, as early as 22nd March, 'our airmen sent us (303rd Siege Battery) the reassuring and heartening report that we were inflicting terrible casualties on the advancing hordes'.

6. Jones, Vol. IV, p. 358.
7. Edmonds, *History of the Great War, 1918*, Vol. II, pp. 273, 274.
8. Lieutenant-Colonel P.K. Wise commanded the 1st Balloon Wing.

CHAPTER 14

1. Liddell Hart, p. 545.
2. Jones, Vol. VI, pp. 435, 436.
3. Jones, Vol. VI, p. 463.
4. *FK8,* a new reconnaissance biplane.
5. Jones, Vol. VI, pp. 463, 464.
6. Later Marshal of the Royal Air Force Sir John Slessor.
7. In a footnote he excluded the roles of the Corps squadrons from this statement.
8. Slessor, pp. 173–175.
9. Slessor, p. 164.
10. See Jones, Vol. VI, pp. 482, 483, for examples of a contact patrol pilot making good use of the procedures for calling for artillery fire. See *ibid,* p. 501, for statistics of artillery response to air calls in First and Third Armies.
11. Jones, Vol. VI, pp. 497, 498.
12. See Jones, Vol. VI, pp. 515 and 519. On p. 515 he gives an interesting example of the detailed orders of XVII Corps of Third Army to No. 13 Squadron, R.A.F. which helped to achieve such success.
13. Jones, Vol. VI, pp. 521, 522.
14. Edmonds, *History of the Great War, 1918, Vol. V,* p. 577.

CHAPTER 15

1. See Jones, Vol. III, pp. 263–283 and Vol. VI, Chapter I.
2. Collier, *A History of Air Power,* p. 72.
3. Published as Appendix 2 to Jones, Vol. VI, in separate volume.
4. Haig's comments will be found in Appendix 3 to Jones, Vol. VI, in separate volume.
5. O'Brien, pp. 16, 96, 677–678.
6. Army Co-operation Report, 1929, p. 17.
7. Army Co-operation Report, 1928, p. 8.
8. See, for example, articles in the *R.A. Journal,* by Major R.G. Cherry, July 1925, p. 548, Lieutenant A.P.C. Hannay, April 1929, p. 67 and Major K.V.B. Benfield, July 1934, p. 151.
9. Lecture to the Royal Artillery Institution of 21st October, 1924, – *R.A. Journal,* April 1925, p. 18.

10. Purists will say that the term 'autogiro' was a trade-name of Cierva's and should not be used to describe, in general, all machines with freely rotating blades. For years, however, the term has been used in the latter sense and the author unrepentantly so uses it in these pages.
11. De Guingand surprisingly suggests (pp. 28–30) that the Army had no say in these matters. Air Force officers often blame the Army for the *Lysander,* however.
12. *Royal United Service Institution Journal,* August 1933, p. 601.
13. For further details of their Air O.P. concept see an essay by Bazeley in *R.A. Journal,* October 1939, pp. 313–334.

CHAPTER 16

1. Probably *Lysanders* and one or two of the *C30* autogiros.
2. *Battle,* a single-engined monoplane, obsolescent as a bomber-reconnaissance aircraft.
3. The first R.A.F. monoplane figher of this era, the prototype of which flew in 1935.
4. *Spitfire:* single-engined monoplane fighter, of which the prototype flew in 1936 and which, in successive versions, remained the outstanding British fighter throughout this war and was also used for a number of other roles, including reconnaissance.
5. Pemberton, p. 37 and *PRO* AIR 27/47.
6. Fuller, *The Second World War, 1939–45,* p. 71.
7. Ellis, *The War in France and Flanders, 1939–1940,* p. 98.
8. Bryant, *The Turn of the Tide,* p. 105.
9. Ellis, *The War in France and Flanders, 1939–40,* pp. 116, 117.
10. See Chapter 14.
11. Fuller, *The Second World War, 1939–45,* p. 81.
12. *PRO* AIR 2/5251.
13. See Babington-Smith for a full account of this organisation.
14. Parham and Belfield, p. 21.

CHAPTER 17

1. Wavell, Despatch, London Gazette, 2nd July, 1946.
2. Playfair, Vol. III, p. 252.
3. Playfair, Vol. III, p. 15.
4. *PRO* AIR 27/1245.
5. Playfair, Vol. III, p. 55.
6. See Playfair, Vol. III, p. 86 and *PRO* AIR 27/1245.
7. Playfair, Vol. III, pp. 114, 150. Air Marshal Broadhurst (letter to the author) has suggested that more use might generally have been made of fighter pilots for reconnaissance without detriment to their

fighter role. Playfair, however (Vol. IV, p. 308 and elsewhere), expressed the opinion that really effective air reconnaissance demands specialised training outside that provided, in those days, to fighter pilots. Perhaps the answer lies between these two, the fighter-bomber pilot's general reports of the presence of vehicles, dust or sand clouds or guns in the area of his sortie offering a good bonus of intelligence to army staffs, who must primarily rely, however, on the more specific and detailed reports of the reconnaissance pilots.

8. The situation and atmosphere of this period in, one must assume, 208 Squadron is well depicted in an article 'An Army Co-operation Squadron in Libya, Winter 1941-2', by Wing-Commander J. W. Stewart, D.F.C., R.A.F.V.R., *Royal Air Force Quarterly*, June 1944, pp. 153–159. The Commander of that Squadron, in a report on the difficulties of obtaining fighter protection (*PRO* AIR 27/1245), wrote: 'It is not to be wondered that a belief arose that the paramount importance of information was not fully appreciated by higher authority.'

9. Brown, *Eagles Strike*, p. 151,

10. Rommel, who was unwell, had handed over to General Stumme before the battle. Von Thoma commanded the German Afrika Korps. Stumme died of a heart attack during the battle and Rommel was recalled. Von Thoma was captured.

11. Playfair, Vol. III, p. 380.

12. *PRO* AIR 27/1241; also Brown, *Eagles Strike*, pp. 237, 238.

13. Playfair, Vol. III, p. 380.

14. Although Owen (p. 118) suggests that a comprehensive German photographic reconnaissance of R.A.F. airfields took place.

15. The tactical reconnaissance squadrons were in course of equipping all their aircraft with cameras – *PRO* AIR 26/402.

16. *PRO* AIR 27/1241.

17. Playfair, Vol. IV, p. 308.

18. Pemberton, p. 158.

19. *PRO* AIR 27/1245.

20. Brigadier General Staff – senior operations staff officer of the Corps.

21. *R.A.F. Quarterly*, June 1944, pp. 153–159.

22. *PRO* AIR 27/417.

23. Letter to the author.

CHAPTER 18

1. Fuller (p. 216) describes this in an ecstatic sentence: 'The campaigns. . .scattered those verbal clouds in which the meaning of air power had been obscured by the so-called experts of 1919–1939, and brought it into the sunshine of the essentials of war.'

2. See Mountbatten, p. 106, para. 341. Tenth U.S.A.A.F. developed many of their systems of close air support during their support of the Chindits' 77th Brigade in June 1944, during its successful operations against Mogaung.
3. Kirby, Vol. II, p. 67.
4. Mountbatten, p. 41.
5. Richards and Saunders, Vol. II, pp. 322, 329.
6. Tulloch, p. 197.
7. Mountbatten, p. 49.
8. Mountbatten, p. 101.
9. *Wirraway* (aboriginal word meaning 'challenge'), a pre-war Australian-built single-engined two-seater 'general purpose' monoplane, armed with three machine-guns and having a maximum speed of 200 m.p.h. and a range of 500 miles.
10. Wigmore, p. 368.
11. *Boomerang,* a wartime Australian production, a single-engined, single-seater aircraft designed as fighter and army co-operation aircraft. Armament two cannon, maximum speed 290 m.p.h., range 930 miles.
12. Dexter, p. 711.
13. Wigmore, p. 368.
14. Kohima: Sixty miles north of Imphal and farthest Japanese penetration.
15. At the end of 1944 a special commendation to the squadron was received from General Sir Oliver Leese, who commanded the land forces of South-East Asia Command, in the unusual form of a signal by radio. It included the words: 'Everywhere I go I hear praise from everyone on the work the Air OP is putting in.' Parham and Belfield, p. 131.
16. Letter to the author.
17. Parham and Belfield, p. 135.
18. Land artillery orders from the pilots were translated into naval terms at a relay-station in the ships.
19. Brigadier Daniell – letter to the author.
20. Jarrett's full description of this affair will be found in the *Royal Artillery Commemoration Book,* 1939–1945, pp. 560–565 and also in Parham and Belfield, pp. 132, 133.

CHAPTER 19

1. *Mosquito:* De Havilland aircraft and one of the successes of this war. Of wooden construction and twin-engined. Speed 415 knots, range 2450 miles, no armament in the photo-reconnaissance role.
2. *Mustang:* Single-engined and single-seater, speed 450 knots, range 950 miles, armament four cannon.

3. 225 Squadron and a detachment of 40 Squadron were based in Corsica, supporting the Allied landings in the South of France, between July and September, 1944.
4. Molony, Volume V, p. 299.
5. *PRO* AIR 26/403 – Eighth Army letter of 27th November, 1943.
6. This example is taken from the article by Staff Sergeant B. C. Gluning, R.A. on pages 25–29 of the *Journal of Army Aviation* of 1973. The procedure is that devised by Jack Parham in 1940 and was described briefly in Chapter 17.
7. Molony, volume V, p. 754.
8. *PRO* AIR 27/418.
9. *PRO* AIR 27/1398.
10. *PRO* AIR 27/1242.
11. *PRO* AIR 27/1711.
12. For further details of artillery-air co-operation in this battle see Pemberton, p. 214, the *Royal Artillery Commemoration Book, 1939–45,* p. 315, Owen, p. 220 and the Squadron Operational Record books, *PRO* AIR 27/418, 1242 and 1398. Pemberton writes that 134 such missions were carried out between 12th and 25th May, 1944, of which 127 were successful.
13. Chapter 5.
14. Royal Artillery Notes, No. 15, 15th Arpil, 1944.
15. It also provided for a rear-facing observer to give warning of impending fighter attack, although this was not very relevant in northern Italy.
16. Chapter 10.
17. Letter to the author from the Air O.P. Squadron Commander.
18. Several congratulatory signals from Eighth Army headquarters to 285 Wing are in *PRO* AIR 26/402.
19. Royal Artillery Notes No.17, 15th June, 1944.
20. *Royal Artillery Commemoration Book,* p. 612. The Squadron concerned was, however, No.40, South African Air Force, commanded, from August 1944 by Lieutenant-Colonel R. H. Rogers.

CHAPTER 20

1. Allied Expeditionary Air Force 'Overall Air Plan', Section 1, Part II (*PRO* AIR 25/699).
2. Letter to the author.
3. 'Flak' – anti-aircraft artillery fire.
4. The *Mustang,* particularly Marks IA and II, was an outstandingly good reconnaissance aircraft but, because of its long range, was much coveted for other roles.

5. One of the *Austers* of No. 653 Air O.P. Squadron had been presented to the British forces in January 1944 by Mrs. W. Gordon in memory of her brother, Captain Bertram Dickson, one of the three pioneer pilots of army aeroplane reconnaissance (see Chapter 5).

6. Parham and Belfield (p. 76) quote some complimentary remarks by General von Runstedt about the activities of the 'air spotting pool'.

7. These were the first British squadrons to operate from French soil since Dunkirk, and not the fighter squadrons which landed on the 10th, as suggested by Leigh-Mallory's despatch, paras 331, 332.

8. Parham and Belfield, p. 78.

9. Policy decision published by Headquarters XXX Corps, 6th July, 1944, (*PRO* WO 171/338).

10. Ellis, *Victory in the West, Vol. I*, p. 335.

11. Published in 21st Army Group's Intelligence Summary No.158 (*PRO* WO 171/132).

12. Leigh-Mallory, para. 263. Some of the missions classified as 'photo-reconnaissance' were probably for bombing assessment. Cameras, furthermore, were increasingly carried and used on tactical-reconnaissance missions, so these figures cannot be regarded as exact.

13. *PRO* AIR 26/54.

14. G. S. Jackson, pp. 47 and 133.

15. *PRO* AIR 26/51.

16. *PRO* AIR 26/61.

17. Parham and Belfield, pp. 79, 80.

18. Eventually a few R.A.F.-piloted *Austers* appeared in communication flights.

19. See *PRO* WO 171/223 (Second Army), WO 171/341 (XXX Corps) and AIR 26/61 (39 Wing).

20. This seems clearly established, in spite of Ellis, *Victory in the West, Vol. II*, p. 55. See Ryan, p. 109, Gregory, p. 113 and Urquhart, pp. 9, 10, 22–24.

21. The air O.P.s, however, were not Canadian; the Canadian Army and air force made an even slower start than their British counterparts and the first Canadian Air O.P. squadron became operational in Europe only a month before the end of the war.

22. Ellis, *Victory in the West, Vol. II*, p. 245.

23. *PRO* AIR 25/722. Philologists will be interested in this early use – in this context – of the term 'swanning'.

24. Royal Artillery Notes, No.28.

25. Pemberton, p. 278. See also paper by A.O.C. 84 Group of 15th April 1945, 'Operation Veritable' (*PRO* AIR 25/722). A considerable number of artillery sorties seem to have been planned but cancelled owing to bad weather; in planning them, conflicts of priority arose between artillery and tactical reconnaissance.

26. On the 21st March weather conditions were particularly good and 400 Squadron produced no less than 10,679 photographs (*PRO* AIR 26/61). Their programme of photography of the Rhine, as an assault river-crossing problem, had been well under way in January 1945.
27. *PRO* AIR 25/716.
28. Letters to the author.
29. 'Recce' – abbreviation for 'Reconnaissance'.
30. *PRO* AIR 25/715, 716.
31. A remarkable example of this strange attitude on the part of Second Army's intelligence staff will be found in their Intelligence Summary No.279 of 10th March 1945 (*PRO* WO 171/3958), where it is remarked that 'only two sorties' (and there were sixty-six *reconnaissance* sorties during the period summarised) 'were really eventful – one a tactical reconnaissance sortie which destroyed one enemy aircraft and damaged another, the other an armed reconnaissance mission which claimed two engines and one rail truck destroyed and eight rail trucks damaged. . .' It is fair, however, to mention also the comment of Squadron-Leader G. Wonnacott, of 414 Tactical Reconnaissance Squadron, R.C.A.F. at 83 Group, after recording the destruction of enemy aircraft during a reconnaissance mission (*PRO* AIR 27/1810): 'The above victories were incidental to the observation of the state of the bridges, movement of enemy transport, enemy gun positions and marshalling yards.'
32. *Roundel,* June 1953: short account of 430 Squadron.

CHAPTER 21

1. Jac Weller, article in 'British Army Review', December, 1969.
2. In the period 1939–41 it was widely supposed that pilots of slow, unarmed light aircraft, flying in the forward battle area, would suffer intolerable casualties. The British Air O.P. squadrons, however, eventually twelve in number comprehending some three hundred pilots, lost between 1942 and 1945 thirty-seven operational casualties, the greatest single cause being the trajectories of their own artillery shells, and only six being due to attack by enemy aircraft and seven due to the fire of enemy anti-aircraft or other weapons. Parham and Belfield, p. 161.

Bibliography

◇

PERIOD UP TO 1914

PUBLISHED BOOKS

ALEXANDER, Brigadier-General E. Porter, *The Great Charge and Artillery Fighting at Gettysburg,* from *Battles and Leaders of the Civil War, Vol. III,* Century Co., New York, 1884.

ALISON, Archibald, *History of Europe during the French Revolution, Part II,* Blackwood, 1833.

BECKE, Captain A. F., *An introduction to the History of Tactics, 1704–1905,* Hugh Rees, London, 1909.

BELLOC, Hilaire, *Six British Battles,* Arrowsmith, Bristol, 1931.

BISMARCK, Count Von, *Lectures on the Tactics of Cavalry,* translated by Major N. Ludlow Beamish, Ainsworth, London, 1827.

BROKE-SMITH, Brigadier P. W. L., *The History of Early British Military Aeronautics,* Royal Engineers Institution, 1952.

BROOMFIELD, G. A., *Pioneer of the Air, the Life and Times of Colonel S. F. Cody,* Gale & Polden, Aldershot, 1953.

BRYANT, Arthur, *Jackets of Green,* Collins, London, 1972.

BURNE, Alfred H, *The Art of War on Land,* Methuen, London, 1944.

BURNE, Alfred H, *The Battlefields of England,* Methuen, London, 1950.

BURNE, Alfred H, *More Battlefields of England,* Methuen, London, 1952.

BURNE, Alfred H, *The Crécy War,* Eyre & Spottiswood, London, 1955.

CHANDLER, Charles de Forest, *Free and Captive Balloons, Parts I and II,* Ronald Press, New York, 1926.

CHURCHILL, Winston S, *Marlborough, His Life and Times, Vols. I to IV,* Harrap, London, 1933 to 1938.

COXWELL, Henry, *My Life and Experiences,* W. H. Allen, London, 1887.

CREASY, Sir Edward S., *The Fifteen Decisive Battles of the World,* J. M. Dent, London, 1851.

DENISON, Colonel G. T., *A History of Cavalry (Second Edition),* Macmillan, London, 1913.

DOYLE, Arthur Conan, *The Great Boer War,* Smith, Elder & Co., London, 1902.

EADY, Major H. G., *Historical Illustrations to Field Service Regulations,* Sefton Praed, London, 1930.

EDMONDS, Brigadier-General Sir James, see WOOD, W. Birbeck.

EGE, Lennart, *Balloons and Airships,* Blandford Press, 1973.

FULLER, Colonel J. F. C., *British Light Infantry in the Eighteenth Century,* Hutchinson, London, 1925.

GAMBLE, C. F. Snowden, *The Air Weapon,* Oxford University Press, London, 1931.

GIBBS-SMITH, C. H., *The World's First Aeroplane Flights,* H.M.S.O., 1965.

GUEDALLA, Philip, *The Duke,* Hodder & Stoughton, London, 1931.

HARRISON, Professor R. K., *A History of Old Testament Times,* Marshall, Morgan & Scott, London, 1957.

HART, Clive, *Kites, an Historical Survey,* Faber & Faber, London, 1967.

HEADLAM, Major-General Sir John, *The History of the Royal Artillery from the Indian Mutiny to the Great War, Vols. I to III,* Royal Artillery Institution, Woolwich, 1931 to 1940.

HISTORICAL SECTION, COMMITTEE OF IMPERIAL DEFENCE, *Official History of the Russo-Japanese War (Naval and Military), Vols. I to III,* H.M.S.O., 1910 to 1920.

HODGSON, J. E., *The History of Aeronautics in Great Britain,* Oxford University Press, London, 1924.

JOMINI, Lieutenant-General, *Histoire Critique et Militaire des Guerres de la Révolution, Vols. V and VI,* Anselin & Pochard, Paris, 1820.

KELLER, Werner, *The Bible as History,* translated by William Neil, Hodder & Stoughton, London, 1956.

KELLY, Fred C., *The Wright Brothers,* Harrap, London, 1944.

LACROIX, Désiré, *Les Aérostiers Militaires du Château de Meudon, (1794–1884),* Auguste Ghio, Paris, 1885.

MACMILLAN, Norman, *Sir Sefton Brancker,* Heinemann, London, 1935.

MARSHALL-CORNWALL, General Sir James, *Napoleon as Military Commander,* B. T. Batsford, London, 1967.

MAURICE, Major-General Sir Frederick, *History of the War in South Africa, 1899–1902, Vols I to IV,* Hurst & Blackett, London, 1907 to 1910.

MONTGOMERY, Field-Marshal Viscount, of Alamein, *A History of Warfare,* Collins, London, 1968.

MONEY, Major-General John, *A Short Treatise on the use of Balloons and Field Observators in Military Operations,* Military Library, Whitehall, London, 1803.

MUFFLING, Baron C. von, *History of the Campaign of the British, Dutch, Hanoverian and Brunswick Armies, and of the Prussians, in the year 1815*, translated by Sir John Sinclair, T. Egerton, Military Library, Whitehall, 1816, republished S. R. Publishers, Wakefield, 1972.

MUNSON, Kenneth, *Helicopters and other Rotorcraft since 1907*, Blandford Press, London, 1968.

NAPIER, Major-General Sir W. F. P., *History of the War in the Peninsula and in the South of France 1807–1814, Vols. I to VI*, Frederick Warne, c. 1850.

PEMBERTON, W. Baring, *Battles of the Boer War*, B. T. Batsford, London, 1964.

PENROSE, Harald, *British Aviation, The Pioneer Years, 1903–1914*, Putnam, London, 1967.

PHIPPS, Colonel Ramsay Weston, *The Armies of the First French Republic, Vol. II*, Oxford University Press, London, 1929.

REDWAY, Major G. W., *The War of Secession, 1861–62*, Swan Sonneschien, 1910.

ROBINSON, Major-General C. W., *Wellington's Campaigns, Parts I to III*, Hugh Rees, London, 1905 to 1911.

ROLT, L. T. C., *The Aeronauts*, Longmans, London, 1966.

SUMNER, Captain P. H., *Streamline Kite Balloons*, Crosby, Lockwood & Son, London, 1920.

TISSANDIER, G., *Histoire des Ballons et des Aéronauts Célèbres, 1783–1800, Vol. I*, Librairie Artistique, Paris, 1887.

WALKER, Percy B., *Early Aviation at Farnborough, Vols I and II*, Macdonald, London, 1971, 1974.

WEBB, Alexander S., *The Peninsula, McClellan's Campaign of 1862*, Charles Scribner's Sons, New York, 1902.

WOOD, W. Birbeck, with EDMONDS, Lieutenant-Colonel J. E., *A History of the Civil War in the United States, 1861–5*, Methuen, London, 1905.

PAMPHLETS

French Pamphlet – Revue Historique No. 49, La Campagne de 1794 à l'Armée du Nord, incomplete, Library of the Royal Aeronautical Society.

War Office Pamphlets

Russo-Japanese War, Reports from British Officers attached to the Japanese and Russian forces in the Field, Vols I to III, 1908.

Field Service Regulations, Part I, Operations, 1909.

Memorandum on the Training of the Royal Garrison Artillery, 1913.

Field Service Regulations, Part I, Operations, 1909, with amendments, 1914.

Field Artillery Training, 1914.

Training Manual, Royal Flying Corps, Part I 1914 and Part II, Military Wing, 1914.

UNPUBLISHED MANUSCRIPT

WALLER, Colonel S., *A History of the Royal Engineers Operations in South Africa, 1899–1902,* Royal Engineers Library.

1914–1918

PUBLISHED BOOKS

ASPINALL-OGLANDER, Brigadier-General C. F., *History of the Great War, Military Operations, Gallipoli, Vols. I and II,* William Heinemann, London, 1929, 1932.

BRUCE, J. M., *War Planes of the First World War – Fighters,* Macdonald, London, 1965.

CHURCHILL, Winston S., *The World Crisis, Vols I to IV,* Thornton, Butterworth, London, 1923 to 1927.

COLE, Christopher, *Royal Flying Corps, 1915–1916,* William Kimber, London, 1969.

COLE, Christopher, *Royal Air Force, 1918,* William Kimber, London, 1968.

COOPER, Duff, *Haig, Vols I and II,* Faber & Faber, London, 1935–6.

COURTNEY, Frank, *Flight Path,* William Kimber, London, 1972.

DAVIES, Major-General H. R., see EDMONDS.

DELAP, J. O. K. Editor, *With a Siege Battery in France – 303 Siege Battery, R.G.A., 1916–1919,* Royal Artillery Institution, Woolwich, 1919.

EDMONDS, Brigadier-General Sir James E., *History of the Great War, Military Operations, France and Belgium, many volumes,* with collaboration in some cases of Captain C. Falls, Lieutenant-Colonel R. Maxwell-Hyslop and Captain W. Miles, Macmillan or H.M.S.O., London, 1933 to 1947.

EDMONDS, Brigadier-General Sir James E., *History of the Great War, Military Operations, Italy, 1915–1919,* with Major-General H. R. Davies, H.M.S.O., London, 1949.

FALLS, Cyril *History of the Great War, Military Operations, Egypt and Palestine, Vol. I* (with Lieutenant-General Sir George MacMunn) *and Vol. II, Parts I and II,* H.M.S.O., London 1928 to 1930.

FALLS, Cyril, *History of the Great War, Military Operations, Macedonia, Vols. I and II,* H.M.S.O., London, 1933 to 1935.

FALLS, Cyril, see also EDMONDS.

FRENCH, Sir John, *Despatches, Mons, Marne and Aisne,* the Graphic, London.

HART, Liddell, *A History of the World War, 1914–18,* Faber & Faber, London, 1934.

HORDERN, Lieutenant-Colonel Charles, *History of the Great War, Military Operations, East Africa, Vol. I,* H.M.S.O., London, 1941.

INSALL, A. J., *Observer,* William Kimber, London, 1970.

JACKSON, A. J., *Avro Aircraft since 1908,* Putnam, London, 1965.

JONES, H. A., *The War in the Air, Vols II to VI,* Clarendon Press, Oxford, 1928–37. See also RALEIGH.

JOUBERT DE LA FERTÉ, Air Chief Marshal Sir Philip, *The Third Service,* Thames & Hudson, 1955.

LEWIS, Cecil, *Sagittarius Rising,* Peter Davies, London, 1936.

LEWIS, Cecil, *Farewell to Wings,* Temple Press, London, 1964.

LEWIS, Peter, *The British Bomber since 1914, Second Edition,* Putnam, London, 1974.

LONGSTREET, Stephen, *The Canvas Falcons,* W. H. Allen, London, 1971.

MACMILLAN, Norman, *Sir Sefton Brancker,* Heinemann, London, 1935.

MACMUNN, Lieutenant-General Sir George, see FALLS.

MARSHALL-CORNWALL, General Sir James, *Haig as Military Commander,* B. T. Batsford, London, 1973.

MAURICE, Major-General Sir Frederick, *Forty Days in 1914,* Constable, 1919.

MAXWELL-HYSLOP, Lieutenant-Colonel R., see EDMONDS.

MILES, Captain Wilfrid, *History of the Great War, Military Operations, France and Belgium, 1917, Part III,* H.M.S.O., London, 1949.

MILES, Captain Wilfrid, see EDMONDS.

MOBERLY, Brigadier-General F. T., *History of the Great War, Military Operations, The Campaign in Mesopotamia, 1914–18, Vols 1 to IV,* H.M.S.O., London, 1923–27.

MORRIS, Alan, *The Balloonatics,* Jarrolds, London, 1970.

MUNSON, Kenneth, *Bombers 1914–19, Patrol and Reconnaissance Aircraft,* Blandford Press, London, 1968.

NEUMANN, Major Georg Paul (Editor), *The German Air Force in the Great War,* translated by J. E. Gurdon, Hodder & Stoughton, London, 1920.

NORRIS, Geoffrey, *The Royal Flying Corps: a History,* Frederick Muller, London, 1965.

RALEIGH, Sir Walter, *The War in the Air, Vol. I,* Clarendon Press, Oxford, 1922. See also Jones, H. A.

SLESSOR, Wing-Commander J. C., *Air Power and Armies,* Oxford University Press, London, 1936.

SUMNER, Captain P. H., *Streamline Kite Balloons*, Crosby, Lockwood & Son, London, 1920.

THOMPSON, Sir Robert, *The Royal Flying Corps*, Hamish Hamilton, London, 1968.

TOWNSHEND, Major-General Sir Charles, *My Campaign in Mesopotamia*, Thornton Butterworth, London, 1920.

WOOLLCOMBE, Robert, *The First Tank Battle*, Arthur Barker, London, 1967.

PAMPHLETS

War Office Pamphlets

Co-operation of Aircraft with Artillery, December, 1916.

Co-operation of Aircraft with Artillery, Revised December, 1917.

British Expeditionary Force, France, Pamphlets

SS170, Notes on co-operation between Aircraft and Artillery during recent operations on the Second Army front, 1917.

SS553, Experience of the German First Army in the Somme Battle, by General von Below (Translation of German document of 30th January, 1917), 1917.

SS135, Co-operation between Aircraft and Infantry, 1918.

SS139/3, Artillery Notes No.3 – Counter-Battery work, 1918.

SS139/7, Artillery Notes No.7 – Artillery in Defensive Operations, 1918.

SS649, The Artillery Aeroplane and the Artillery Balloon (Translation of a German document), 1918.

40/WO/2884, Notes on Artillery observation from Kite Balloons, 1918.

Training Leaflet 9, Artillery Notes for Pilots and Observers, R.A.F., 1918.

Training Leaflet 10, Questions and Answers on the Practical Application of SS131 for the Training of Pilots and Observers, R.A.F. 1918.

UNPUBLISHED MANUSCRIPTS

ANSTEY, Brigadier-General E. C., *The History of the Royal Artillery, from 4th August, 1914*, Royal Artillery Library.

HUSSEY, Brigadier-General A. D., *War Diary, 1914–18*, Royal Artillery Library.

MACLEOD, Colonel R., *An Artillery Officer in the First World War*, Royal Artillery Library.

RAWLINS, Colonel S. W. H., *A History of the Development of the British Artillery in France, 1914–18*, Royal Artillery Library.

THOMPSON, Brigadier W. F. K., *Contemporary documents of his father, orders and other papers relating to 'Counter-Battery' and 'Air Shoot' arrangements.*

1918–1939

PUBLISHED BOOKS

ALLEN, Wing-Commander H. R., *The Legacy of Lord Trenchard*, Cassell, London, 1972.

ALLWARD, Maurice F., see TAYLOR, John W. R. and ALLWARD.

BOYLE, Andrew, *Trenchard – Man of Vision*, Collins, London, 1962.

DOUHET, Giulio, *The Command of the Air*, 1921, translated by Dino Ferrari, Faber & Faber, London, 1943.

MASON, Francis K., *Hawker Aircraft since 1920*, Putnam, London, 1961.

MUNSON, Kenneth, *Helicopters and other Rotorcraft since 1907*, Blandford Press, London, 1968.

NESBITT-DUFORT, John, *Scramble – Flying the aircraft of World War II*, Speed & Sports Publications, London, 1970.

SEVERSKY, Alexander P. de, *Air Power – Key to Survival*, Herbert Jenkins, London, 1952.

TAYLOR, John W. R. and ALLWARD, Maurice F., *Westland 50*, Ian Allan, London, 1965.

THETFORD, Owen, *Aircraft of the Royal Air Force since 1918, Fifth Edition*, Putnam, London, 1971.

PAMPHLETS

War Office Pamphlets

Artillery Training, Vol. II, Gunnery, 1934.

Field Service Regulations, Vol. II, Operations (General), 1935.

The Employment of Air Forces with the Army in the Field, 1938.

Air Ministry Pamphlets

Army Co-operation Reports, 1927 to 1939.

A Lecture by the Deputy Chief of the Air Staff at the Imperial Defence College, April 1933 (Air Staff Memo. 52 of June 1933).

A Selection of Lectures and Essays from the Work of officers attending courses at the R.A.F. Staff College, 1923 to 1927.

UNPUBLISHED MANUSCRIPTS

ROYAL AIR FORCE, *Operational Record Books and Air Ministry documents of historical importance*, Public Record Office.

1939–1945

PUBLISHED BOOKS

AIR HISTORIAN OF THE ROYAL CANADIAN AIR FORCE, *The R.C.A.F. Overseas – The Fifth Year* and *The R.C.A.F. Overseas – The Sixth Year*, Oxford University Press, Toronto, 1945 and 1949.

AIR MINISTRY, *Wings of the Phoenix (The Official Story of the Air War in Burma)*, H.M.S.O., London, 1949.

ALEXANDER, Field Marshal Viscount, of Tunis, *Despatches, Africa, Sicily, Italy, London Gazette, 3rd and 10th February, 1948, 6th June, 1950*, H.M.S.O., London, 1948, 1950.

ALLEN, Wing-Commander, H. R., *Who Won the Battle of Britain?*, Arthur Barker, London, 1974.

ANDERSON, Lieutenant-General K. A. N., *Despatch, North-West Africa, London Gazette, 5th November, 1946*, H.M.S.O., London, 1946.

ANON., *6 Army Group, Royal Artillery*, privately published.

AUCHINLECK, General Sir Claude J. E., *Despatches, Middle East, London Gazette, 20th August, 1946 and 13th January, 1948*, H.M.S.O., London, 1946 and 1948.

BABINGTON-SMITH, Constance, *Evidence in Camera*, Chatto & Windus, London, 1958.

BELFIELD, E. M. G., see PARHAM, Major-General H. J. and BELFIELD.

BLAXLAND, Gregory, *Destination Dunkirk*, William Kimber, London, 1973.

BROOKES, Andrew J., *Photo Reconnaissance*, Ian Allan, London, 1975.

BROWN, James Ambrose, *South African Forces, World War II, Vols. II and IV*, Purnell, Cape Town, 1970 and 1974.

BRYANT, Arthur, *The Turn of the Tide, 1939–43*, Collins, London, 1957.

BRYANT, Arthur, *Triumph in the West, 1943–46*, Collins, London, 1959.

BUCKLEY, Christopher, *Norway, the Commandos, Dieppe*, H.M.S.O., London, 1951.

CHURCHILL, Winston S., *The Second World War, Vols I to VI*, Cassell, London, 1948 to 1954.

CLARK, General Mark, *Calculated Risk*, Harrap, London, 1951.

COLLIER, Basil, *The Battle of Britain*, B. T. Batsford, London, 1962.

COLLIER, Basil, *The War in the Far East, 1941–1945*, Heinemann, London, 1969.

DEXTER, David, *Australia in the War of 1939–1945, The New Guinea Offensives*, Australian War Memorial, Canberra, 1961.

DUNCAN, Brigadier W. E. and others (Editors), *The Royal Artillery Commemoration Book, 1939–45*, Royal Artillery Benevolent Fund, 1950.

ELLIS, Major L. F., *History of the Second World War, The War in France and Flanders, 1939–40*, H.M.S.O., London, 1953.

ELLIS, Major L. F., *History of the Second World War, Victory in the West, Vols. I and II*, H.M.S.O., London, 1962 and 1968.

FALLS, Cyril, *The Second World War, a Short History*, Methuen, London, 1948.

FERGUSSON, Bernard, *The Watery Maze*, Collins, London, 1961.

FRANKLAND, Noble, see WEBSTER, Sir Charles.

FULLER, Major-General J. F. C., *The Second World War, 1939–45*, Eyre & Spottiswood, London, 1948.

GILLISON, Douglas, *Australia in the War of 1939–45, Royal Australian Air Force, 1939–42*, Australian War Memorial, Canberra, 1962.

GREATOREX, Wilfred, see URQUHART, Major-General R. E.

GREGORY, Barry, *British Airborne Troops*, Macdonald and Jane's, London, 1974.

GUINGAND, Major-General Sir Francis de, *Operation Victory*, Hodder & Stoughton, London, 1947.

HAY, Ian, *The Battle of Flanders, 1940*, H.M.S.O., London, 1941.

HORROCKS, Lieutenant-General Sir Brian, *A Full Life*, Collins, 1960.

JACKSON, Lieutenant-Colonel G. S., *Operations of Eighth Corps*, St. Clement's Press, London, 1948.

JACKSON, W. G. F., *The Battle for Italy*, B. T. Batsford, London, 1967.

KIRBY, Major-General Woodburn, *History of the Second World War – The War against Japan, Vols I to V*, H.M.S.O., London, 1957–69.

LEIGH-MALLORY, Air Chief Marshal Sir Trafford, *Despatch, North-West Europe, London Gazette, 31st September, 1946*, H.M.S.O., London, 1947.

LONGMORE, Air Chief Marshal Sir Arthur, *Despatch, Middle East, London Gazette, 17th September, 1946*, H.M.S.O., London, 1946.

MACMILLAN, Norman, *The Royal Air Force in the World War, Vols. I to IV*, Harrap, London, 1942 to 1950.

MARR, Flight-Lieutenant D. S. B., *A History of 208 Squadron*, privately published.

MCCARTHY, Dudley, *Australia in the War of 1939–45, South-West Pacific area, First Year, Kokoda to Wau*, Australian War Memorial, Canberra, 1959.

MILLINGTON, Air Commodore G., *The Unseen Eye*, Anthony Gibbs & Phillip, 1961 (footnote references are to Panther Books edition, 1965).

MOLONY, Brigadier C. J. C., *History of the Second World War, the Mediterranean and Middle East, Vol V*, H.M.S.O., London, 1973.

MONTGOMERY, Field Marshal Viscount, of Alamein, *Despatch, North-West Europe, London Gazette, 3rd September, 1946*, H.M.S.O., London, 1946.

MOUNTBATTEN, Vice-Admiral Earl, of Burma, *Report to the Combined Chiefs of Staff by the Supreme Allied Commander, South-East Asia, 1943–45*, H.M.S.O., London, 1951.

MUNSON, Kenneth, *Bombers, Patrol and Transport Aircraft, 1939–45*, Blandford Press, London, 1969.

MUNSON, Kenneth, *Aircraft of World War II, Second Edition*, Ian Allan, 1972.

O'BRIEN, Terence H., *History of the Second World War, Civil Defence*, H.M.S.O. and Longman's Green, London, 1955.

ODGERS, George, *Australia in the War of 1939–45, Air War against Japan, 1943–45*, Australian War Memorial, Canberra, 1957.

ORPEN, Neil, *South African Forces in World War II, Vol. I, East African and Abyssinian campaigns*, and *Vol. III, War in the Desert*, Purnell, Cape Town, 1968 and 1971.

PARHAM, Major-General H. J. and BELFIELD, E. M. G., *Unarmed into Battle – The Story of the Air Observation Post*, Warren & Son, Winchester, 1956.

PEMBERTON, Brigadier A.L., *The Second World War, 1939–45, Army, Development of Artillery Tactics and Equipment*, War Office, 1950.

PLAYFAIR, Major-General I. S. O., *History of the Second World War, The Mediterranean and Middle East, Vols. I to IV*, H.M.S.O., London, 1954 to 1966.

RICHARDS, Denis, *The Royal Air Force, 1939–45, Vols. I to III*, with Hilary St. George Saunders, H.M.S.O., London, 1944–53.

RYAN, Cornelius, *A Bridge too Far*, Hamish Hamilton, London, 1974.

SAUNDERS, Hilary St. George, see RICHARDS, Denis.

SHORES, Christopher F., *2nd T.A.F.*, Osprey, Reading, 1970.

TAYLOR, Jeremy, *This Band of Brothers – a History of the Reconnaissance Corps of the British Army*, White Swan Press, Bristol, 1947.

THETFORD, Owen, *Aircraft of the Royal Air Force since 1918, Fifth Edition*, Putnam, London, 1971.

TULLOCH, Major-General Derek, *Wingate in Peace and War*, Macdonald, London, 1972.

URQUHART, Major-General R. E., *Arnhem*, with Wilfred Greatorex, Cassell, London, 1958.

WAVELL, General Sir Archibald P., *Despatches Middle East, Western Desert, East Africa, London Gazette, 11th and 25th June, 2nd and 9th July, 1946*, H.M.S.O., London, 1946.

WEBSTER, Sir Charles, *History of the Second World War, the Strategic Air Offensive against Germany, 1939–45, Vols. I to III*, with Noble Frankland, H.M.S.O., London, 1961.

WIGMORE, Lionel, *Australia in the War of 1939–45, The Japanese Thrust*, Australian War Memorial, Canberra, 1957.

WILMOT, Chester, *The Struggle for Europe*, Collins, London, 1952.

WINDROW, Martin C. (Editor), *Aircraft in Profile, Vol. VII*, Profile Publications, Windsor, 1967.

WINTERBOTHAM, F. W., *The Ultra Secret*, Weidenfeld and Nicolson, London, 1974.

PAMPHLETS

War Office Pamphlets

Royal Artillery Training Memorandum (Field Branch and Anti/Tank), War, No. 1, December, 1939.

Royal Artillery Notes, 1942–46.

Army/Air Operations Pamphlets 1 (General Principles and Organisation) and 2 (Direct Support), 1944.

First Canadian Army, 84 Group, R.A.F. and 35 Reconnaissance Wing, R.A.F. Pamphlets

35 days in 35 Wing, 28 July to 31 August, 1944.

From Normandy to Hanover, June 1944 – June 1945.

Air Recce, c. 1946.

83 Group, R.A.F. and 39 Reconnaissance Wing, R.C.A.F. Pamphlets

A Short Historical Account of No. 83 Group, 1st April 1943 to the end of the War in Europe (Compiled Squadron Leader D. R. Morgan, B.A.). 1957.

'Flap' (39 Wing), December 1944 – July 1945.

UNPUBLISHED MANUSCRIPTS

ALLIED CENTRAL MEDITERRANEAN FORCE, *Artillery Lessons of the Campaign in Italy, 1943–45*, Royal Artillery Library.

ARMY, *War diaries and other documents of historical importance*, Public Record Office.

BURNAND, Wing-Commander L. G., *Greek Interlude, April 6th to 26th, 1941*, Geoffrey Burnand.

DANIELL, Brigadier A. J., *Contemporary documents from the Arakan theatre of Burma, 1945, concerning the lessons of the 1944–45 operations and the use of Visual Control Posts.*

V CORPS, *Artillery Lessons, Tunisia, from notes of Commander, Corps Royal Artillery*, Royal Artillery Library.

FIRST ARMY, *Lessons from operations in North Africa, November 1942 to May 1943*, by Lieutenant-General K. A. N. Anderson, C in C, dated 16th June 1943, Royal Artillery Library.

FIRST ARMY, *Artillery Notes on the Battle of the Medjerda Valley, May 1943*, Royal Artillery Library.

FIRST ARMY, *Artillery Lessons of the Campaign in North Africa, 4th June, 1943, by the Brigadier, Royal Artillery*, Royal Artillery Library.

PARHAM, Major-General H. J., *Brigadier, Royal Artillery, Second British Army, notes for historical record prepared before the landings on the Continent of 4th June, 1944*, Royal Artillery Library.

ROYAL AIR FORCE, *Operational Record Books, including those of Air O.P. Squadrons, and Air Ministry documents of historical importance*, Public Record Office.

ROYAL AIR FORCE SQUADRONS, *Short Histories, 40 (S.A.A.F.), 208, 225 Squadrons*, Ministry of Defence, Air Historical Branch and Adastral Library.

ROYAL ARTILLERY, 46th DIVISION, *Account and Lessons of Operations in Tunisia*, Royal Artillery Library.

COVERING SEVERAL PERIODS

PUBLISHED BOOKS

BIDWELL, Shelford, *Gunners at War*, Arms & Armour, London, 1970.

COLLIER, Basil, *A History of Air Power*, Wiedenfeld & Nicolson, London, 1974.

MONDEY, David, see TAYLOR, John W. R.

SIMS, Charles, *The Royal Air Force – the First Fifty Years*, Adam & Charles Black, London, 1968.

TAYLOR, John W. R., *Spies in the Sky*, with David Mondey, Ian Allan, London, 1972.

JOURNALS AND REVIEWS

AERO MAGAZINE, 1910–13, Iliffe & Sons.

AERONAUTICAL JOURNAL (retitled 1922 JOURNAL OF THE ROYAL AERONAUTICAL SOCIETY).

AEROPLANE, Temple Press.

AIR O.P. OFFICERS ASSOCIATION REVIEW.

AIR PICTORIAL, The Air League, London.

ARMY AIR CORPS ASSOCIATION JOURNAL (retitled 1972 ARMY AIR CORPS JOURNAL).

ARMY REVIEW, 1911–14, H.M.S.O., London.

AUSTER QUARTERLY.

BRITISH ARMY REVIEW, Ministry of Defence, London.

FIGHTING FORCES JOURNAL, 1946–9, London.

FLIGHT, Dorset House, London.

ROUNDEL, Royal Canadian Air Force, Ottawa.

ROYAL AIR FORCE QUARTERLY JOURNAL, Gale & Polden, London.

ROYAL ARTILLERY HISTORICAL AFFAIRS COMMITTEE (retitled 1967 ROYAL ARTILLERY HISTORICAL SOCIETY) PROCEEDINGS, Royal Artillery Institution, Woolwich.

ROYAL ARTILLERY, JOURNAL OF THE, Royal Artillery Institution, Woolwich.

ROYAL ENGINEERS JOURNAL, Institution of the Royal Engineers, Chatham.

ROYAL ENGINEERS, PAPERS ON SUBJECTS CONNECTED WITH THE DUTIES OF THE CORPS OF, Institution of the Royal Engineers, Chatham

ROYAL ENGINEERS, PROFESSIONAL PAPERS OF THE CORPS OF, Institution of the Royal Engineers, Chatham.

ROYAL UNITED SERVICES INSTITUTION, JOURNAL OF THE.

UNITED SERVICE INSTITUTION OF INDIA, JOURNAL OF THE.

UNITED SERVICES MAGAZINE, 1897–1911, William Clowes, London.

Assistance given to the Author

—◇—

I acknowledge with gratitude the assistance and advice I have received from the following individuals, many of them busy people with manifold commitments who could ill afford the time they devoted to my affairs. Where, in correspondence, an individual has not used his service rank, I have thought it best to omit it here.

Group Captain A. F. Anderson
Mrs E. B. Ashmore
Cedric Atkinson
Major E. M. G. Belfield
Mrs L. L. Blake
Squadron Leader Cal D. Bricker
Air Chief Marshal Sir Harry Broadhurst
Lady Brooke-Popham
Geoffrey Burnand
Guy M. Burnand
Lieutenant-Colonel Charles Carrington
J. D. Cass
Basil E. Catchpole
Squadron Leader F. E. Clarke
Sir John E. L. Clerke, Bt.
L.A.C. E. E. Colman
Brigadier D. W. Coyle
Brigadier A. J. Daniell
A. G. Davey
Air Commodore P. L. Donkin
Myles Eadon
Lieutenant-Colonel J. C. Edelmann
Henry Edmunds
Mrs Fraser Evans
Air Commodore A. J. W. Geddes

General Sir John Gibbon
Wing Commander Peter Gover
Wing Commander A. H. Hill
C.W.O. F. O. Honey
Air Chief Marshal Sir Edmund Hudleston
Group Captain T. Humble
G. G. Hunter
Squadron Leader R. T. Hutchinson
Laurence Irving
Lieutenant-Colonel C. J. B. Jarrett
George Keeping
Flying Officer F. R. Loveless
Air Chief Marshal Sir Theodore McEvoy
Dr. Malcolm MacEwan
Colonel R. Macleod
Frank McMath
Major-General J. M. McNeill
Group Captain A. S. Mann
Air Commodore E. G. L. Millington
Brigadier C. J. C. Molony
Group Captain E. H. G. Moncrieff
Major-General R. C. Money

Lieutenant-Colonel John H. H.
    Mooney
Major R. W. V. Neathercoat
W. H. Odell
Serjeant Robert J. Ohs
Lieutenant-Colonel D. P. D.
    Oldman
W. L. Palk
Major-General H. J. Parham
Mrs Parham
Harald Penrose
Lieutenant-General R. H.
    Rogers
Brigadier-General R. H.
    Rohmer
Air Chief Marshal Sir Frederick
    Rosier

Charles J. Rushhon
Group Captain G. H. Sellers
Mrs D. Sole
Squadron Leader C. T. P.
    Stephenson
George T. Sutherland
Brigadier W. F. K. Thompson
D. L. Thornton
Lieutenant-Colonel F. C. Tracey
R. H. Walker
Air Commodore R. H. G.
    Weighill
Major-General G. P. L. Weston
H. C. Wilkins
Professor T. C. Willett
Lieutenant-General Sir John
    Woodall

I wish also to thank the Directors, Commanders and Staffs of the
following establishments, units or other organisations for the facilities,
help and kindness they have accorded me.

The Public Record Office, in particular the Staff of the West Room,
    Portugal Street, London.
The Air Historical and AR 8 branches of the Ministry of Defence.
The Directorate of Army Air Corps. Middle Wallop.
The Directorate of History, National Defence Headquarters, Ottawa.
The Directorate of Personnel Services, Department of Defence,
    Canberra.
The Australian War Memorial, Canberra.
La Service Historique de l'Armée de l'Air Française.
The Imperial War Museum, Departments of Photographs, Printed
    Books and Sound Records.
The Ministry of Aviation Technical Library, Boscombe Down.
The Ministry of Defence Central and Adastral Libraries.
The Museum of Army Flying.
The Airborne Forces Museum.
The Royal Aeronautical Society Library.
The Royal Artillery Institution and Library.
The Royal Engineers Institution and Library.
The Library of the Royal United Service Institute.
The South African National Museum of Military History.
No.400 Air Reserve Squadron, Canadian Forces.
The University of Keele, Department of Geography.
Flight International magazine.

I cannot sufficiently thank Gillian Cox for the manner in which she produced the final draft of my manuscript for the printer, demonstrating an uncanny knack for detecting errors and great accuracy at the end of many a long day's work.

PETER MEAD

Index

Printed in England for Her Majesty's Stationery Office
by Hobbs the Printers of Southampton
(1370) Dd716845 C39 12/82 G381